The Mounted Police
of Natal

Major-General Sir J. G. Dartnell, K.C.B.

The Mounted Police of Natal

The Zulu War, the Boer War, Zulu Rebellion and Policing the Colonial Frontier in South Africa 1873-1906

H. P. Holt

LEONAUR

The Mounted Police of Natal
The Zulu War, the Boer War, Zulu Rebellion
and Policing the Colonial Frontier
in South Africa 1873-1906
H. P. Holt

First published under the title
The Mounted Police of Natal

Leonaur is an imprint of Oakpast Ltd

Copyright in this form © 2010 Oakpast Ltd

ISBN: 978-0-85706-385-4 (hardcover)
ISBN: 978-0-85706-386-1 (softcover)

http://www.leonaur.com

Publisher's Notes

The opinions of the authors represent a view of events in which he
was a participant related from his own perspective,
as such the text is relevant as an historical document.

The views expressed in this book are not necessarily
those of the publisher.

Contents

Preface

I am asked to write an introduction to this work telling something of the very early days of the Natal Mounted Police, and I have much pleasure in doing so, for it is the history of a corps which I raised and commanded for nearly thirty years, and which is now losing its identity as the Natal Police by becoming absorbed in the South African Constabulary under the South African Union Government.

I have practically been connected with the corps from "start to finish," for since my retirement in 1903 I have kept up a correspondence with many of the officers, and have taken a great interest in the changes which have since taken place in the corps I commanded so long and loved so well.

I sold out of Her Majesty's Service in 1869, and went out to Natal with the intention of settling there, not with any idea of taking up a semi-military life again, but as a farmer. However, after I had purchased a farm, stock, etc., and lived upon it for a couple of years or more, my wife, who had just returned from a trip to England, at the end of 1873, refused to return to the farm, saying the life was too lonely and that I must try something else.

I didn't quite know what else to try! But the Government of Natal, after their experience of the Langalibalele Rebellion, were about to raise a mounted police force, so I put in an application offering to raise the force for them, not anticipating that I should be given the appointment, but telling my wife of my application and adding that if it failed she would have to go back to the farm.

To my surprise, about a week after I had sent in the application, the Governor of the colony, Sir Benjamin Pine, rode out one afternoon to the house where I was living and told me he had selected me, from the list of applicants, to raise the mounted police. I replied that I was very much obliged to him for his confidence in me and that I would do my best to deserve it, but that I might tell him at the same time that I knew nothing about police work.

"You probably know as much as any of the other applicants," he said, "and should at all events know something about discipline, having been in Her Majesty's Service."

I then asked his permission to proceed to the Cape Colony to learn something of police work, for they had had a mounted police force there for some few years called the Frontier Armed and Mounted Police. The Governor kindly gave his consent to my going, so I went to the headquarters of the F.A.M.P. at King William's Town and stayed there a week or two, learning all I could of the organization of the force from its then commander, Colonel Bowker. I then returned to Natal and presented my report to the Governor, and started almost immediately to raise the force which was called the Natal Mounted Police at first, but was afterwards called the Natal Police, in 1894, when the whole of the police forces of the colony were organized into one body.

I wanted to send home for men, but this the Government would not sanction, so I had to start recruiting from amongst the flotsam and jetsam of the colony, and a very rough lot they proved to be, being principally old soldiers and sailors, transport riders, and social failures from home, etc. They were, however, a very fine, hardy lot of men, ready to go anywhere and do anything, and very willing and cheerful if a little troublesome in town; but in the country, away from temptation, they were excellent men, who grumbled occasionally, of course, but were more inclined to laugh at and make light of discomfort and hardship.

Three officers were appointed to assist me, *viz.*, Mr. G. Mansel (afterwards Colonel Mansel, C.M.G., who later raised and commanded the Zululand Native Police), Mr. F. Campbell (a relative of the Speaker of the Legislative Council), and Mr. F. Phillips (son of Judge Phillips of the Supreme Court of the colony). Later on I got the Government to consent to all promotions in the corps being made through the ranks, in order to avoid any undue political influence being brought to bear in the appointment of officers; I also wanted to induce a good class of men to enlist in the force by the prospect of promotion, and I achieved my object, for after a few years about a third of the men were gentlemen. Some of them were University men, and there were boys from nearly every public school in England.

The constitution of the force was, at first, 50 Europeans and 150 natives, but when I proposed to arm the natives, as well as the Europeans, there was an outcry at once, and the numbers were practically transposed. Some few years afterwards the strength of the force continually fluctuated, being increased when times were good and cut down when the treasury was getting low, so I described the police, in one of my reports, as the financial barometer of the colony, and was taken to task by the Governor for using such a simile.

I was assisted in the training of the men by a first-rate sergeant-major—Stean—who had been a colour-sergeant in the Cape Mounted Rifles, and was the very best man I could possibly have got to lick a rough lot into shape, for he was strict and at the same time good-tempered. Although he used to shout at the men in a deep bass voice, and turn them out before daylight in the morning to clean barracks and groom their horses, preparatory to riding-school, in which he delighted, he was much liked by them, and they used to speak of him familiarly behind his back as "Puffy." Some years later, when he became adjutant, he was spoilt, for he never had his heart in his work as he had when sergeant-major, and missed not being able to shout at the men and take them out to riding-school, where his language was free and his vocabulary often very quaint.

One morning I was looking on from a little distance at the squad undergoing instruction, and out of the ken of the sergeant-major, who had not noticed me, when I saw him suddenly draw his sword and make a dash for a man who promptly tried to gallop off. He soon overtook him, however, and flourishing his sword over the man's head said: "By God, I'll cut your —— head off!" The poor terrified recruit was clinging to the pommel of his saddle like a monkey, with his forage-cap at the back of his head and his chin-strap under his nose, saying, "Please, sir! Oh, sir!" and after a particularly vicious flourish of the sword, "Don't, sir!"

I was very much amused, and some of the men in the squad laughed loudly. That took the sergeant-major back angrily, but, perceiving me, he came up and saluted, saying: "That —— fellow"—pointing to the still shaking recruit—"wouldn't keep his horse in the ranks, sir, so I was just giving him a little lesson."

I could repeat many similar stories of him, but have said enough to show what the sergeant-major was like and what his methods of instruction were.

At first we were encamped beyond Fort Napier, the military barracks at the upper end of the town, which was a very inconvenient spot, and I repeatedly asked to be allowed to move into some permanent building where we should have more shelter and better convenience, but was always put off by one excuse or another, so, finding a vacant house at the very top of the town, next to Government House, which had been an hotel, I believe, and where there was some stabling, I took it upon my own responsibility, and we continued to occupy it for the following sixteen or seventeen years, though it was rather a tumble-down old place, and very insanitary.

I was both paymaster and quartermaster myself for some time, and had great difficulty in getting an advance from Government for the purchase of horses, saddlery, uniforms, etc., for the men had to pay for everything out of their consolidated pay of 5s. 6d. a day; but by dint of hammering away and flooding the treasury with vouchers for payment of these things, to be recovered afterwards from the men, I was at last given an advance for which I was made responsible, and upon which I continued to work for nearly thirty years.

The clothing was at first the same as that worn by the Frontier Armed and Mounted Police, *viz.*, brown corduroy jacket and breeches, black leather boots coming nearly to the knee and buckled down the side, and a leather peaked cap with a white cover. It was a stinking uniform, however, which caused the men to be nicknamed "The Snuffs," but anything in the shape of uniform was hard to get in the colony at that time. Afterwards, as more suitable uniform was obtained, the men began to put on a little "side" when walking out, and the then Governor said to me one day: "Your men swagger too much. We don't want swashbucklers."

To that I replied: "If you knew the difficulty I have had to make them forget the name of 'snuffs' and instil a little swagger into them, you wouldn't wish to see it reduced."

A little later on another Governor said, with reference to his orderly at Government House: "I wish you wouldn't send a prince in disguise as my orderly, for he looks so spick and span that I am almost ashamed of my own get-up whenever I pass him."

The following year, 1875, the Government said they could not afford a Commandant of volunteers as well as a Commandant of police, and that I would have to do the double work and they would allow me an extra £100 a year for it. I remonstrated, but it was no use. They gave Major Giles, the then Commandant of volunteers, who had been adjutant of his regiment; the 14th Light Dragoons (now Hussars), and served in Sir Hugh Rose's force with me during the Mutiny, a magistracy; and I was appointed.

I have exceeded the limits of a preface, I think, so will conclude with the hope that the old force of Natal Police will be as successful and distinguished in their new role of South African Constabulary.

J. G. Dartnell
(Major-General)

Folkestone,
1st March 1913.

Introduction

The Natal Police have a fighting record second to that of no similar body of men in the world, and on two occasions they have had the distinguished honour of covering the retreat of British troops. The first was during the retirement of Lord Chelmsford's force from Isandhlwana to Rorke's Drift, on the 23rd January 1879. And the second was after the disaster at Laing's Nek in the Boer War of 1881, when the column under General Colley retired to Mount Prospect on the 28th January. The corps has had its ups and downs, but it is today, (at time of first publication), the best organized police force in South Africa. In a little while all the various police bodies in the Union will be merged into one, but though the Natal Police will cease to exist under that name the men will remain at their various stations.

Though certain modifications are to be made in the regulations, the force will continue to work substantially as it does today. Few men have a more exciting life than those in the corps, for their work takes them to remote, semi-civilized stations, where life is not as sacred as it is in Piccadilly; but they are modest and retiring, nearly always regarding thrilling adventures that are over in the light of a jest. Hard as nails with constant exercise and fresh air, they are good soldiers and clever policemen, and they discharge their duties just as conscientiously when posted in the far north or remote west of Zululand as they do at headquarters.

My thanks are due to General Sir John Dartnell, who founded the corps in 1874, and remained its centre prop for many years, for his assistance in tracing the early history of the force. I also have to express thanks to Colonel W. J. Clarke, the present Chief Commissioner, for the valuable aid he gave me, and his kindness in personally conducting me to remote out-stations which I visited in both Natal and Zululand. But for his wonderful diary, which he has kept faithfully since he joined the corps as a trooper in 1878, I should have had great difficulty in tracing the movements of the corps. I must also acknowledge with thanks the permission given by Sub-Inspector Esmonde-White to reproduce some of the photographs which he took during the rebellion of 1906; and finally I have much pleasure in expressing my appreciation of the kindness of my many friends in the force who aided me in every possible way in delving into the past, so enabling me to compile this book, which I hope has at least the merit of being historically accurate.

H. P. Holt.

Pietermaritzburg, Natal,
1st March 1913.

CHAPTER 1

The Days of Savagery

For more than half a century prior to the formation of the Natal Mounted Police human life was sacrificed in South Africa as though it were of no account. Intertribal warfare was continuous, and but little is known, or ever will be known, of some of the appalling carnivals of bloodshed which were the fruits of fanaticism and savagery.

An era of comparative peacefulness in Natal ended about the year 1812, when the first of two great Zulu chieftains began to train his men for battle systematically. They had fought as untutored savages until Dingiswayo, a natural leader of fighters, took his tribe, the Umtetwas, in hand. It was perhaps by sheer luck that Dingiswayo ever stumbled upon the art of organizing troops properly. Having grown weary of seeing his father, Jobe, reign, he had a little consultation with his brother, and the two sons decided to expedite matters by attending their father's funeral.

But Jobe was astute as he was decisive in acting. The old man gathered a small force in the dead of night, intent on wiping out this dangerous section of his family. In accordance with the usual custom on such occasions a number of people were killed, including Dingiswayo's brother, but the future leader of the Zulus crawled away with an *assegai* in his back. Probably he too would have perished but for the bravery of his sister, who tracked him in the bush, took the terrible weapon out of his back, nursed him for a while, and then sent him on life's road rejoicing.

Dingiswayo became a wanderer, being uncertain of his reception if he returned home; and it was assumed that he was dead. He went to the far west of Africa, mixed with the tribes near the boundaries of the civilized settlements at the Cape, and there quietly studied the white man's methods of making war. It was there that the Umtetwa outlaw gained the knowledge which ultimately led to bloodshed involving the death of countless thousands of men. When the days of Jobe were ended, Dingiswayo returned in state on a white charger to the home of his ancestors, killed the chief who had become temporary ruler, to save further dispute, and established himself at the head of the Umtetwas. Like his father, Dingiswayo lost no time in acting once he had formed his plans.

Nature had endowed him with the brains of a great chief, and chance had enabled him to learn how to deal with his forces. Without delay, he began to emulate the white chiefs by organizing his men into regiments, and appointing officers of various rank. Many officers were dispatched to the outlying districts—the first Zulu recruiting sergeant—in order to make certain that every man was enrolled. It was typical of Dingiswayo that he did not let obstinacy amongst the men stand in his way. Those who did not care to join were merely killed, as indeed were those who were suspected of not desiring to join. So thorough was the chief that he even organized the girls into regiments.

Drills were instituted, and in a little while this notable son of Jobe found himself at the head of an army so powerful that all the neighbouring tribes were at his mercy. Fortunately for them, Dingiswayo was not cruel, as they would have understood the word, but he could not withstand the temptation to test his power. Instant success attended all his preliminary battles, and he reduced the lesser tribes to a state of subjection, fighting more with the idea of showing his own superiority than with the lust for blood. He never allowed the women and children to be killed, but he demanded substantial toll from those whom he vanquished. His method consisted of attacking a tribe in order to acquire their stores of grain, to feed his men. When the corn was exhausted he would move on to fresh territory, with similar designs, leaving the conquered as his acknowledged vassals.

At this time there was a youth named Chaka,[1] who had an unfortunate domestic difference on the subject of bloodshed, which was the turning-point in his career. He was the son of Senzangakona, chief of a tribe conquered by Dingiswayo, and his habits of violence became so objectionable that he had to flee for his life. Chaka was a genius in his way, a genius with such a hideous capacity for brutality that the civilized mind reels at the memory of his doings. He enlisted with Dingiswayo, and at a very early stage showed that he was no ordinary

1. Otherwise spelt Tshaka.

18

warrior. His gallant conduct in the field soon earned distinction for him, and he began to study the fighting methods of his chief very closely.

While Dingiswayo was opposed to unnecessary cruelty, Chaka was ruthless, and he saw a weakness in his chief's forbearance. Although the Umtetwas were victorious wherever they went, they left the vanquished tribes free to join together and form an invincible foe; so he decided that when his chance came he would adopt the policy of smashing the power of beaten tribes to such an extent that they would never be able to rise against him subsequently.

Chaka's opportunity came with the death of his father, Senzanga-kona. The diplomatic Dingiswayo, convinced that the forceful Chaka would make a better friend than an enemy, placed him at the head of the weaker tribe; and this arrangement worked excellently, the young chief fighting in many campaigns side by side with the man who had taught him how to fight systematically. The very possibility which Chaka had foreseen ended in the undoing of Dingiswayo. Some of the smaller tribes combined and made a frantic raid, and the old chief fell amongst the victims. Chaka, true to his genius, rose to the occasion, and by sheer generalship beat off the enemy with such judgment and skill that he was accepted as joint ruler over the Umtetwas and his own kinsmen.

Once he was in supreme command he set to work carrying out his own ideas, and establishing the unquestionable supremacy of the Zulus. From that moment onwards he appears to have had an unquenchable thirst for blood which amounted to a mania. His first act was to mobilize his entire army and fall upon his neighbours. As the other tribes were vanquished he murdered their women, children and old men, and absorbed the young men into his own force. Tribe after tribe he attacked in this way, each victory adding to his own power enormously; and all the time he continued to develop his own ideas of the correct way to conduct warfare. Instant death was the penalty for every warrior who returned from battle without his *assegai* or shield, or with a stab in the back, and any regiment under his command which fared ill in battle was wiped out, lest the same thing should occur again, and as a warning to others.

Driven thus by fear of death, the Zulus became an implacable power, scattering destruction southwards from Delagoa Bay to the banks of St. John's River. The hosts under Chaka gave no quarter, and a vast area in the course of a few years became desolated. The scattered tribes in Natal were crushed so completely that terror prevented them from existing together in numbers, and thousands were reduced to living in the *kloofs* and subsisting on roots. Starvation caused hundreds of deaths, and to escape this miserable end batches of men would occasionally make their way as far as the Tugela River in the hope that they would be permitted to join the terrible band of Chaka. It was a desperate measure to adopt, for the unfit were at once slain, only the capable men being allowed to join the force.

Probably the most appalling butchery ever organized and carried out by Chaka was when his mother died. The scene was witnessed by Mr. H. F. Fynn. Chaka was, in his way, very fond of the woman who bore him, and tears rained down his cheeks for a quarter of an hour after he was told of her death. He stood still, unable to speak all that time; and then the brutality in him asserted itself, and his feelings became ungovernable. Knowing what to expect with their chief in a particularly dangerous mood, his people instantly tore every ornament from their bodies and flung them to the ground, at the same time beginning to howl and yell dismally.

The screams reached the ears of natives in the *kraals* all over the district, and a great stream of Zulus came running to the side of the chief, each man doing his best to howl. By dawn there were fully 60,000 men there, all wailing. Scores of oxen were sacrificed, but Chaka ordered that nobody was to eat or drink; and gradually hundreds sank to the ground exhausted. These Chaka killed off first, adding to them all the people who were not howling loud enough to suit his fancy.

During the morning Chaka worked the multitude up into a perfect frenzy, and a general slaughter began, 7000 victims being killed before the middle of the afternoon.

Still nobody was allowed to eat or drink, and the melancholy wailing was kept up until ten o'clock on the following morning by those who valued their lives.

On the third day following the death of Chaka's mother a hole was dug near the spot where she expired, and ten women were buried alive with her, the earth being thrown on the top of them until they were suffocated.

When Mr. Fynn visited the great Zulu king he found him sitting under a tree decorating himself. Round him were about a couple of hundred of his subjects, a servant standing at his side holding a shield as a sunshade for the monarch.

Round his forehead Chaka wore a turban of otter skin, and in it a crane's feather, quite two feet long, standing straight up. Ear-rings of dried sugar-cane, carved round the edge, and an inch in diameter, were let into the lobes of his ears, which had been cut to admit them. From shoulder to shoulder he wore bunches of the skins of monkeys and genets, which hung half-way down his body. Round his head were a dozen bunches of red feathers, tied to thorns which were stuck in the hair. On his arms he wore white ox-tails, cut down the middle to allow the fur to enircle his arms.

He had a petticoat, somewhat resembling a Scottish plaid, tied round his waist. This garment was made of skins, with small tassels hanging round the top; and there were white ox-tails about his legs and dangling round his ankles.

The great Zulu chief's power was at its height in 1824, when a little party of Britishers landed at the place now known as Durban, pitched a camp, and endeavoured to negotiate with Chaka for permission to settle and trade there. Some of the scattered tribesmen started to collect round the British camp in search of food, and these natives formed the nucleus of the repopulation of Natal by the native tribes. Chaka refused to grant the Englishmen an interview, although presents were sent to him by the Cape Government. These negotiations were still in progress when Chaka's extraordinary career came to an abrupt end.

His brother Dingaan, tired of waiting for authority, assassinated him while he was talking to some of his headmen near the Umvoti River. Full of treachery, Dingaan sent for the British settlers, but they refused to go, whereupon the new chief sent an army down to exterminate them. Having been warned, the settlers left hurriedly for the south, taking with them their natives. There was some fighting, but the Englishmen got across the Umzimkulu River, and from that position concluded their negotiations with Dingaan, who, in 1831, appointed Mr. Fynn as "The Great Chief of Natal Kafirs."

Not long after this, some of the Dutch inhabitants of the Cape set out to explore Natal, and finding that Dingaan had already made certain terms with the Englishmen established there, endeavoured to persuade the chief to give them facilities for settling. Dingaan politely made pleasing promises, stipulating only that the Boers should recover for him certain cattle which had been stolen. The Boers pluckily attacked the thief, recovered 700 head of cattle and 60 horses, and took them to Dingaan—who rewarded them by killing every man of the party. The chief, not content with this act of treachery, sent an *impi* to kill every white man in Natal.

One party of Dutch immigrants was exterminated, but the rest of the Boers collected, formed fortifications with their wagons, and successfully withstood the attack of an enormous force of Zulus. The Boers lost about 700 lives in the massacres. Having added fresh immigrants to their ranks, the Dutchmen, burning for revenge, persuaded the English settlers to join in a punitive expedition, and this led to terrible bloodshed. The English, who had about a thousand armed native followers, crossed the Tugela River near the coast and walked into an ambuscade; and the entire party were killed. The Dutch, taking a different route, advanced on Dingaan, but were also trapped; and very few of them escaped. Finally the victorious Zulus swept down the coast again, killing and destroying everything they could find, but fortunately some of the settlers escaped on a ship.

Shortly afterwards the Boers again returned to Durban in larger numbers and beat off a fresh attack very successfully. Andries Pretorius, with 460 trained men and a few stragglers, attacked the Zulus near the Umhlatoos, the enemy being about 12,000 strong. In spite of the enormous difference in the two forces, the Zulus could not overcome the gallant little band, and Pretorius, at the exactly correct moment, made a master-stroke by sending a couple of hundred mounted men to attack the natives' flank. Utterly taken by surprise, the Zulus fell into a panic and bolted, leaving 3000 dead warriors behind. The Dutch settlers then laid out the towns of Durban and Pietermaritzburg, the latter place consisting of six houses in 1839.

In still another direction ill-luck awaited Dingaan. He had a younger brother whose nature was entirely unlike that of his own. This youth, Umpanda, was a lover of peace, and a number of Zulus who had grown weary of constant battle became his adherents. He got into communication with the English and Dutch settlers, their forces were joined in 1840, and 5000 men attacked Dingaan, whose army fled, Dingaan himself being assassinated while seeking shelter amongst some tribes which he had beaten at an earlier date. Umpanda was then proclaimed chief, and the Dutch took possession of a large tract of land which did not become the British colony of Natal until the Boers surrendered to a force sent out by the Cape Government. From that time onwards the population of Natal began to increase rapidly, the white settlers numbering over 17,000 in 1874—the year the Natal Mounted Police came into being.

Umpanda, meanwhile, continued his peaceful rule for thirty-two years, and gradually developed such a huge figure that when he desired to move from one place to another the front wheels of a wagon had to be removed and the royal body was slid into the vehicle. Umpanda's troubles, like those of many another South African chief, began when his sons were growing up. His first-born, Cetewayo, was hot-headed and restless; and he soon had a following of kindred spirits. In the year 1856 another of his sons, Umbulazi, gathered round him a considerable force, and a memorable battle was fought near the Tugela River between the armies of the rival sons, Cetewayo's men forming the attacking body.

Hundreds of Umbulazi's army fell at the point of the *assegai*, and a great many more were drowned in attempting to cross the flooded river. Incidentally Umbulazi and five of Umpanda's other sons were killed in the battle. Gradually Cetewayo gained influence, and in 1873 he was formally pronounced ruler in place of his too-massive parent when that worthy was gathered to his fathers. The ceremony was performed by an expedition sent by the Natal Government, and Cetewayo was given clearly to understand that he would find himself in trouble unless he exercised prudence, moderation, and justice in his authority.

A series of events was occurring at this time which demanded very serious attention. Firearms possessed a powerful fascination for the *kafirs*, and in order to prevent the natives from arming themselves an Act was passed making it illegal for anyone to possess a gun that was not stamped and registered at a magistrate's office. The natives working on diamond fields found that if they refused their labour unless they were paid with guns some unscrupulous employers would supply them with firearms. The news of this quickly spread amongst the *kafirs*, and numbers of them left Natal for the Vaal River, where they worked for a gun and then returned to Natal. One tribe in particular, the Amahlubi, led by a chief named Langalibalele, was known to be conspicuous in this movement, and the difficulties experienced in checking it during the year 1873 led to the formation of the Natal Mounted Police.

Langalibalele was called upon to appear before the resident magistrate, and subsequently before the Secretary for Native Affairs, but he ignored the messages and insulted the messengers. The Amahlubi at that time, after various movements, were settled near the sources of the Bushman's River, close under the Drakensberg. Land had been given to them there on condition that they gave protection against the

LANGALIBALELE.

thefts made by small colonies of bush-men who lurked in the caves of the mountains and were troublesome on occasions. Langalibalele was a somewhat haughty chief who was believed by the *kafirs* to control the weather. On more than one occasion Cetewayo has asked for his services when rain was required.

As Langalibalele did not display the slightest intention of complying with the orders sent to him, a formidable force, which included 5000 armed natives, set out to fetch him, but the wily chief was forewarned, and disappeared with a small party over the Bushman's River pass of the Drakensberg, leaving instructions that the cattle were to follow in charge of the young men. As he had been previously sending messages to Molapo, a Basuto chief, it was inferred that his object was to hand the cattle over to the Basutos for safety. A party of volunteers from the attacking army hastened to stop the Bushman's River pass, and found all the cattle being driven by armed men. The Amahlubi secreted themselves behind the rocks and opened a steady fire on the volunteers, who were compelled to retire after losing several men. The flight with the cattle was resumed, the natives rejoining Langalibalele in Basutoland, where the chief was soon after captured, together with his five sons, his brother, and three of his head men.

A trial was conducted according to native law, the charges being high treason and rebellion, and severe sentences were passed. Although it was held that Langalibalele had earned the penalty of death he was banished for life, his property being confiscated. One of his sons, for having fired on the representatives of the Government, was transported for five years, while six other sons and more than 200 of the tribe were imprisoned with hard labour for various terms ranging from two to twenty years.

Langalibalele and one of his sons were to have spent the period of their sentence on Robben Island, off Cape Town, but a powerful appeal against the sentence on the chief was made by the Bishop of Natal, largely on the ground that he was not a conspirator and had merely been the victim of the turbulent spirit of his young men who had a harmless and boyish desire to possess a gun. The appeal eventually came before the Secretary of State for the Colonies, and as it was decided that there was some little doubt on certain matters the deposed chief was not sent to Robben Island, but was banished from Natal and placed under police surveillance.

CHAPTER 2

The Founding of the Corps

In its earliest days the existence of the Natal Mounted Police was so precarious that nobody was absolutely certain that it actually did, or would, continue to exist. The Langalibalele Rebellion had clearly demonstrated the urgent necessity for a semi-military police force, for the loss of life that took place at the Bushman's Pass would probably have been obviated had the Government had a trained, mobile force ready to march into the Puniti Location when the first signs of trouble became visible. It was announced by the Colonial Treasurer, in the Legislative Council of Natal, that the Government had decided to organize a fully equipped and disciplined force in order to check insubordination in its earliest stages. The force could never be a police force in the English sense of the word, as the conditions were, and still are, so utterly dissimilar to those in a fully civilized place. In 1873 there were nearly half a million blacks and fully 30,000 Indians spread over a vast area of mountainous country, some parts of which were almost inaccessible.

It was fortunate for the future history of the force that General (then Major) Dartnell, a fine, hard soldier and an Indian Mutiny veteran, was chosen to control its destinies. He was a fighting man, with real grit, and the determination of a bulldog.

He was leading the comparatively simple life, farming, near the Umvoti River, after a strenuous career in the army, when the call came for him to take charge of the Natal Mounted Police. He had entered as an ensign in the 86th Regiment in 1855, became Lieutenant the following year, Captain in 1859, and Brevet Major in 1865. He was appointed to the 2nd Battalion 16th Regiment in 1859, and exchanged to the 27th Regiment three years later, retiring by sale of commission ten years afterwards.

While with the 86th Regiment he served with the Central Indian Field Force, under Sir Hugh Rose (afterwards Lord Strathnairn), during the Indian Mutiny in 1857-8, and was present at the storm and capture of Chandaree.

The stern old warrior was always disinclined to speak of his own achievements, but probably the most exciting moment in his life was when as a subaltern and a mere boy he led the only escalade attack on the fortress of Jhansi, and escaped almost miraculously with his life.

At the assault on this fortress he was with the left escalade attack, under Major Stuart, of the 86th Regiment, consisting of the light companies of the 86th and 25th Bombay Native Infantry, and a few sappers carrying four escalading ladders.

Upon arrival under the walls, which were 30 feet high, the Engineers tried to place the ladders in position, but they were continually thrown down again and otherwise damaged by big stones and logs of wood thrown from the walls.

At last one was placed, and up it young Dartnell at once rushed and dropped from the top of the wall into a bastion, alighting in the midst of a crowd of astonished rebels.

These men hacked at him with their *tulwars* (native swords), whilst he defended himself as best he could with his sword for a few moments, but was soon overpowered and fell to the ground. Lieutenant Fowler, and other officers following closely after him, shot some of his assailants, and the rest bolted. There had been too many of them, and they had been in each other's way, otherwise they would undoubtedly have killed the brave young subaltern.

He received five wounds, four of them sword cuts, one of the latter nearly severing his left hand. The fifth wound was from a bullet from a match-lock, which luckily struck the plate of his sword-belt. The latter deflected it and it only grazed his body.

Today he bears deep scars showing how savage the attack upon him was. For his gallantry he was recommended by Major Stuart for the treasured V.C. The medal was not awarded, but Dartnell was promoted to an unattached company upon the recommendation of Sir Hugh Rose.

The wounded man was invalided home for six months, and he left Bombay by the overland route for England. At the expiration of five months he applied for an extension of leave, as he heard the regiment was on the march down to Bombay to embark for home. The leave was refused, however, because he had been appointed adjutant, so he returned again to Bombay, overland, and was there only three days when he embarked for England with the headquarters of the regiment, and was four months on the voyage home.

For his services he received the Mutiny medal, a Captaincy, and Brevet Majority. In the Bhotan Expedition, in 1865, he served as A.D.C. to Major-General Sir Henry Tombs, and was present at the capture of Dewanjeri, for which he received the medal with clasp.

This, then, was the record of the man who was appointed to make and drill, out of the best material he could find, an efficient force of semi-military police; and in the course of years he found himself at the head of as fine a body of men as anyone could wish to command. At first he held his new post in conjunction with that of Commandant of Volunteers, receiving £150 a year for the latter work, this salary including his travelling expenses.

Unfortunately the authorities, after deciding to establish the new force, and putting an officer at its head, seemed to think that was all that was necessary. Even a model Commandant cannot carry on a corps of mounted regulars without money and horses, and the authorities paid a painful disregard to such material points.

At first Major Dartnell was allowed to go to King William's Town in Cape Colony and study the methods of the Frontier Police there, so that he could model his own corps on somewhat similar lines. The Frontier Police had then been established many years, and had done good work. He returned in about a month, and drew up his scheme for developing the new force. In the first instance, he had been authorized to raise a corps of 50 Europeans and 150 natives, and the first man enrolled joined on the 12th March 1874.

These were indeed days of strenuous endeavour for the mutiny veteran. For many years he was his own paymaster, quartermaster, and adjutant, the first officers appointed being G. Mansel and F. A. Campbell as sub-inspectors, with W. Stean, late of the Cape Mounted Rifles, as sergeant-major. Having established a mounted police force, the Government would not sanction the purchase of horses for the men lest the animals should die of horse-sickness! Few men other than the iron-willed Major would have fought on and eventually won in such baffling circumstances. He has since stated that the task in front of him was so heartbreaking that on more than one occasion he was on the point of sending in his resignation.

When the uniform was at last procured, or rather a section of it, it was hideous, no suitable material for clothing being obtainable then in the colony. It consisted of a dark brown corduroy tunic and breeches, the substance being the same as that which is used for railway porters' clothing in out-of-the-way places in England. The odour of it alone was enough to spread discontent amongst the thin line of recruits. To make matters worse, the uniforms were all ready-made, a ship's sailmaker being employed as tailor. His simple method of adjusting the uniform to the men was to pull it in until it was skin-tight. The head-dress, also, was a wonderful construction of leather, with a peak, a white cover falling from the back. This grotesque uniform resulted in the corps being dubbed "The Snuffs"; but at a later date it was changed to a dark grey woollen cord with white helmet—a neat and serviceable uniform.

The major's official letter-book, giving copies of all the forceful missives which he had to send to the Colonial Secretary during the first year of the corps' existence, had lain buried away and forgotten until a few months ago. These communications alone show the stern fight the commandant had to keep things going in any sort of fashion. A fortnight after the first man had been enlisted at Pietermaritzburg, at which the "headquarters" were stationed, the major wrote in somewhat bitter terms to the Colonial Secretary concerning recruits. He had already written recommending that the European portion of the force should be raised from 50 to 150 or 200 men, and that an officer should be sent at once to England to enlist men and to order and send out as soon as possible the arms, clothing, and appointments required by the corps, as they could not possibly be obtained in the colony. Notices had appeared offering candidates for the force pay at the rate of 5s. 6d. per day—a wage which would bring a scornful smile to the face of a *kafir* who can put a wagon on the road. An ordinary mechanic could then earn more than that without the risk of life involved by being in the corps, and a steady skilled *kafir* labourer would have expected as much.

In his letter to the Colonial Secretary Major Dartnell added:

In answer to these notices about twenty men have applied personally and by letter, but several were ineligible, so that up to the present time I have only enlisted twelve men.

It was, I think, imagined that a sufficient number of recruits could easily be procured in the colony, and of a better stamp than could be enlisted in England, but I doubt if such will be found to be the case. The men who have applied to me, and who have now been enlisted, are:

(1) Young men of respectable families in England who have only been in the colony a short time, have spent the little money they brought out with them, and are unaccustomed or unable to turn their hands to any laborious occupation, so join the police merely for the sake of a temporary living and not with any desire of remaining in the service.

(2) Colonial born men who have led an unsettled life for years, such as transport riding, varied by occasional working at some trade, but never sticking to anything long.

(3) Ex-soldiers and ex-sailors and loafers of divers sorts. All these are addicted to drink more or less, but they are the only men who offer themselves, and I do not think any better class is likely to be procured in the colony, for the rate of pay offered is too low, and the chances of promotion are too uncertain in a small force to induce well-to-do men to join the service.

Unless an influx of men takes place from the diamond or gold fields I doubt if 50 recruits will be obtained in the colony within the next six months, so I still think it advisable that an officer should proceed to England at once to recruit men there, if the police force is to be increased; but if the colony cannot afford it, or if the Legislative Council will not vote sufficient funds to support a force of 150 or 200 men, then the sooner the few already enlisted are dismissed and the whole scheme knocked on the head, the better; for a force of 50 Europeans cannot possibly do the work expected, *i.e.* 'Patrol the whole colony, etc.'; and there is nothing useful in the country having to pay for an inefficient force.

The commanding officer further pointed out that he was quite in the dark also as to what was to be done with the native section of the force in the matter of arming and drilling. He continued:

I think they should be armed with a rifle of some sort; for if they be only armed with assegais, and another outbreak takes place like the late Langalibalele affair, or they are employed to hunt men out of broken ground or bush, they will certainly refuse to go in against men armed with guns, and will then have to be armed in a hurry with a weapon about which they know nothing. I do not think there would be the slightest danger in arming and drilling 100 or 150 natives if they be enlisted for three years or more.

I dare say it will be said that I am losing sight of a police force and wish to establish a defence force for the colony, but I have no such wish (though the two must be combined to a certain extent). All I desire is to see a properly organized and sufficiently numerous body of police formed so that they can carry out their proper duties of patrolling the colony, executing warrants, etc., and also to have sufficient men in hand to nip any outbreak in the bud, or make a stand until the volunteers could be called out.

It seems to me absurd to enlist men unless I have authority to mount, equip, and render them efficient.

At this period the "barracks" consisted of a few tents at the back of Fort Napier, Pietermaritzburg, and the early recruits were of that peculiar type known in South Africa as "hard cases." The colonial "hard case" must be met to be understood. They were notorious in their way, but were hard workers and, on pay day, hard drinkers. Hardships they were never without, according to their own story. The fashionable drink was "square face" taken in all its neat glory, often with maddening effect. But though the trooper police of those days were occasionally a little wild, they never brought the corps into disrepute. They had at their head a strict disciplinarian who had very distinct ideas on the subject of his men's behaviour, and he enforced his ideas in a very pointed fashion.

He had a peculiarly commanding personality, and one which instantly gave men a sense of confidence in him. By some he was spoken of as a martinet, but everybody loved him in a soldierly fashion. Old troopers who served under him long ago, when blood stained the slopes of Africa red, have told the writer, with a touch of grimness in their eyes and voice, that had he given the word they would cheerfully have "followed him to Hades."

There was no nonsense, either, about Sergeant-Major Stean, upon whose shoulders fell the unenviable task of training the wild rankers. He made his reputation in the Cape Mounted Rifles, and improved upon it when he discovered the sort of material he had put before him in Natal to turn into soldiers. Always popular—your "hard case" has neither respect nor obedience for the namby-pamby drill instructor— he is still spoken of as the best man the corps ever had for putting recruits through their paces.

The sergeant-major was universally known as "Puffy." He was a soldier from the tip of his pith helmet to the soles of his boots, and he knew to a nicety exactly when to pour forth a stream of invective when the drill grew ragged. A man of tireless energy, he expected his men to keep up to his own pitch, and his methods of training were severe. No recruit ever born had such a thick skin that he did not feel the bitterness of the sting when "Puffy" chose to bestow his choicest expletives on him.

One man who "went through it" under "Puffy" at the riding-school in 1879 has put on record an example of the remarks the sergeant-major used to let drop while drilling his men. They ran like this:

Prepare to mount. By numbers—One—two—there's a man putting his wrong foot into—he's got the right one now. Mount. Keep your heels well down, and your toes turned in. Don't look at me, my man; do as I tell you, not as I do. Heels well down, Ilberry—you look like a ballet girl. Squad! March. Left hand in a line with your confounded elbow, Jenkins. Look at him! Look at him! You're the man who told me you'd hunted with the Oakleighs, are you? Sit up—you look more like a monkey on a piece of crockery than anything I've ever seen. When I give the word to trot, break into a gentle trot. Squad! Trot.
Now, idiots! Let go those lifebuoys, Ilberry. Look at him hugging that horse round the neck. That's a horse, Ilberry, not a girl. I'll have you off if you ride like that. You're off, are you? Halt. Get up again. That's right. You're a beauty. Get into the ranks. March. Trot. Sit up in your saddle, Ilberry. You're slipping under the horse's belly—he might hurt you if you stop there. What a crew! There's Jenkins again. Nearly off. Sit up straight in your saddle, Simpson. It's 'here's my head and my boots are coming' with you—sit upright, man. I saw you in the Park on Saturday, on foot, with Ada. You'll never be able to take her out for a ride if you don't learn to ride better than that. Lord, there's Ilberry off again—and Jenkins as well—Halt!

Then "Puffy" really would begin to talk.

He was promoted to the rank of adjutant later, but that removed him from the sphere in which he shone, and the later recruits never knew what it was to hear the biting sarcasm that could fall from his lips on parade. He spent the last year or two of his service keeping a letter register, which became a sort of hobby, and finally he retired to Bristol on pension.

When the commandant received a brief note from the Colonial Secretary stating that the purchase of horses was to be deferred until the sickly season was over, and therefore stables would not be necessary "for the present," he wrote pointing out that the sickly season was practically over, and continued:

> I applied for a stable because I considered Maritzburg a more or less unhealthy place for unstabled horses at all seasons of the year; and as the men have to buy their own horses out of their pay I think it hardly fair that they should be obliged to run unnecessary risks. But if stables are not to be allowed at all it would be better to let me know at once, and allow me to purchase horses as required, for unless I am soon allowed to get the horses, teach the men to ride, and instruct them in mounted drill, I should never have been told to start recruiting, as it is only paying men for nothing keeping them three or four months over drill when it might be done in a much shorter time.

A more anomalous position than that then occupied by the commandant could not easily be imagined. It was almost like a comic opera regiment, though the chief saw little humour in it. Not only was he without barracks, uniforms, horses, and stables after the recruits had been signed on, but he even had no firearms. At the end of March he wrote:

> The only arms I have been able to get for the force are six Snider carbines which have been handed over to me by the Volunteer Department. The same department has in store about twenty Terry rifles (which are unserviceable) and a lot of muskets and short Enfield rifles, none of which will do for the police force.

In spite of the miserable conditions that faced the recruits, and the poor rate of pay, considering what was expected of them when they did get to work, fresh arrivals were slowly added to the ranks of Europeans, the total at the end of April reaching the noble proportions of twenty-four; but the commandant was still having a battle royal with the Colonial Secretary on the subject of the provision of horses or stables or both. He stuck to his guns valiantly, urging first one suggestion and then another with as little effect as though he had been talking to the four winds of Heaven.

At the end of April he wrote to the Secretary for Native Affairs urging him to secure fifty *kafirs* for the force, stipulating that they should be young, active fellows, willing to enlist for three years. Their pay was to be fifteen shillings a month, and in addition they were to have their food (*mealie* meal, and meat once a week), one suit of clothes a year, and one blanket and one greatcoat a year. Six non-commissioned officers were to be appointed from amongst these men, namely, three corporals and three sergeants, who were to be paid at the rate of 17s. and 22s. a month each respectively. He pointed out that if men speaking English or Dutch could be selected that would be an advantage.

Affairs in Weenen County were still very unsettled, following on the passage-at-arms with Langalibalele, and the Commandant, still leaving no stone unturned to get some sort of equipment for his men, saw that there would be trouble unless the district were patrolled, and he was curtly told that the matter must stand over.

At length a dozen undersized and aged animals arrived at the "barracks," one of them immediately being pronounced as utterly hopeless. These, it must be remembered, were to be the unhappy beasts that had to carry the raw troopers over wild country, and on their decrepit legs the lives of the soldiers would depend in case of emergency. The men were not going out on pleasure, but with the prospect of having to fight a horde of wild, ruthless *kafirs*, who were past-masters in the act of arranging an ambush. Added to this, the commandant had the unpleasant knowledge that the men would have to pay for the animals out of their wages, but these were the only horses forthcoming, so he offered to keep them until the danger of horse-sickness was over, after which he would take over such of them as could be used for the police work; and this course was adopted. Three of the animals died in the interval.

The first useful work done by the force began on the 6th of May 1874 when a detachment of sixteen men left Maritzburg on their sorry steeds to do or die in the Weenen County. They were under Sub-Inspector Mansel, who long afterwards became commandant of the corps. Excepting their leader and Private Corbett, all these pioneers have since died. The recently discovered official record states that the little band consisted of Corporal Ellis, Lance-Corporal Jackson, and Privates Babington, Corbett, Crallan, Johnson, Maddock, Saulez, Smith, Sullivan, Thompson, Vear, White, Faddy, Abbott, and Hughes.

The officer in charge was given careful instructions not to over-fatigue either men or horses, for both were green at the work. As the crow flies they had fifty-five miles to cover before they reached Est-

34

court, and all the roads were hilly and winding. The commandant was compelled by circumstances to give the following order to the officer in command:

You will make the best arrangements you can for provisioning the men and horses on the road, but you must clearly understand and explain to the troopers that the Government will not bear any portion of the expenses incurred on this account.

The men were armed with the antediluvian muzzle-loading weapon known as the Terry rifle, but these, it was understood, were to be exchanged, as soon as they reached Estcourt, for a number of Westley-Richards carbines which had been served out some time previously to a small Basuto force living on the frontier. The superintendent of the Weenen County was advised by the commandant, in view of the men being still imperfectly drilled, to see that they were not broken up into small parties "when they would be under no supervision and soon lose the few habits of discipline they had already acquired."

On the arrival of the small force the men were placed on patrol, five natives accompanying them. Although the unrest amongst the *kafirs* continued for some time, there appears to be no record of any actual fighting, although that, perhaps, was fortunate, considering the raw condition of the men and their inadequate equipment. In June they were stationed in a vacated house on the farm Ellestby, and were ordered to patrol along the valley of the Ingesuti up to the heights of the forest between the Ingesuti and Table Mountain towards Cathkin Peak, and to prevent any native from going through the locations without a pass.

The commandant protested that this task was too much for sixteen men and five natives to undertake, but a score or so of Zulus were added to the force, and the police patrolled the district named, the object being to prevent any of Langalibalele's men returning to Natal and settling in the location.

To add to the discomforts of the troopers the weather was terrible. The Drakensberg was perpetually covered with snow, and the men suffered very badly from exposure, as there were no tents then. Those whose duty kept them away from their temporary headquarters had to make the best shelter they could under a tree and a blanket.

"The men who are at present serving in the force," writes Col. W. J. Clarke, who joined in 1878, and was in close association with many of the pioneers for years:

. . . . . will scarcely realize the discomfort of *veldt* life which was experienced in the early days. Even when I joined, such luxuries as waterproof sheets, waterproof coats, pack-horses, etc., were unknown. We received no travelling allowances, had no kit-bags or kit-boxes, and everything we possessed in the way of kit had to be carried in saddle-bags on our horses. *Mufti* was almost unknown, and I believe that in a detachment of seventy-one men, with which I served at Estcourt, we had not one suit of plain clothes among us. Our boxes were left in Pietermaritzburg at our own risk, and most of these were stored at a confectioner's shop in Church Street. So opposed to the wearing of mufti was the sergeant-major that we made all haste to dispose of such articles of attire as we possessed. For six and a half years I never wore any dress but uniform.

In 1874 the patrol tent was carried in two portions, which buttoned together along the top, each man carrying half a tent, and a tent pole lashed to his carbine.

The first pack-horse purchased for the force was known by the name of 'Cracker,' and he spent many years of his life at headquarters, being employed chiefly as a punishment mount for obstinate recruits. Many of us who rather fancied ourselves as horsemen were considerably taken down when the sergeant-major gave us a dose of 'circle' at the trot, with the stirrups crossed, on this horribly rough animal. We used to take the beast out of the stable at night and tie him up to a tree in the square in the hope that he would contract horse-sickness, but he only thrived on an outdoor life. A man named Haynes tried to shoot the animal one day at mounted pistol practice, but missed his mark and was unseated owing to the animal shying. Any man who gave his horse a sore back was mounted on 'Cracker,' so it is easy to imagine how we nursed our steeds.

Perhaps the officers were not aware of all our difficulties and discomforts. As far as I can judge, there is no comparison between the conditions of service then and now.

Towards the end of May the Commandant at last secured barracks in Pietermaritzburg for his growing corps. He was able to rent a house in Church Street at £5, 10s. a month for them, and the strength of the force stood at thirty-eight. The barracks were very primitive. One room was orderly room and pay office, one room was a volunteer office, one a quartermaster's store, and one was occupied by the commandant. This was the home of the police for seventeen years.

It was a rough life for the men when they were at headquarters. Most of them had to sleep in tents in which there were bed-boards—without mattresses. For years the men all had to do their own fatigues, and no non-commissioned officer below the rank of sergeant (in those days they had corporals and lance-sergeants) was allowed a native servant.

Messing was one huge picnic prepared by very amateur cooks. No native servant was allowed in the kitchen, and the mess-room was like a bear-garden, the food being badly prepared. One of the oldest members of the corps, recalling this rough-and-ready way of living, writes:

> At one time we had a system of private messing, each man, or group of men, being allowed to make any arrangement about food. The messing was so bad when I reached Estcourt that I went into a private mess with a companion. He catered and I cooked. We clubbed our money on payday, and he went down to the village to order supplies, while I fixed up a paraffin tin as a cooking stove and laid in a stock of firewood.
>
> My mess chum was brought back by a picket with a haversack containing two bottles of beer—my month's rations—and as we could get no credit we spent the rest of the month living on doves and *mealie* meal, the *mealies* being purchased as 'extra forage' and ground by the cook (myself), who also had to shoot the doves.
>
> I borrowed a confiscated rifle from the magistrate's court, took the powder out of my cartridges, and stalked doves that came to the thorn trees near the fort. Ammunition was so scarce that I never fired at anything on the wing. At a later date private messing was tried at Fort Pine, and proved an utter failure. For seven months I endured it, and can safely say that I never had a satisfactory meal during the whole of that time.

Further trouble occurred at Estcourt, a *kafir* attempting to stab Mr. Mellersh, the resident magistrate, and a further force of fifteen police had to be sent, to mount guard. There was great difficulty in getting uniforms for them, and they only had an old Terry rifle each besides six revolvers between them. These were all the revolvers the commandant could procure in the colony. By the end of June there were forty-five troopers in the force, a number of men having been dismissed for misconduct. They were nearly all on patrol in Weenen County, and they were all perpetually hard up owing to the very heavy expenses which they had to incur there, and which they had to defray out of their slender pay. Hay, for instance, could not be got under £5 a ton.

On the 25th July 1874, it being considered that there was no immediate danger of unrest amongst the natives, the bulk of the men at Estcourt were ordered down to headquarters.

There was a *kafir* chief named Umgwapuni in Alfred County who had obstinately refused for two years to "move on" with his wives and followers when ordered to do so. As soon as the newly raised force arrived from Estcourt it was sent with Mr. John Shepstone, Acting-Secretary for Native Affairs, to deal with the chief. They trekked to the south *via* Stoney Hill, reaching Murchison, where Umgwapuni was ordered to appear before Mr. Shepstone. He declined absolutely to have anything to do with that gentleman, whereupon the police, keenly anxious for the "fun." to start, were sent to persuade him. Umgwapuni, alarmed by this show of strength, left his kraal hurriedly, and his removal was effected without any further difficulty.

The first recorded instances of cattle-stealing reported to the police occurred during August of that year, near Pietermaritzburg. Two men chased one thief to Umvoti and captured him. The second thief, a Hottentot, was followed to Kokstadt and caught. Both were imprisoned.

Nothing particularly exciting happened for some weeks, and an attempt to form a police camp at Harding—then a desolate, out-of-the-world place—proved impossible. Huts were erected there, but sufficient food for twenty-five men and horses could not be found, and the detachment was withdrawn to Pietermaritzburg .

There is splendid testimony to the fact that the police did not work in a slipshod way in those days, for those mud huts have stood the storms and heat of all these years, and are as sound today, (at time of first publication), as they ever were.

Up to this time there had been a certain amount of friction between the police and the press. Accusations had been made from time to time imputing serious misconduct to the force. A doubtless well-meaning, but wrongly-informed, missionary did much to foster the ill-feeling. During the march into Alfred County the greatest difficulty was experienced in finding food for the troopers in a country where at that time stores were unknown. When the force got south of Umzinto meat could only be obtained from the natives. A large figure was asked for an ox and the impoverished troopers could not, and very rightly would not, pay the man's price. Without taking the trouble to inquire into the circumstances the missionary rushed into print as soon as he heard of the dispute, accusing the troop of "commandeering supplies."

An official inquiry followed, and the matter came before the Legislative Assembly, when the Acting-Colonial Secretary stated that the charges were unfounded.

"This perpetual blackening of the characters of the men," he said, "is not only unjust to them but most injurious to the force in other ways. They become disheartened and reckless, and serious injury to the public service is the result. Good men who would otherwise join are deterred from doing so. They are nothing but a body of colonists enrolled for the protection of their fellow-colonists, and I think it the duty of every one to uphold them in the proper discharge of their task. Do not let wrong be done to what is as precious to the members of this force as to ourselves—their good name, their character, and their honour."

This apparently went home to the newspapers. A few days afterwards the *Times of Natal* contained an article which spoke in glowing terms of the value of the force.

In justice to the missionary it should be explained that after he discovered his errors he apologized in writing for making misstatements, though this did not remove the stigma that stuck to the corps for a long time afterwards. One of his inaccuracies, scattered broadcast, was to the effect that in commandeering food the men shot two goats belonging to natives. They did shoot two goats, but not until after they had paid for them, and were told that they would never catch the animals unless they used their guns.

It was still impossible for the commandant to obtain necessary equipment, although he bullied the authorities politely daily on behalf of his men. All his heroic efforts were practically ignored, and he grew weary of righting for the very existence of his corps without effect; so at last he carried out a frequently repeated threat and tendered his resignation. This occasioned alarm, even amongst the newspapers which had done most to vilify the corps. They now said they had always entertained the highest opinion of his fitness for the important position he held, and added that it was just because he was capable and declined to be perpetually hum-bugged that he had resigned from a position which he could not hold with credit to himself or benefit to the colony.

Even those who had spoken ill of the corps were bound at this juncture to admit the wonderful grit and determination of the man who had made the force, though only those who were working with him, such as "Puffy" Stean, ever knew what a fine fight he made against heavy odds.

"Major Dartnell stands out," said the *Natal Witness*, "as an example worthy of imitation by many of our officials, but we are afraid it will be a long time before we see one of them have the manliness to follow a similar course. We hope the day is not far distant when his services will be secured by a Government better able to appreciate them."

Fortunately for the Government, however, the services of the Commandant were appreciated, and on a promise being made by the authorities that his efforts for the improvement of the force under his control would not be frustrated, he withdrew his resignation.

Here is an instance of the curious relations that existed between the police and public, who had not at this time grown to appreciate the force properly. The news reached Sub-Inspector Campbell that a number of sheep had been stolen from a farmer. He immediately sent two men to the farm to make inquiries and recover the animals if possible, but to their astonishment the man told them it was no good their trying to discover anything about it from him, as he would tell them nothing. With this uncivil reply on his lips the farmer turned his back on the police officers, whose only course left was to retire gracefully and wonder what they were paid for.

Prisoners had a playful habit of escaping from gaol at Pietermaritzburg occasionally, and two men, one of whom was a soldier, gave the police a stern chase. On breaking away from the gaol one of them, a desperate character, stole a revolver, and the pair lost no time in getting well into the country. It was several days before the police heard which direction they had taken, and then Sub-Inspector Mansel, together with a trooper, rode out on their track. A long way from headquarters they came to the place where the men had left the main road, and here the pursuers were in difficulties for a time.

At last they picked up the convicts' spoor on a *kafir* track. Following this for fifteen miles they came to a lonely part of the country, and there was danger at every step, for it was known that the men were armed. After a long and trying search they came upon the pair in a swamp. One of them held out a revolver, but the police were ready with their weapons, and the convicts were called upon to surrender or be shot. Seeing that the odds were against them the fugitives surrendered sulkily and were taken back to Pietermaritzburg.

CHAPTER 3

The Early Days

There being some dread, on the part of the colonists, at the idea of employing too many armed and disciplined natives—the Hottentots in the old Cape Mounted Rifles had mutinied in Cape Colony some years before—it was decided to reduce the number of blacks in the Natal Police from 150 to 50. At the same time the full strength of the Europeans in the force was raised to 115. The Defence Committee had recommended that the Europeans should number 150, but on financial grounds this suggestion was not adopted. Although powers were granted to bring the strength up to 115, the actual number of men enrolled did not come to anything like that figure for a very long time.

Suitable members of the corps could not be got at the price. At the close of 1874 the strength all told was 45, and it only reached 72 by the end of 1875. Even the men who offered their services and were chosen could not be relied upon to remain with the force. A few enlisted each month, but there were constant desertions, and nearly every month one or two were dismissed for misconduct, or as being physically unfit. Several members died or were killed during the first eighteen months of the force's history.

Gun-running had at this time become a profitable pastime, and early in 1875 Sub-Inspector Campbell with three troopers, had a long chase after a man who left Greytown with a wagon supposed to contain firearms. The wagon had gone three days before the police heard of the affair, but they caught it up near the Buffalo River. There was some delay, owing to the difficulty of getting a search-warrant, and when the police pounced on the wagon it was empty. Afterwards it was discovered that the man had had fifty guns in his cart, but while the police were being detained for the warrant he heard that they were after him and buried the weapons about half an hour before the search was made.

In several other instances the police made important captures of guns and ammunition which would otherwise have been sold to the natives.

Chasing cattle-raiders and going out on patrol constituted the chief work of the force at this time, many exciting days being spent in trekking after the thieves in wild, semi-civilized districts.

It was admitted in 1876 that the slowly growing body of Natal Police formed, to all intents and purposes, the finest and most valuable military force there was in the colony. Hard as nails with constant drill and no luxury in the way of food, they were beginning to come up to the standard which their stern commander had intended they should reach. The ramifications of the force were spreading also, for the camp at Harding was reoccupied, and there were other out-stations at Greytown and Estcourt, patrols keeping in constant touch with these places.

By August there were 94 men on the books, and of this number 62 officers, non-commissioned officers, and troopers were sent off on a general patrol over the east of the colony, which lasted about two months. Each man was mounted. No wagons were taken, as much rough country had to be traversed, and a dozen pack-ponies formed the only available transport.

Leaving Pietermaritzburg, the men passed over the Noodsberg to the coast, and then turned south to Durban, where a halt was made for three days.

In the region of Umzinto there was a chief named Umkodoya who, three years previously, had settled without permission, and who took not the slightest notice of all official messages to the effect that he had to go. The magistrate, tired of being defied, sent down to Durban for the services of the patrol. The men moved to Umzinto. Umkodoya promptly deserted his *kraals* and trekked for dear life when he saw the police. The detachment occupied the huts until all the chief's household goods had been removed and he had settled down with his tribe on the land allotted to them.

A week's drill was put in at Park Rennie, and from there the men moved down the coast to the Umzimkulu River, there being rumours of unrest amongst the natives in East Griqualand. Their services were not required, however, and the force marched up the banks of the river to Middle Ford, and thence to Pietermaritzburg.

The grand tour had proved useful in several ways, and from an educational point of view had been excellent for the men. But the *Natal Witness*, which for many years pursued a steady policy of nagging the police, ridiculed the patrol, said it had been purely ornamental, and declared it was absurd to teach policemen to act as a concentrated force. As a matter of fact, it was of vital importance that they should learn to act in a body, and so be able to crush an insurrection at its birth before it had time—even a few days—to assume such proportions that it would have been beyond the power of the slow-moving regular troops and half-disciplined volunteers to subdue.

The first police law was published in 1876, and it was the custom to read portions of this law to the men on every full-dress parade. Not until the following year were the regulations issued to the men in printed form.

When, towards the end of 1876, Sir Theophilus Shepstone was appointed Special Commissioner to annex the Transvaal, he applied for an escort of the Natal Police, and, permission having been given by the Governor, the following members of the corps were detailed for this special duty: Sergeant Abbott; Corporals Cushing, Faddy, Champ, McQueen; Trumpeter Knott; and Troopers Allison, Barclay, Bradshaw, Grissair, Jenkins, Holmes, Husband, Mathie, Myers, McDonald, Owen, Pleydell, Rafter, Scrivener, Sparks, W. H. Sharp, R. M. Sharp, Ward, and Whitwell. This force, under the command of Sub-Inspector Phillips, left Estcourt on 14th December 1876, and joined the Special Commissioner at Newcastle a week later.

The Transvaal was in a very unsettled state, there being strong opposition to the annexation. When the party reached the Transvaal border a number of Boers had an interview with the Special Commissioner. At Standerton, a week later, an address of welcome was read, and parties of mounted Boers fired volleys in honour of the occasion, there being another enthusiastic reception at Heidelberg.

President Burger's carriage went out to meet the Special Commissioner as he neared Pretoria; the horses were taken out of the vehicle, and the crowd drew him through the streets. A camp was pitched in the market square, and the Union Jack was hoisted. But in spite of these demonstrations of delight, the general body of Boers were bitterly opposed to the movement, and Sir Theophilus was perfectly aware that at any moment the scenes of enthusiasm might change into scenes of strife. There is no doubt that there would have been fighting had not the leaders of those who opposed the movement persuaded the men to trust to an appeal to the British Government. Two deputations were, in fact, sent to England, but they were unsuccessful.

Throughout the time the police were in Pretoria a disturbance was hourly expected. While a special meeting of the *Volksraad* was being held the police were confined to camp. Sentries with loaded arms were posted round the building in which the Special Commissioner was staying, and the police camp was removed into the enclosure for greater security. On the 12th April the proclamation annexing the Transvaal was read, and although everything passed off quietly the police had to be kept under arms all day. A week afterwards the Commissioner was sworn in as Governor. The 13th Regiment was hurried up from Pietermaritzburg, and on their arrival the police were released from further duty. They were played out of Pretoria by the band of the 13th Regiment and marched down country, reaching their barracks three weeks later.

In some quarters the opinion had been expressed that the little force which accompanied the Special Commissioner was inadequate, and that Sub-Inspector Phillips was not sufficiently experienced to take charge of a detachment for such an important duty. Before leaving Pretoria Sub-Inspector Phillips received the following letter:—

Government House, Pretoria,
28th May 1877.

The Administrator of the Government desires me, on the occasion of your returning to Natal with the detachment of the Natal Police under your command, to convey to you the high sense he entertains of the manner in which you have discharged the duties of the officer commanding his escort, and his thanks for the ready cheerfulness with which you have always complied with his wishes.

He requests you to express to the non-commissioned officers and men of the escort the pleasure it has given him to observe their orderly and praiseworthy conduct, which has won for them the good opinion of the inhabitants.

They have been engaged on a mission the results of which will permanently, and, His Excellency trusts, beneficially affect the history of South Africa; and to have been connected with such a mission will hereafter, he hopes, be a continually increasing source of gratification to them.

It is recorded that on the return journey all the horses stampeded excepting two, and the troopers had to do part of their trek on foot until they came upon the animals at Newcastle.

Fresh signs of insubordination were showing in Pakadi's location in Weenen County, and for two months a patrol kept the natives quiet, after which every available man of the corps was rushed off to Pretoria, as it was stated that an attack on the Special Commissioner was contemplated. The attack was not made, however, and the force returned to headquarters.

The first small station (as distinguished from troop stations) was opened in 1877 at Karkloof, a corporal and six men being posted there. It came to a sudden end not very long afterwards, a grass fire which swept over the whole district burning it to the ground; and the place was not rebuilt.

There was still the utmost difficulty in getting recruits for the corps in South Africa and, as it was considerably under strength, thirty men were sent out from England in 1877 and twenty-five the following year.

Some trouble was caused at this time by Smith Pommer, a Griqua who had the idea that he could run a rebellion with advantage to himself. Both the police and the 3rd Buffs were ordered down to the East Griqualand border in a hurry. The Buffs left Pietermaritzburg two and a half days before the police, who were encamped at the Noodsberg when the call arrived. By making forced marches they overtook the Buffs on the road near Ixopo. Smith Pommer was eventually shot on the slopes on the Ingeli Mountain.

Colonel Clarke, the present chief commissioner, joined the corps before the troops returned from the East Griqualand border, and his own story of his arrival at Pietermaritzburg shows that in those days they were not by any means armchair soldiers.

"I cannot remember a more miserable night," he writes:

. . . . . than the first I spent as a trooper. I was served out with two blankets, a bed-board and two trestles, a *pannikin*, and a combination knife and fork and spoon. Three of us were put in a bell tent with no mattress or pillow, and the cold—it was the end of April—was intense. Our private effects had not come from Durban, and did not arrive for several days, so we had no extra covering.

We had arrived in the city by the omnibus which ran between Durban and Maritzburg. Our dinner was handed out to us in a mess-room, lit by one solitary candle, and the appetising food, served on the bare table, consisted of tough steak and rice.

After dinner we strolled down to see what sort of a place we had struck in our travels, and I hardly need say that our youthful spirits sank to zero. Open *sluits* ran down the sides of the principal streets, and one or two faint oil-lamps only intensified the darkness. Every shop was closed, and not a soul was to be seen in the streets. We sat on the railings at the corner of Longmarket Street and Commercial Road, and cursed our folly in coming to such a place.

When the bulk of the men returned to headquarters, things became somewhat livelier, and the presence of Sergeant-Major Stean infused some animation into us. We were always at the riding-school in the Zwaartkop Valley, near the entrance to the Botanical Gardens, by dawn, and until 6 p.m. we could never find a moment's rest.

We had military saddles, with a heavy steel curb bit, a bridoon bit, steel stirrups, brass bosses on curb bit, crupper and breast-plate, white helmets with spike, chin chain and monogram of brass, black boots with metal buckle up the sides, and black cord uniform. All this superfluous kit had to be kept in a high state of polish, and by the time we had got through our physical drill, rifle exercises, goose step and stables, we felt we had earned a night's rest.

Riding-school meant a six-months' course, for we had riding on *numnahs*, single and double ride to go through, and then each man had a turn at drilling the squad. To make men feel contented with headquarters, the sergeant-major constantly held out threats to those who were awkward that he would send them to an out-station, until we dreaded the very thought of it.

The mention of white cotton gloves should bring a smile to the face of men who were serving in the corps in its infancy. The greatest offence a man could commit, according to the view of "Puffy" Stean, was to go out in the town on Saturdays or Sundays without these gloves. Many men were sent back to camp under arrest for having committed the awful crime of being abroad in bare hands. Men who had passed through the riding-school were permitted to take their horses out on Saturday, but it was a sorrowful moment for any man if he was seen rising in his stirrups at the trot.

At 9.30 p.m. every man had to fall in to answer his name, and the eagle eye of "Puffy" glanced along the ranks when "Right turn, dismiss" was given. The troopers under him were not angels, and occasionally he would order men to stand fast while the night parade was being dismissed, in order that he might put them through their turnings "by numbers"—to see whether they were sober or not.

CHAPTER 4

The Tragedy of Isandhlwana

The saddest day in the history of the Natal Police occurred in the Zulu War of 1879; and yet it was the day on which the corps acquitted itself with more glory than ever it has had the opportunity of doing before or since. That was at the last tragic stand at Isandhlwana.

The corps has been involved in more fighting than any other police force in the British Empire, and yet even in its records there is no instance of gallantry that approaches the way in which the men faced slaughter and fought to the finish under the shadow of that gloomy hill.

The great struggle of '79 was threatened for many months before it actually came about. Cetewayo, who had been the king of the Zulus since 1872, is said to have excelled in dissimulation, fraud, and cunning, which have been characteristic qualities of practically every Zulu ruler. His vast army was well organized, and it became a standing menace to both Natal and the Transvaal. After a barbarous murder of women a remonstrance was sent to the king, whose reply to the Natal Government was intensely insolent. The beginning of the end came when the High Commissioner, Sir Bartle Frere, sent an ultimatum to Cetewayo, couched in very drastic terms.

The surrender of certain Zulu offenders was asked for, the disbandment of certain Zulu regiments was insisted upon, and Cetewayo was informed that there must be a British Resident. This step was taken in December 1878, and the warning was uttered that if the requests were not complied with, forcible measures would be adopted.

Zulu regiments were moving about on unusual and special errands, several of them organizing royal hunts on a great scale in parts of the country where little game was to be expected and where the obvious object was to guard their border against attack by the white men. The

ISANDHLWANA HILL

hunters were said—according to a report by the High Commissioner to the Imperial Government—to have received orders to follow any game across the border, which was, according to Zulu custom, a recognized mode of provoking or declaring war.

Unusual bodies of armed natives were reported to be watching all drifts and roads leading to Zululand; these guards occasionally warned off Natal natives from entering Zulu territory, accompanying the warning with the intimation that orders had been given to kill all Natalians who trespassed across the border. Zulu subjects went hastily into Natal to reclaim cattle which they had sent out to graze, and very alarming rumours of coming trouble increased the excitement and agitation on both sides of the border.

The Government has done its best to avoid war by every means consistent with honour, and now feels bound to use the power with which it has been entrusted to secure peace and safety.

Thus wrote Sir Bartle Frere at this critical juncture. There are people today who say that the war was an unjust war, and that Cetewayo was little worse than an injured innocent; but the High Commissioner considered it necessary, in the interests of self-preservation and self-defence, that an army should enter Zululand.

There was much delight amongst the ranks of the Natal Police at Estcourt when the welcome news arrived that, with the exception of the Harding detachment, they were all to be placed under the orders of the military authorities, and had to go straight to the Zululand border. Their horses were in a shocking condition, for there was not a blade of grass within miles of the camp, and neither *mealies* nor forage could be procured excepting at exorbitant rates. Free forage, however, was sent by the authorities, and in a few days the animals were fit to trek. The men from Pietermaritzburg received orders to go to Helpmakaar, picking up the Greytown troopers *en route*, while the Estcourt men, consisting of 2 officers, and 64 non-commissioned officers and men, were ordered to join the rest of the force *via* Ladysmith and Dundee.

The Estcourt detachment had a couple of transport wagons allowed to them on condition that they provided their own drivers. There were many adventures with those wagons before the destination was reached, partly because the oxen were untrained; and so were the drivers—Corporal Jordan and a trooper.

The main body started off in a cheerful frame of mind and off-saddled at midday at the Blauw Krantz River at noon. Night came along, but the wagons did not, and then came the news that one of them was in difficulties in the Little Bushman's River. The men were getting painfully hungry, so some of them were sent back in the dark for food, and at midnight they all went on foot to Moord Spruit, where the wagon was found capsized in a *donga*,[1] its unhappy driver being unable to move it without assistance.

At Colenso there was no bridge over the Tugela River, and most of the day was spent in the tiresome task of pulling the wagons through the water. The oxen managed to cover eighteen miles next day, reaching Ladysmith late at night. The men had to bivouac on the market square. The next morning there was a grand hunt for fresh oxen, which were as wild as buck. The whole detachment went out on horseback and the new teams were driven into a *kraal* and lassoed.

The drivers found their troubles were only just beginning when the performance of in-spanning started. Spirited mules require quite careful handling before they become a harnessed team, but very fresh oxen are considerably worse; and the drivers found they had many advisers and few helpers. At last the detachment started, reaching Sunday's River in the afternoon, but the wagons were toiling along far behind, and did not catch the men up until after dark, in pouring rain which made the preparation of anything but a most primitive meal impossible. The night was a wretched one, but the sun shone the next morning, and the wagons were hauled across the water at Sunday's River Drift.

From there the roads were so heavy that only eight miles were covered that day; but, being full of enthusiasm, the men got up sports at Meran and had a great time. After this interlude they pushed on in the rain through the black soil in the thorns of the Washbank Valley. Transport was ever associated with heartbreaking difficulties, and many detachments have had similar experiences, but the police had a rough time before they reached Dundee. The rain came down in torrents, and the oxen wallowed in black, sticky mud. Time after time they came to a dead stop, the wagons sunk to the axles. There was very little occasion for jesting as the men dismounted, sinking up to their knees in the ooze and pulling and tugging at the unruly team. It was hard work, and there was plenty of it; and the only alternatives were to pull—or stop there in the wilderness of slime.

At the foot of the Biggarsberg every package had to be taken off

---

1. A hollow, washed out by heavy rain.

the vehicles and carried to the top of the hill. Hungry—for they had no food with them—sweating and tired, the men toiled up with the kits, ammunition, and bales of fodder, and then pulled the wagons to the summit of the hill.

Disappointment awaited them at Dundee, which in those days consisted of a solitary store. It had been expected that rations would be sent there for them by the authorities, but something had gone wrong, and there was nothing to eat at the store. One man named Hifferman went out with his carbine and returned triumphantly with two geese and a leg of a calf which he had found dead on the veldt. He tried to make everybody believe that the calf's leg was the leg of a buck that he had shot, but they refused to touch it, and the detachment of sixty odd men dined more or less sumptuously off two geese.

Breakfast was naturally out of the question next morning, when an early start was made. The men were ravenous by the time they reached Peter's farm, and they were served with boiled dumplings made entirely of flour and water, and so hard that the memory of them still remains with everybody who joined in the feast. Partly refreshed, they hurried on through heavy rain to Helpmakaar, where; to their joy, they found bell tents had already been pitched for them by the men from headquarters and Greytown. The total strength of the police was 110.

An unfortunate incident occurred on the following morning. After being tethered in the cold all night, 120 horses were turned out to graze, without being knee-haltered. Exercise was just what they wanted, so the whole lot began to gallop about, and in a few minutes were out of sight. The task of recovering the animals was not made any simpler by the fact that the troopers were on foot, but everybody turned out, expressing their view of the situation in very warm language, and during the morning forty of the truants had been taken back to camp. The rest had scattered far and wide. A number of men were selected to scour the country for them, but it was more than a fortnight before they were all recovered. As soon as they got their horses the men were put through special drills in preparation for warfare with the natives.

The police who were at Helpmakaar have good reason to remember their Christmas Day. They had decided to celebrate it with a sort of banquet, and ordered a wagon-load of all manner of luxuries from Pietermaritzburg. The wagon got as far as Keate's Drift, but the river was in flood, and carried the vehicle with the Christmas dinner away.

Six oxen were drowned, and Quarter-Master Sergeant Hobson had a narrow escape of losing his life. A few of the stores were subsequently saved, but the remnants of the banquet did not arrive until the 8th January. Such things as plum puddings, sausages; and jam had not been spoilt in the Mooi River, and the troopers were thankful to get such luxuries, even though they were late and had been rather roughly handled in their adventures.

The ultimatum to Cetewayo expired on the 11th January 1879, and as no communication was received from him the invasion of Zululand was started. Four columns were formed, the third being the headquarters column. This was the one at Helpmakaar, to which the police were attached. Commanded by Colonel Glyn, it was exceptionally strong, consisting of:

132 Royal Artillery, with six 7-pounder guns,
320 Cavalry,
1275 Infantry, and
2566 Native Levies,

Lord Chelmsford, the General Commanding, arrived at Helpmakaar before the advance was made. Addressing the police after Church Parade he said that during the short time they had been under his command he had every reason to be satisfied with their conduct and appearance. He added that it would give him great pleasure to take them with him into Zululand, where they must expect to meet a foe outnumbering the British forces by twenty to one. He spoke of the many hardships they had in store, with days and nights of constant watching and some severe fighting. "But," he concluded, "I feel sure you will give a good account of yourselves and sustain the high reputation which has always attached to your corps." That such proved to be the case is a matter of history.

Some dissatisfaction was caused by Major Dartnell having been superseded in his command of the police and volunteers by the appointment of Major Russell, of the 12th Lancers, to the command of the cavalry, with the local rank of Lieut.-Colonel. Major Dartnell's men expressed their disinclination to cross the border excepting under their own officer's command, and they offered to resign in a body. It was only upon Major Dartnell's strong remonstrance that they agreed to serve under Major Russell, and the former officer was placed on the General's Staff as the only way out of the difficulty. Inspector Mansel took charge of the police.

At Rorke's Drift all superfluous stores were disposed of, and the baggage was cut down to the lowest possible limit, the incessant rains having made the roads very bad. The task of crossing the Buffalo was a dangerous and difficult one, the river being swollen, but the column got over without mishap. A strong escort of police and volunteers was chosen to accompany Lord Chelmsford to Itelezi Hill, where he held a consultation with Colonel Evelyn Wood, who was in command of another column. The escort paraded at 2 a.m. and marched to the punt on the Buffalo, where the men deposited their arms, haversacks, and belts, it being feared that they might, if unduly hampered, be carried down the river.

The infantry, who also crossed before dawn, had to undergo being searched, each man's haversack and water-bottle being examined, the former for cigars and the latter for alcohol. A Greytown man had arrived in camp the previous day with two wagons laden with liquor, and this had been looted by the men of the 24th Regiment during the night. The number of empty bottles left lying about indicated that a good many of them had taken part in the affair. The Greytown man was rewarded with a message from the general that unless he cleared off at once his wagons would be pitched into the river.

The infantry crossed first in the punt, to cover the unarmed advance of the cavalry, and the native contingent crossed next, doing so hand in hand, some of them being washed off their feet. Men were stationed at the point below the drift to help anyone who was swept away, but only one of the police met with such a mishap, although the water was high up the saddle flaps and the current rapid. Everybody had got over safely by 4 a.m. The infantry and natives were left to guard the drift, and Lord Chelmsford set off to Itelezi Hill, the police forming the advance and flank guards. The route lay over an open, undulating country, but a dense mist overhung the ground. The men could only see each other in a dim way, and two of the police, who were flank skirmishers, lost touch with the party altogether. They had a trying time, and did not reach camp again until late at night.

During the forenoon the fog cleared, and a number of the Frontier Light Horse, under Colonel Redvers Buller, were met. After the conference the police formed the advance-guard for the return journey, and incidentally seized a group of Zulu cattle, taking them into camp. Several *kraals* were passed, and Lord Chelmsford informed the occupants of one that he was making war against Cetewayo and not against the people, but if they wished to retain their arms and cattle they must go into the British lines.

A violent storm knocked many of the tents down at the camp during the night, and at 3.30 a.m. the whole force was ordered out to reconnoitre the road. Part of the force went on to attack the stronghold of Sirayo, at the head of the Bashee Valley, and the volunteers and police went to the right to cut off the retreat of the enemy, who could be seen on the top of a mountain near a *nek* over which they had to pass. The thorn bush was thick, and progress consequently slow, and the natives had plenty of time to assemble for an attack. No opposition was shown at the *nek*, and the volunteers, who were ahead, had just passed out of sight round the bend, when the police were attacked as they were crossing a deep *donga*.

At a range of a couple of hundred yards the Zulus, who were posted under cover of a hill, began to let off their old blunderbusses with a noise like the discharge of field-guns. Their aim, like their fire-arms, was bad, and before they had time to reload, the police had dismounted.

While one-half of them looked after the horses, the other half advanced in skirmishing order, firing as they rushed up the steep slope, but the Zulus retired precipitately with their antique weapons. At the top of the hill the flying forms of the natives could be seen, and the police had a few moments' shooting before the enemy all disappeared. The Zulus had about ten men killed, one of them being a son of Sirayo.

In the meantime the infantry had destroyed Sirayo's *kraal* in the valley, and captured a large herd of cattle, which were sold to the butchers at 30s. each and bought back by the contractor at £18 each to feed the troops. This low price for the captured cattle was a sore point amongst the men, because though they made many large hauls some of them did not get a sovereign as their share at the end of the campaign.

The country into which the British force had moved was one in which the hills were pitted with deep dongas and ravines, where the undergrowth of prickly cactus, aloe, and euphorbia formed vast natural defences for the natives. In small bands the Zulus loved to lie in wait on such ground, but this method was not employed by the large *impis*[1] in the open field, where they relied upon victory by advancing in a solid body, and by sheer weight of numbers crushed the enemy by stabbing them at close quarters, utterly regardless of their own losses.

1. Zulu armies.

The road through the Bashee Valley was so sodden with the rain that a strong force of men had to be sent to repair it, otherwise the wagons would never have been able to get through. On the morning after the attack on Sirayo's *kraal* the troops were turned out again at 3.30, and were kept out on the hills all day watching the country towards Ulundi, from which direction an attack was regarded as probable. After a tiring day they returned to camp to find another patrol was ordered for 3.30 a.m. On this occasion a reconnaissance was made to the Isipezi Mountain, passing over the *nek* of Isandhlwana. Wagon tracks were carefully examined and the country sketched, for this was to be the column's route to the interior of Zululand. About forty miles were covered this day—the 14th January.

Patrols and *vedette* duties were continuous from early morning until dark, sometimes in a heavy downpour of rain, and a few of the men began to think that there was very little romance about active service. There was a good deal of justifiable grumbling concerning the issue of bully beef in two-pound tins. One half-section had to carry the beef and another the biscuits. This worked very satisfactorily when the men were able to find one another, but they generally got separated, and there was many an unhappy mortal on outpost duty who had to dine off plain biscuits or plain bully beef, according to his luck. As they left camp long before the fragrant odour of coffee was in the air, and did not get back until "lights out" had been sounded, the man who had only had biscuits felt he had fairly good grounds for complaint.

Taking fifteen days' supplies on ox wagons, the column moved on to Isandhlwana on the 20th January. A month's supplies were left behind at Rorke's Drift, where a number of sick and wounded remained in hospital. The men paraded at 4 a.m. and the police acted as advance-guard. Some of them had to scout the country, keeping at least a mile from the road. They climbed up and down stony hills for miles, coming out on the plain where the Isandhlwana church now stands, the troops being halted on the *nek* below Isandhlwana Hill.

The police had had a hard task, and were anticipating rest and food for themselves and their beasts when a staff officer rode up and ordered Inspector Mansel to place outposts on all the commanding hills on the east. Colonel Clarke recalls the fact that his troop was sent to an outlying ridge, and it was left there until long after dark, when a non-commissioned officer rode out and explained apologetically to the ravenous men that they had been forgotten by the staff officer. It was then 8 p.m., and they did not reach camp until an hour later, when dinner (which consisted of biscuits and bully beef) was over.

At 9.30 "Fall in for orders" was sounded, and the police were informed that they had to parade at 3 a.m. with the volunteers to reconnoitre in the direction of Matyana's stronghold. The news that Major Dartnell was to be in command was received with cheers. The police, having only a few hours in which to rest, did not trouble to find their kits, and they never saw them again. All but thirty-four members of the police went off before dawn. They took no rations, being informed that they would be back at noon, when a hot meal would be provided for them. There was many a man wished, sorrowfully, afterwards, that he had put something to eat in his pocket.

They covered a considerable extent of the country during the morning without getting a glimpse of the enemy, and after midday met the Native Contingent, under Colonel Lonsdale. The troopers off-saddled for a while, and then received sudden orders to move in an easterly direction, away from the main camp, where small bodies of the enemy had been reported. On a ridge near the Isipezi Mountain a few Zulus were seen, whereupon the force dismounted, while Inspector Mansel, with a small number of police, Sergeant-Major Royston, and a few of the *carbineers*, galloped out to reconnoitre.

It was soon seen that the enemy were there in large numbers, for they opened out until they covered the whole ridge, and dashed down the hill in an attempt to surround Inspector Mansel's party, who, however, wheeled back and escaped the *impi*. A trooper named Parsons, in attempting to load his revolver, accidentally discharged the weapon. His horse shied and he fell off. As a reward he was sent back to camp in disgrace, the incident causing a good deal of merriment. Parsons was killed during the attack on the camp the next day.

The *impi* returned to the ridge when the reconnoitring party escaped from them, and Major Dartnell decided not to make an attack with mounted men alone, the Native Contingent being reported by Colonel Lonsdale to be too tired and hungry to be relied upon. It was afterwards discovered that the enemy had contemplated rushing down on the British force, but hesitated to do so because they thought the Native Contingent, most of whom wore red coats, were Europeans.

In order not to lose touch with the Zulus, Major Dartnell decided to bivouac with the police, volunteers, and Native Contingent on the ground he had taken up, and two staff officers, Major Gosset and Captain Buller, returned to the main camp to report the presence of the enemy and ask approval of the bivouac. In many accounts of the

Zulu war it is stated that he appealed for reinforcements, but this is incorrect. He had decided to attack the *impi* at dawn, adding that a company or two of the 24th Regiment might instil confidence in the Native Contingent, but whether they came or not the attack would be made at 6 a.m.

The promised hot dinner having long gone cold, far away, the men had a cheerless prospect. They were without blankets, and the night was bitterly cold. Moreover, there was the ever-constant dread of a surprise attack. The troopers hitched up their belts, and bids up to ten shillings were made for a single biscuit; but nobody had any to sell. The horses were linked, one man in each section of fours being left on guard over them, and the Native Contingent provided outlying pickets.

In several ways it was a night never to be forgotten. Captain Davy, adjutant of volunteers, had gone back to the camp, and it was anxiously hoped that he would return with some food. He returned late at night with a very inadequate supply of provisions, which quickly disappeared.

Quietness reigned during the early hours of the night, but just before the 'witching hour a shot was fired by one of the outlying pickets. Instantly there was terrible confusion. The whole Native Contingent, consisting of 1600 men, stampeded into the bivouac, rattling their shields and *assegais*. The sudden awakening from sleep, the din, the hoarse cries of the natives, the knowledge that a large body of the enemy was in the vicinity, the difficulty of distinguishing friend from foe in the darkness, and the confusion that invariably follows a stampede, would have been sufficient to startle the best troops in the world. The natives crouched down near the white men for protection, and for a time nobody knew what had caused the panic.

The wonder is that many of the native soldiers were not shot by the white troopers. The discipline of colonial troops has rarely been put to a more severe test. The small body of police and volunteers, miles away from support, fell in quietly and quickly, and remained perfectly steady.

Some of the natives declared that an *impi* had passed close to the bivouac, and was going to make an attack. The troopers were ordered out to the brow of the hill to feel for the enemy. Suddenly shots began to ring out, and bullets whizzed past the white men. The scared Native Contingent, blundering again, had opened fire on the troopers, who were not sorry to get the order to retire. It was so dark that the force would have been practically helpless had a large *impi* rushed down on them, and the majority of them never expected to see daylight again; but the Zulus did not come, and the natives were with difficulty driven to their own bivouac.

A couple of hours afterwards the weary troopers were awakened by another similar panic, and again shots were sent flying by the natives, who almost got beyond control. Their officers and their European non-commissioned officers were so disgusted that they spent the rest of the night with the police.

The experience was a striking proof of the unreliability of undisciplined native troops in the hour of danger. It is a wonder that the whole force was not exterminated, for from what Mehlogazulu, a son of Sirayo, afterwards told General Wood, it appeared that the chiefs of the neighbouring *impi* decided to postpone such an easy task until they had first "eaten up" the main camp.

There were many pale, haggard faces when daylight broke on the morning of the eventful 22nd January. The colonial troops were not destined to fight a battle on their own account, for at 6 a.m. Lord Chelmsford joined them with Mounted Infantry, four guns of the Royal Artillery, and six companies of the 24th Regiment.

The Zulus had retired from the ridge before dawn, so the British force moved into the valley in search of the *impi*. Small parties were seen about four miles away, and several hours were spent in chasing them. There was some skirmishing, and about sixty Zulus, who took refuge in caves and amongst the boulders on a hill, were surrounded and killed. The *dongas* running down from the hills offered a very serious obstacle to the passage of guns and ambulances, and greatly retarded the men's movements, so a halt was called at midday, when a rumour was circulated that fighting was going on at the Isandhlwana camp. The firing of heavy guns could be heard, and the General decided to return with the Mounted Infantry and volunteers, leaving the police and men of the 24th Regiment to bivouac with part of the Native Contingent—a prospect which was not at all appreciated after the experience of the previous night.

The general had promised to send out rations, and firewood was being collected from a deserted *kraal* when a Staff officer galloped up with instructions that the whole force had to return to camp instantly.

The disastrous battle of Isandhlwana was in progress, and a man on a spent horse had come out with the following thrilling message:—

For God's sake come, with all your men; the camp is surrounded and will be taken unless helped.

Still worse was a report from Colonel Lonsdale. He had unsuspectingly ridden close to the camp, and was within a few yards of the tents, when he was fired at. He then recognized that all the Zulus near were wearing soldier's clothing, and that the camp was entirely in the enemy's hands. He turned back quickly and escaped the bullets.

The smoke of the infantry fire had been seen, and the occasional boom of the 7-pounder field-guns was heard. Thousands of the enemy could be seen in the distance, retiring from the camp to the hill which they had occupied previously. It was late in the afternoon when Lord Chelmsford briefly addressed the force under him, prior to the dash back to the camp, at a *spruit*[2] about two miles from the tents. The situation was as bad as it could be, he said, but they must retake the camp. He expressed his confidence in them to avenge the death of their comrades and uphold the honour of the British flag.

The column gave three cheers, and then advanced in the deepening gloom upon what appeared to be a most desperate venture. Ammunition was scarce, there was no food, the greater part of the men had marched for two days and had passed a sleepless night, while over and above these material disadvantages there was the depressing knowledge that the enemy which could annihilate one-half of the force in the daylight might, favoured by night, with equal certainty demolish the other half.

Much has been written about the ghastly massacre at Isandhlwana in which Cetewayo's overwhelming army of about 20,000 men killed 689 officers and men of the Imperial troops and 133 officers and men of colonial volunteers, Natal Police, and Native Contingents; and scarcely any one has denied that the colossal tragedy was due to blundering. It was the intention of Cetewayo to drive the third column back to Natal, but he never contemplated an attack on the 22nd January until he found his enemy had split up, spreading itself over a great area and practically delivered itself into his hands. The state of the moon was not propitious, according to Zulu tradition, and the inevitable sprinkling of medicine before a battle had not taken place, but when the king saw an obvious opportunity staring him in the face he made his attack and won.

The Zulus were not seen from the camp until 9 a.m., when a small

---

2. Stream.

number were observed on the crests of the hills. An hour later Colonel Durnford arrived from Rorke's Drift, and went out with a body of mounted natives. Everyone was utterly ignorant of the fact that such a huge *impi* was near, and forces were sent out in several directions. A large body of Zulus attacked Colonel Durnford, who retired to a *donga*, disputing every yard of the way. When reinforced by two-score mounted men he made a stand, every shot appearing to take effect amongst the solid mass of black some hundreds of yards away.

The natives employed their usual well-organized method of attack, being formed into a figure roughly resembling that of a beast, with horns, chest, and loins. A feint is generally made with one horn while the other, under cover of a hill, or bush, sweeps round to encircle the enemy. The vast chest then advances

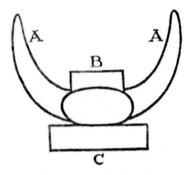

A, The Horns. B, The Chest.
C, The Loins.

and crushes the foe. The loins are left a little distance behind, ready to join in pursuit where necessary. It was the left horn of Cetewayo's army that was held in check by Colonel Durnford. The chest, or main body, became engaged with the force at the camp, and the right horn was swinging round the hills to the rear of Isandhlwana. The Zulus were fast surrounding the camp, when the Native Contingent and camp followers fled in all directions, seized by panic. Steadily, remorselessly, the *impi* closed in, a hungry sea of Zulus of overwhelming strength. Then followed the ghastly butchery. With short stabbing assegais the naked savages rushed straight on, treading underfoot those in their own ranks who were shot. Mercy was neither expected nor granted during that brief scene of slaughter.

Fighting like demons, a party of the 24th men, the Natal Police, and volunteers rallied round Colonel Durnford and held their ground gallantly, attacked on all sides by a shrieking mass of blacks, until their last cartridge was fired. Then they were stabbed to death. Twenty-five of the police were amongst the victims, and of these a score were afterwards found lying round the body of Colonel Durnford. They had fallen where they fought, and died fighting. Practically nothing is known of what happened in that awful few minutes at the finish, for the Zulus were not very communicative on the subject for many years afterwards.

While in prison Mehlogazulu, who had been in command of one portion of the *impi*, made the following statement:—

We were fired on first by the mounted men, who checked our advance for some little time. The rest of the Zulu regiments became engaged with the soldiers, who were in skirmishing order. When we pressed on, the mounted men retired to a *donga*, where they stopped us, and we lost heavily from their fire. As we could not drive them out we extended our horn to the bottom of the *donga*, the lower part crossing and advancing on to the camp in a semicircle.

When the mounted men saw this they galloped out of the *donga* to the camp. The main body of the Zulus then closed in. The soldiers were massing together. All this time the mounted men kept up a steady fire, and kept going farther into the camp. The soldiers, when they got together, fired at a fearful rate, but all of a sudden stopped, divided, and some started to run. We did not take any notice of those who ran, thinking that the end of our horn would catch them, but pressed on to those who remained. They got into and under the wagons and fired, but we killed them all at that part of the camp.

When we closed in we came on to a mixed party of mounted men and infantry, who had evidently been stopped by the horn. They numbered about a hundred, and made a desperate resistance, some firing with pistols and others using swords. I repeatedly heard the command 'fire,' but we proved too many for them, and killed them all where they stood.

When all was over I had a look at these men, and saw an officer with his arm in a sling, and with a big moustache, surrounded by *carbineers*, soldiers, and other men I did not know. We ransacked the camp and took away everything we could, including some ammunition which we got out of boxes.

Before the living ring finally closed round the doomed men, a rush was made by those who could escape in the direction of the Buffalo River. These were followed by a section of the enemy, who hacked the fugitives as they ran. Of the 34 members of the Natal Police who had been left at the camp by Major Dartnell, only 9 escaped. The bodies of three were found a couple of hundred yards away, and one was lying in Fugitives' Drift.

The members of the force who were killed at Isandhlwana were: Corporal Lally, Lance-Corporal Campbell, and Troopers Banger, Berry, Blakeman, Capps, J. Clarke, Daniells, Dorey, Eason, Fletcher, Lloyd, McRae, Meares, Niel, Pearse, Parsons; Pollard, Pleydell, F. Secretan, Siddall, Stimson, Thicke, C. White, and Winkle.

The men who escaped were: Lance-Corporal Eaton, Trumpeter Stevens, and Troopers Collier, Doig, Dorehill, W. Hayes (died of fever at Helpmakaar), Kincade, Shannon, and Sparks.

So sharp and terrible had been the onslaught that the police who survived were unable to say much about the last scenes. They had been sent out with all the mounted men to hold the main Zulu army in check, which they did until their ammunition was exhausted. Messengers galloped back frantically for more cartridges, but did not return, so the whole body retired. It was then learnt that the messengers had found the cartridges, tightly screwed up in boxes, and it was impossible to get at them. The practice of screwing down the lids was abolished when the news of this incident reached England.

At the moment the mounted men fell back to the camp the right horn of the *impi* appeared on the *nek*, closing the road to Rorke's Drift. Even then, had the troops been concentrated, and ammunition available, it is possible that the position might have been held, but the infantry were split up, and it was too late to move away.

As the final rush came, Colonel Durnford clearly saw that death was inevitable for nearly everyone.

"Get away as best you can," he shouted to the police and volunteers near, but very few heard or obeyed him.

To escape along the Rorke's Drift road was impossible, and those who left could only make a dash over terribly rocky ground where even horsemen had the greatest difficulty in avoiding the pursuing natives. Scarcely a single person on foot reached the Buffalo River alive. The river was in flood, but the Zulus pressed hard behind, and there was no time to look for a ford. Each man dashed into the stream as he reached it. Trumpeter Stevens, of the police, was washed off his horse, which swam across. The trumpeter owed his life to a native constable, who caught the animal and bravely took it back, enabling Stevens to cross the river before the Zulus attacked him.

While the historic tragedy was in progress the force under Lord Chelmsford was approaching. They did not get close to the camp until it was dark, and merely the black outline of the hills could be seen. Shrapnel shells were sent bursting over the camp, but not a sign came from the desolate place, and the force advanced cautiously up the slope. When within three hundred yards of the *nek* they opened fire again, and a detachment was sent to take a *kopje* on the south.

Not a Zulu was seen, and the force moved up to the place where dead men only were encamped. Stumbling over the bodies of white men and natives in the darkness, they made their way, awestricken, to the *nek*. Every man was knocked up with continual marching and lack of food, and they lay down; weary and almost broken-hearted amidst the debris of the plundered camp and the mangled corpses of men and horses. It was a night of horror. The men who lived through it do not care to recall the memory. Bright fires were seen in the distance, so the horses were not unsaddled but were ringed, and stood uneasily all night with the bodies of dead men lying round them.

"I had charge of thirty of the horses during part of the night," writes Colonel Clarke in his diary.

> There were the corpses of four men of the 24th Regiment in the ring, and others under the horses' legs, which caused the animals to surge to and fro so that it was almost impossible to control them. At one time we were on top of the adjoining ring, which brought curses on my head. I was not sorry to be relieved.
>
> There were several false alarms, with some firing. In the middle of the night someone found a commissariat wagon and called out 'Roll up for biscuits,' but there was no response so far as we were concerned.
>
> The night seemed endless, but at break of dawn we were able to realize the horrors of our situation. Mutilated bodies were lying everywhere, some naked, some only in shirts; and nearly all without boots. The Zulus had done their plundering very thoroughly.

Most of the fallen men were mutilated, but with few exceptions the members of the police had been killed with one or two stabs. Everything in the camp was broken; sacks of *mealies* and oats were ripped open, tins of bully beef were stabbed, bottles were broken and tents destroyed. Even the wagons had been overturned into dongas in the mad carnival of wrecking.

In the numerous descriptions of the battlefield very little mention is made of the fact that the police shared with an equal number of volunteers the honour of having made the last stand on the *nek* of the hill. At the crest where the dead men were lying thick, a large proportion of them were in the uniform of the Natal Mounted Police. In a patch of long grass, near the right flank of the camp, lay Colonel Durnford's body, a central figure of a knot of brave men who had fought it out around their chief to the bitter end.

Around him lay 14 *carbineers* and 21 of the police. Clearly they had rallied round the colonel in a last despairing attempt to cover the flank of the camp, and had stood fast from choice when they might have essayed to fly for their horses, which were close by at the picket line.

On the 30th June 1879 the *Natal Mercury* contained the following:—

There is one branch of the army that is now spreading itself over our frontiers, and over Zululand, to which scant justice has been done in the records of this campaign. It is a force which, to us in Natal, ought to, and we believe does, possess particular interest, for it represents the future army of Natal, and the contribution of Natal in some approaching time, to the future army of South Africa. We refer to the Natal Mounted Police.

That body occupies a peculiar position. It is not Imperial in any sense of the term, although the Government which has created it owns the supremacy of the Queen. It has played an effective and very honourable part in an Imperial campaign. It consists in the main of men recruited in England, and although there are amongst its ranks several colonists, its ranks are from time to time filled up by men who have enrolled themselves at home. Only the other day over sixty such additions came to fill up the gap left by the cruel losses at Isandhlwana.

We have always felt it both a pleasure and a duty to uphold the ●
reputation of Major Dartnell's force, and we do so the more heartily now because it has, during the eventful and trying times of the last six months, earned every right to be regarded with respect and admiration. That the men played the part of true soldiers at Isandhlwana, the bodies of their slain comrades

grouped round the last rallying point sadly testify. The records of the campaign show that whenever their services have been called into action they have behaved with gallantry and distinction.

This is no more than we might have expected of any corps led by Major Dartnell, than whom, we believe, a more devoted, daring, and yet discreet leader will not be found in South Africa. The trumpet of fame has not sounded their praises, but that is due to circumstances rather than to intention. Whatever the Natal Mounted Police have had to do they have done well; and the fine young fellows who have come out to join its ranks may take just pride to themselves in thinking that they belong to a force that enjoys, in an especial degree, the appreciation of the community they serve. The corps must and will be our chief defence force of the future. What we want in Natal is a mobile, effective body of men ready on short notice to operate at any point where insurrectionary tendencies display themselves, and such a body we have in the police.

CHAPTER 5

Zulus Repulsed At Rorke's Drift

Shortly after dawn on the morning following the disaster of Isandhlwana, January 23, 1879, Lord Chelmsford's force received orders to march, the police being given the rear-guard. The column had cleared the *spruit* below the *nek*, and the police were moving after it, when a violent fusillade was started in front of them. Unable to tell for a few seconds what was happening, the police "closed up," and then they saw the Native Contingent charging valiantly up a hill, where they cut to pieces a solitary Zulu who had had the temerity to open fire on the column. Some hundreds of shots were fired at him.

Another shock followed a little later. A number of natives were seen on the left, and an attack was feared, but orders were passed round to save ammunition as much as possible, because it was feared the Zulus had captured the depot at Rorke's Drift. The natives came very close to the rear-guard, where the police were, and shouted, but they did not attack. It was afterwards found that there had been fighting at Rorke's Drift, where a gallant stand was made by the British force, and these Zulus were the men who had been repulsed.

The column marched straight on to Rorke's Drift. Figures were seen moving about, and as the hospital had been burnt down it was feared there had been a fresh disaster. It was impossible to see whether the men at the depot were Europeans or natives, but at last one of them sprang on to the wall. The garrison had held the place. The column under Lord Chelmsford became so excited that ranks were broken by men, heedless of commands, and they rushed up the slopes anyhow to congratulate everybody there.

Some tinned beef and bread were found, and the column ate the first decent meal they had had for several days. The police and the rest of the men were thoroughly knocked up, some of them having been without food for sixty hours—and sixty very strenuous hours. To the joy of every one, rum was issued to each man who merely passed with his can. This was an opportunity far too good to be missed, for the troopers had almost forgotten what a canteen looked like, so a number of them changed their names several times that morning. Blessings were showered on the lance-corporal who served out the rum. Perhaps he saw what was happening and closed one eye to it: at any rate, according to the list more than 6000 Europeans had returned with the General. The actual number was nearer 1000. The deficiency in rum was possibly "written off."

The battle at Rorke's Drift had been a bitter one, the bodies of the Zulus' dead round the building numbering 375. Fatigue parties were employed all day burying them. Three members of the Natal Police had taken part in the defence, the total force there not numbering over fourscore. The police there were Trooper Hunter, who was killed; Trooper Green, who was slightly wounded; and Trooper Lugg, who afterwards became Lieut.-Colonel and magistrate at Umsinga.

All three had been left in the hospital when their comrades moved off to Isandhlwana, but they were able to take a very active part in the defence. The Zulus made straight for the hospital, swarming on to the verandah. The soldiers barricaded the doors as firmly as possible, and then knocked holes in the walls, from room to room, passing the sick men through to the adjacent store. Each aperture was defended by soldiers while this was going on, and one or two Victoria Crosses were won in this way.

When the last room was reached and nearly all the invalids had been removed, a dash had to be made across the open space to the store, a few yards away.

Here Hunter lost his life. He had almost reached shelter when a Zulu lunged at him with an *assegai*. He was badly wounded, but he had strength to kill his assailant before he fell. Their bodies were found close together afterwards.

Some of the sick men had to be left in hospital as the enemy set fire to the thatched roof and were crowding round. One invalid was burnt to death; others were carried by the natives over a ridge, out of range of bullets, and were dreadfully mutilated.

It is a favourite method of warfare with Zulus to burn any building they attack. One native raised a bundle of burning forage to the thatched roof of the store. Had he set it alight, probably nobody in the British force would have been left alive, but a bullet bored its way

RORKE'S DRIFT DEPOT AFTER THE BATTLE OF 22ND JANUARY 1879.

THE PLACE WHERE THE PRINCE IMPERIAL WAS KILLED,
AS IT WAS JUST AFTER HIS DEATH.

through his brain while he was in the act, and the enemy were eventually beaten off under a hail of lead.

When the column to which the police were attached arrived they found the bodies of natives lying all round the hospital and store. There were many wounded Zulus, but none recovered, and several who tried to escape were shot. One actually got back across Rorke's Drift, although dozens of shots were fired at him, but he was followed by a mounted infantryman and killed.

Great preparations were made in readiness for another attack. The defences were strengthened, the parapets were raised, and four field-guns were dragged into the laager. Scouts were sent out to look for signs of the enemy, but they reported that there were no Zulus anywhere near.

In the evening the police and volunteers were told off to occupy an old cattle *kraal*. They threw in a lot of loose forage to make the place more comfortable, and for a while had a good rest.

The Native Contingent, which supplied the out-lying picket, also supplied their usual false alarms. Shortly after midnight the word was passed round that an *impi* was coming on in immense numbers. The European officers with the outposts followed up the report promptly by joining those inside the walls, and remained there without troubling to verify the statement. As soon as the natives with the British force heard the rumour, however, they disappeared in twos and threes; and most of them were never heard of again. But the *impi* never arrived, and after a while the men turned in again.

They were called early the following morning, and one of the police, in searching for part of his kit, turned over the forage in the *kraal*. Under it he discovered the body of a dead Zulu. A further examination showed that one group had slept comfortably on seven of the enemy's dead.

At dawn on the 24th January, the sergeant-major selected a party of twenty of the police to act as escort to Lord Chelmsford, who was going to Pietermaritzburg for reinforcements, Major Dartnell accompanying him. The best horses were picked for the journey, and there was keen rivalry amongst the men to be included in the escort, which, however, had a rough experience. The animals were exhausted after the hard work they had done, and an attempt to reach Ladysmith ended in one horse falling dead, while two others collapsed, and one had to be left on the road. To make matters worse, when night came the party missed the road, finally arriving at the post-cart stable at Mod-

THE RORKE'S DRIFT MEMORIAL.

der Spruit, where men and beasts rested for a few hours. Ladysmith was reached the next day, and the police remained there awaiting the return of Major Dartnell, who went on to arrange about further supplies of clothing and equipment to be forwarded to Helpmakaar.

Ten men of the police had meanwhile remained at Rorke's Drift for patrol duty, and the rest went direct to Helpmakaar, where most of the survivors from Isandhlwana were found. One of them, Trooper Sparks, of the Natal Police, had conveyed the General's dispatches to Pietermaritzburg, being about the first person to arrive there with news of the disaster.

Amongst the party left at Rorke's Drift was the present Chief Commissioner, Colonel Clarke, who recalls that they had a terribly hard time. Food was not too plentiful, and they had neither tents, blankets, nor a change of clothing. Few of them had any eating utensils, which is not surprising considering their movements for several days before, and most of them had to draw their rations in empty bully beef tins. They had to "sleep rough," and carried nearly as much mud as kit about with them.

Every morning at three o'clock the police were called out, and while the other troops stood to arms inside the *laager* they were sent away into the surrounding country to make certain there was no *impi* within five miles before this morning parade was dismissed. There was a *mealie* field through which they often had to ride in the darkness, always with the prospect of being *assegaied*; and the dongas in the district were possible death-traps, for it was never known when the Zulus would return.

Midnight scares were frequent, and whatever the hour, the police were ordered out "to feel for the enemy."

Two of the colours of the 24th Regiment had been lost at Isandhlwana, and ten days after the fight the police accompanied a party which left the *laager* at Rorke's Drift to search for them. They made a quick ride and no natives were seen, until the famous hill was reached. There a few Zulu sentinels were observed standing on the heights. The party hunted for a couple of hours amongst the bodies of the men near the place where the guard tent had stood, but no colours were found, and as the natives on the surrounding hills increased in numbers, Major Black, who commanded the party, deemed it prudent to retire. It was decided not to go back by the same road, as an ambush was feared.

Two troopers of the police had an unpleasant experience when the return journey was started. They had been left on the *nek* with orders to stay there until Major Black fired a shot from the point of a hill in the direction of Fugitives' Drift. The force disappeared, and the isolated troopers remained at their post by no means free from danger, until they realized that they were being left behind. No sound of a shot reached their ears. They waited for a time, and at last, deciding to take the bull by the horns, galloped off to the main party. They afterwards heard that the major had been afraid to fire the promised shot because there were many of the enemy near, and they might have taken it as the signal for an attack.

The route taken was the same as that followed by those who took part in the wild rush from Isandhlwana to the Buffalo River, and everybody had a very trying experience. The descent from a ridge, along which they rode, to the water was almost like riding down a precipice, and as the river was unfordable at this point, they had to swim as the fugitives had done. Once in Natal, they had no fear of being attacked, and while the bank of the river was being examined one of the missing colours was discovered. A messenger was sent on ahead to announce the good news, and there was a moving scene when the little party returned with the tattered, stained colour. The troops turned out and presented arms, and old soldiers with tears in their eyes kissed the flag.

The police at Helpmakaar at this time did not find life a bed of roses. A wagon *laager* was at first formed round the *hartebeeste* sheds in which the stores were kept. This was converted into an earthwork, surrounded by a moat, in which stagnant water gathered, the conditions being most unhealthy. The troops were shut up there every night, and marched out an hour after daylight each morning, the police providing thirty men every day to scour the surrounding hills.

Clothing was painfully scarce, and blankets were badly needed by the police, this occasioning great hardships. When the kits of all the infantry who had been killed at Isandhlwana were sold by auction they fetched astonishing prices. The police were permitted to wear the blue infantry trousers, but although their own tunics were falling into a sad state of disrepair, they were not allowed to wear the red jackets.

So great was the demand for eating utensils that dust-heaps were dug up in search of empty tins. These, carefully polished, served many a trooper as plates for a long time. The unhealthy conditions soon began to tell on the men. There was no shelter from the sun during the daytime, and the troopers were in little better than a sea of mud each night, rotting oats and *mealies* in the store adding to the general unpleasantness. As might have been anticipated, fever broke out, carrying off many of the regulars and half a dozen of the police. These were Corporal Chaddock, and Troopers Bennett, W. Hayes, Ingram, Nagle, and H. Smith.

Prior to the arrival of the 4th Regiment from Pietermaritzburg, one man of each section of fours had been on sentry at night-time, and one or two false alarms occurred. Once a tame baboon, with a steel chain attached to its neck, escaped from its box and, climbing on to the iron roof of the store, made a terrific din, which sounded as though the Zulus were looting the place. Everybody sprang up. The horse lines were close to the *laager*, and orders had been given that in case of alarm the animals were to be released by the guard. On the occasion of the baboon's antics the horses were unfastened. It was soon found that the enemy were not making an attack, but all the horses had disappeared by morning.

There was another false alarm near the *laager*, caused by a stray ox. It is stated that one regiment of infantry fired away 10,000 rounds of ammunition without doing any damage, even to the ox.

While the men were at this time undergoing various hardships, the residents of Ladysmith sent up a wagon-load of useful articles— clothes, food, and luxuries of all kinds—for the police and volunteers. These came as a perfect godsend, and the men eagerly drew lots for them. It was not until the middle of February that tents and blankets for the police arrived from Pietermaritzburg, the road through the Greytown thorns being practically closed. Transport riders, even at exorbitant figures, refused to perform the journey so near to the borders of Zululand. When the wagons did arrive the tents were pitched in the daytime, but the poles were pulled down at nightfall, the men entering the laager.

A nimble-witted lance-corporal of the 13th Regiment made a small fortune by forming a sort of market near the *laager*. Natives brought milk, *mealies*, and pumpkins for sale. These he retailed at his own price, while he paid the natives less than theirs. Milk soon became more plentiful than water, which was supplied by one spring. There were 1600 men in camp, and as the spring began to run dry sentries had to be placed near it to see that water was only drawn for drinking purposes. Men had to do without washing excepting on the occasion of the weekly bathing parade, when they all marched down to the stream. Half of them entered the water at a time to enjoy all the delights of badly needed ablutions, while the other half, fully armed, remained on the bank.

While the police were experiencing the joys of life at the Helpmakaar camp, an attempt was made at Pietermaritzburg to secure recruits for the force by Lieut.-Colonel Mitchell, who had been appointed Acting Commandant in the absence of Major Dartnell. Advertisements were inserted in the local papers asking for men willing to join for six months under Natal Police Regulations, pay being offered at the rate of six shillings a day, with free rations and forage, uniform and equipment being supplied by the Government. Either the prospect was not tempting enough, or the colony had been drained of men by the raising of so many corps of volunteers, for there were no suitable applicants.

On the 20th February, Major Dartnell left Helpmakaar with an escort of police, for Ladysmith, the route taken being *via* the Waschbank Valley. The first night was spent at a farm where there was a garrison of Carbutt's Horse, otherwise known as the "Blind Owls," who lived on rum and dampers. On reaching Ladysmith the following day, the police were quartered in the commissariat store, where they had to sleep on wet sacks of *mealies*. This made every man in the escort ill, and caused the death of Trooper Laughnan, who was buried in Ladysmith. The hotel-keepers were reaping a harvest, charging 25s. a cwt. for forage and 4s. 6d. a bottle for beer. Another night was spent with the hospitable "Blind Owls" on the return journey.

At Helpmakaar they found a great deal of sickness. There were no bedsteads, and the patients, most of them in a raging fever, were lying in tents on a wagon-cover spread on the ground. Milk became scarce, and the sick men for a time could only get rice and arrowroot, without sugar or milk, and an occasional supply of beef-tea. Brandy and port wine was doled out sparingly, but these generally disappeared while the sick men were asleep. Every trooper in the police at Helpmakaar passed through the hospital there, and as the fever patients became convalescent they were removed to Ladysmith. Some went into the hospital, which stood where the magistrate's court now is, and others went into a separate hospital reserved for police and volunteers.

On the arrival of reinforcements from England, a company of the 24th Regiment was left to garrison Helpmakaar, and the police were ordered to join the column under General Newdigate at Dundee, arriving there on the 18th April.

As Lord Chelmsford advanced to the relief of Eshowe, he gave orders for raiding parties to cross the border into Zululand simultaneously. On the appointed day the police and volunteers entered the Bashee Valley, where they burnt several *kraals* and destroyed some crops. This did no good whatever, and caused resentment and retaliation. The police escorted Lord Chelmsford to Baiter Spruit at the end of the month, and then with the volunteers relieved the infantry at Helpmakaar.

There was great disappointment when the news came that the police were not to join the column that was to advance on Ulundi. There Cetewayo's great army of over 20,000 warriors was defeated on the open plain by a force of about 5000 white men.

On relinquishing his command of the cavalry column, Lieut.-Colonel Russell wrote to Major Dartnell:

> As the Natal Mounted Police have now passed from under my command, and I may not come across them officially again, I wish to thank them all for the cordial manner in which they have supported me in every way and on every occasion since the beginning of the campaign. I most sincerely wish you all, individually and as a corps, every good fortune in the future.

The ranks of the police having been considerably thinned by sickness and fighting, the arrival of sixty recruits from England on the 1st June was opportune. Forty more men joined in the colony, and this brought the corps up to its full strength once more. As quickly as possible a score of these troopers were fitted out, drilled, and sent up to Helpmakaar, where the men were chafing badly under the monotony of inaction other than routine work.

Prince Louis Napoleon, who joined the headquarters Staff of Lord Chelmsford, met his death a few miles from Nqutu. He was with a small force when fifty Zulus made a sudden rush The prince was dismounted, and his horse, which was sixteen hands high, was always difficult to mount. On this occasion it became frightened by the sudden rush, and pranced in such a manner that the prince had the greatest difficulty in keeping it under control. The holster partly gave way, and he fell, being trodden on by the excited animal. He was now alone, with a dozen natives close upon him, but he regained his feet and, revolver in hand, faced the blacks and death. The fight was hopeless, and the prince died as he had lived, a brave soldier.

After the body was recovered and conveyed to Pietermaritzburg, the police were ordered to furnish an escort for it to Durban, the coffin being taken by road and placed on a warship which took it to England.

The bodies of those who were killed at Isandhlwana having lain where they fell for five months, a force was sent out towards the end of June to perform the sad task of burial. It was joined at Rorke's Drift by sixty of the police under Major Dartnell.

Nature had softened the scene when they arrived; the dead were there, but in nearly every case they were hidden by the grass and corn that had grown everywhere. It was a heartbreaking task, but all the bodies of the police were identified and buried, their names being written in pencil on wood or a stone near them.

The only victims left untouched were those of the 24th Regiment. These were not moved, at the express desire of Colonel Glyn and other officers, who hoped to be able to inter them themselves at a later date.

The officer commanding was anxious, for more reasons than one, not to prolong the stay on that grim battlefield, and the return journey was started at noon. The English horses' powers of endurance were severely tested on the journey. Several of the Lancers' animals were knocked up on the return trip. The police not only had had the extra distance from Helpmakaar to Rorke's Drift to cover in the morning, but were kept on *vedette* duty all day, and then marched back to Helpmakaar in the evening.

When Sir Garnet Wolseley arrived in the colony to take command of the troops, he was escorted to the front by a detachment of police under Sub-Inspector Phillips. He travelled *via* Pietermaritzburg and Helpmakaar, arriving at Ulundi six days after the battle. A detachment of the police went out and found the two 7-pounder guns taken by the natives from the camp at Isandhlwana.

The Zulu king, Cetewayo, had at this time fled, and immediate steps were taken to secure him. The police left in search of the king, putting in some very hard marching without transport and without rations other than those which each man could carry for himself. They covered fifty miles on horseback the first day, and reached the kraal of one of Mpanda's wives the second day, learning that Cetewayo had spent the night there. On the 15th August a number of the force joined the party under Lord Gifford, who was also hunting for Cetewayo. He had as guide a Dutchman named Vijn, who had lived with Cetewayo during the war.

Sub-Inspector Phillips discovered the king's pet herd of cattle in the valley of the Umona River, and asked permission to take the police with him and seize them. This was given, and the beasts were taken into Ulundi, where they had to be disposed of at 50s. a head, although the commissariat officers were paying £15 to £18 each for cattle. Again the police went out after Cetewayo, and the party to which they were attached got on to his trail. They would have had the honour of taking him, had not a column under Major Marter been a trifle quicker. By making an early morning move into the Ngome Forest the major ran the Zulu king to earth, and this important capture had the immediate effect of pacifying the whole country.

A difference of opinion existed from the first as to the necessity for the Zulu War, and concerning the character of Cetewayo. This became much more pronounced after the disaster at Isandhlwana. There was one section of the public in England who had never even seen a Zulu, but voiced their incorrect opinions loudly. The leader in South Africa of the party who denounced the war was Dr. Colenso, Bishop of Natal. He argued in an able manner in favour of the blacks, but experience has shown time after time that the native leader cannot be dealt with as a white man in the matter of treaties. It had become absolutely necessary that Cetewayo should cease to reign, and that the enormous military power of the nation should be broken.

Writing officially on the subject at the time, Sir Bartle Frere said:

Having lived now for many weeks within a couple of Zulu marches of the Zulu border, amongst sensible Englishmen, many of them men of great sagacity, coolness, and determination, and reasonably just and upright in all their dealings, who never went to sleep without their arms within reach, and were always prepared to take refuge with wives and families at a minute's warning within a fortified post; having talked to *voortrekkers* and their children who had witnessed the massacres at Weenen and Blauw Krantz, and who could thus testify that the present peculiarities of Zulu warfare are no recent innovation, I may be allowed to doubt the possibility of making life within reach of a Zulu *impi* permanently tolerable to ordinary Englishmen and Dutchmen.

They make no prisoners, save occasionally young women and half-grown children. They show no quarter, and give no chance to the wounded or disabled, disembowelling them at once.

The events of the last few months have rendered it unnecessary to prove by argument that the Zulus have been made into a great military power; that they can destroy an English regiment with artillery to support it, or shut up or defeat a brigade six times as strong as the ordinary garrison of Natal unless our troops are very carefully posted and very well handled. The open declarations of their king, no less than the fundamental laws of their organization, proclaim foreign conquest, and bloodshed a necessity of their existence.

They are practically surrounded by British territory. Except that of the Portuguese, there is now no foreign territory they can reach for purposes of bloodshed without passing through British territory. They are separated from Natal by a river easily fordable for the greater part of the year, and not too wide to talk across at any time.

I submit that in the interests of the Zulus themselves we have no right to leave them to their fate. The present system of Cetewayo is no real choice of the nation. It is simply a reign of terror, such as has before now been imposed on some of the most civilized nations of the world. The people themselves are everything that could be desired as the unimproved material of a very fine race. They seem to have all the capacities for forming a really happy and civilized community where law, order, and right shall prevail, instead of the present despotism of a ruthless savage.

They might, by living alongside a civilized community, gradually imbibe civilized ideas and habits. But for this purpose it is necessary that their neighbours should be able to live in security, which, as I have already said, seems to me hopeless unless the military organization and power of Cetewayo be broken down.

There are the means of improvement which may follow conquest and the breaking down of Cetewayo's military system; and this seems to me the only reasonable mode of doing our duty by these people. In the cases of Abyssinia and Ashantee we were compelled by circumstances to retire after conquest and wash our hands of any further responsibility for the future of those counties, but there is no necessity in the case of Zululand—there is nothing to prevent our taking up and carrying the burden of the duty laid upon us to protect and civilize it.

There are still many people who declare that the war on Cetewayo was wicked and unjust, but in the years that have passed since the power of the Zulu was crushed finally at Ulundi it has been seen by those who are in a position to judge how much better off the native now is, and how much more secure is the white settler. True, there were some severe tussles in the rebellion of 1906, but the fighting methods organized by Chaka were practically ended in 1879, and the Zulu is gradually becoming civilized. He is by nature exceedingly happy and easy-going; and takes kindly enough to British rule. Occasional unrest prevails amongst an isolated section of the natives, but it soon blows over, and one can rarely meet a Zulu who does not welcome the presence of the white man in his territory.

If you ask a Zulu why he likes the white men to live amongst them he will smile, roll his brown eyes almost *coquettishly*, and say: "He gives me leekle bit money." But this ignoble reason does not stand alone; he looks up to the white man, and, in towns especially, imitates him to a degree which is at times positively ludicrous. It is an infinite pity that some of the white men with whom he comes in contact are not worthy of being imitated by the despised black, who unfortunately follows an example, be it good or bad, without much discrimination.

Chapter 6

A Captive King

After the capture of Cetewayo the Zulu king was sent to Port Durnford, under an escort of Natal Police, where he embarked on a steamer for Cape Town. He was melancholy and abstracted on the journey, and even the wonders on the steamer—for this was his first sea trip—did not rouse him greatly from his state of lethargy. He showed a childish interest in some things on board, and the machinery inspired him with such awe that he would not go down into the engine-room. He asked how many cattle the vessel cost, and when an effort was made to give him some idea it was quite clear that he thought he had struck a number of particularly untruthful people.

He said he knew from the first that the war would end as it did, and that he himself would be the sufferer. The battle of Ulundi, he declared, was fought against his wish, and he blamed his young men, whom he could not restrain. He knew the power of his nation was broken, and laughed to scorn the idea of any more fighting being possible against British rule.

Cetewayo remained at Cape Town for some considerable time and, before being released, was taken to England. Finally he was sent back to Zululand, where he died, though not before he had been involved in more than one serious quarrel with neighbouring chiefs.

Early in August, Inspector Mansel, with thirty-eight members of the police, left Helpmakaar to join Colonel Baker Russell's flying column, which destroyed the *kraal* of Manyanyoba, whose people had taken refuge in some caves. They were dislodged by dynamite, but not before a sergeant-major and a private of the infantry were killed. At Hlobane earlier in the war a number of irregulars had blundered over a precipice at full gallop, when retiring from the mountain on the day preceding the battle of Kambula. Their bodies were buried by men from the column. The force also punished the chief Sekukuni, in the Transvaal, but the police were not able to take part in this campaign, as the Natal Government asked for them to be returned; so they marched back to Pietermaritzburg, where they had a lively time with kit inspections, from which ordeal they had long been free.

The relatives of a number of deceased members of the police having put in claims, a Commission was appointed to deal with the matter, and it was recommended that the widows and families of Troopers Meares and White should, in each case, be granted an annuity of £54, or a gratuity of £330. Each trooper being the actual owner of his kit, and many of them having lost all their kit during the struggles of the war, it was decided to compensate the men for lost articles at the following rates: officers' kit, £30, spare kit £10, chargers £35 each; non-commissioned officers' and troopers' kit £10, and troop horses £25 each.

The barracks at Pietermaritzburg were so terribly insanitary that an outbreak of fever occurred at the close of 1879. There were no men at headquarters, and a score of them went into hospital, but only one died.

In the early part of 1880 Sub-Inspector Phillips took a detachment of the force to Fort Pine, on the Biggarsberg, eight miles from Dundee, where it had been decided to establish an out-station. When the troopers got there the building was not ready, and for months the men had to live under canvas. This out-station was occupied for many years, and a very useless one it was. Many attempts were made to move the detachment to Dundee, but much opposition was shown to this project. Sir Charles Mitchell, a former Governor, held particularly strong views on the subject, and said that it was highly inadvisable to station men so close to a canteen.

Some of the troopers in those days were very rough diamonds, but such precautions as these were unnecessary, and it often proved awkward to have the men at such inaccessible places. So little confidence was placed in the common sense of the men (who undoubtedly were guilty of little alcoholic indiscretions on such occasions as pay day now and again) that when a canteen was opened at headquarters in September 1880 the sale of intoxicants was not allowed there.

It fell to the lot of the Natal Police to escort the ex-Empress of the French to visit the spot where her son, the Prince Imperial, fell in Zululand. There was keen competition amongst the troopers to be chosen, and three non-commissioned officers and seventeen men were selected. For days before the arrival of the Empress there were daily practices in pitching and striking the tents, which consisted of one large marquee mess tent, two small marquees for the Empress, and six bell tents for the staff. After a few days these could be pitched in ten minutes and struck in three. This was on the soft ground in Government House gardens, and the men looked forward to an easy time.

On the hard *veldt* the same operations occupied two hours, and half an hour respectively; and it was very hard work at that. Whenever the Empress rode she had an escort of two troopers, and as others had to be detailed for different duties, the tents often had to be pitched by a dozen men. The ground was like granite in places, and as they ran out of spare tent-pegs the work became increasingly hard.

As the tour was to extend over a period of seven weeks, in a region where railways were non-existent, all the food for the men, mules, and horses had to be carried by road. Wagons were sent on in advance, dropping supplies at places where the camp would be pitched, but the convoy which accompanied the Empress never consisted of less than twenty-five mule wagons.

On the 29th April 1880, just as the cold weather began, the expedition left Pietermaritzburg. As many of the men who took part in the escort have left the corps, and are scattered all over the globe, it may be of interest to mention the fact that they consisted of: Sergeant Faddy (in charge); Corporals Burgoyne and W. J. Clarke; Troopers Berthold, W. Brown, W. D. Campbell, Cooper, F. Evans, Ford, Green, Heathcote, Hutton, Lockner, Longfield, H. Pennefather, Piers, Ravenscroft, Russ, Stevens, and Wilmot

Throughout the trip the police turned out at dawn and had their tents struck and everything of their own packed on the wagons by sunrise. Immediately after breakfast the other tents and marquees were packed and taken quickly to the next camp, which was generally twenty or twenty-five miles farther on. The tents were pitched there while the Empress travelled leisurely along the road, either riding on horseback or being driven by General Sir Evelyn Wood in a "spider" drawn by four horses.

The first day's trek landed them at Albert Falls, and the week-end was spent at Sevenoaks. The troopers were all down at the *spruit* enjoying a bath when the "dress" was sounded, followed by "trot," so they hurried back to camp to find that General Wood had ordered a church parade. The general expressed astonishment that the men were not ready for it, but they had not expected church parade in peace time.

The route lay through Greytown, Umsinga, Helpmakaar, and Dundee, to Landman's Drift, where the Zululand border was crossed. At this stage Sergeant Faddy was taken ill, and it is recorded that as he was nursed by the Empress's maids and had an abundance of luxuries, besides a medical ration of rum at frequent intervals, his convalescence was somewhat protracted. A keg of rum, by the way, caused sorrow. On the Queen's birthday the general ordered that the police were to have a liberal ration of this liquid, but when the men rolled up with their tins it was found the keg was empty. This was caused by evaporation, the commissariat officer said.

By way of Blood River, the party went to Kambula, to enable the Empress to visit Utrecht, where they experienced such violent wind and rain that the whole camp had to be struck and repitched in a more suitable place. The skeletons of the Zulus who were killed in the Kambula fight were still lying about when the Empress passed the place.

From this point the expedition moved over the ground where Vryheid now stands, and misfortune overtook the convoy. The wagons got badly bogged. The first task that had to be tackled was that of getting the Empress's vehicles out of trouble. The police worked in deep mud all the afternoon, and after a most unhappy and strenuous time were able to pitch the camp late in the day at Fort Piet Uys.

Utterly unconscious of what had taken place, the Empress dined peacefully. The police, however, had worked themselves to a standstill, being too knocked up to go back to the bog and fetch their own wagons. Instead, they bivouacked under the wall of the fort. It was a cold, frosty, moonlight night, and the ravenous troopers, longing for the rations stored away on their own wagons, caught the odour of good things in the large marquee.

Casually taking a stroll after dinner, the Empress caught sight of the recumbent figures near the fort, and asked who the men were. She was greatly shocked on hearing that they were without food or blankets, and took them all into her drawing-room marquee, where they were given food. Then the Empress thoughtfully turned out spare blankets, shawls, petticoats, and dresses to put over them; and in the early hours of the morning when the night air grew cutting those troopers blessed the Empress for her kindness.

There was a French chef with the party, and at Hlobane the chief, Ohamu, with a thousand men, came into the camp as a mark of respect. The chef, glancing out and catching one glimpse of the *impi*, murmured a hasty prayer, shouted to the police to arm, and rushed for his revolver. There was some difficulty in persuading him that his last day had not come.

The widow of Captain the Hon. R. Campbell, Coldstream Guards, had taken from England a very heavy gravestone, and this was carried up the mountain by the *impi* to the place where the officer fell.

Four days later Ityotyosi, where the prince had been killed, was reached, and a halt was made for eight days. The Empress visited the *mealie* garden where her son was trapped, and as the police were able to assemble the natives who took part in the affair she saw exactly how he had been killed. The native who inflicted the final stab was invited to pay a visit to Pietermaritzburg and point out the *assegai* which he used, but on the night the party arrived at Robson's Drift he fled, doubtless fearing the invitation was a prelude to punishment.

From the camp at Ityotyosi two of the police were guided by a Zulu to the remains of Captain Barton of the Grenadier Guards. This officer, when endeavouring to escape from Hlobane, had been followed by three natives for a considerable distance, being overtaken and killed. His fate had remained unknown until his body was pointed out.

There was one curious circumstance which did not add to the happiness of the police during the camp at Ityotyosi. A titled lady was on her way from Natal to pay a visit to the camp, and very strict orders were given that she was to be politely but firmly intercepted when she turned up. Night and day the troopers were stationed at out-posts watching for the lady's approach, and when at last she did arrive, with two police from the Fort Pine detachment whom she had persuaded to act as escort, she was guided to a mission station some miles away. There she remained until after the camp was struck.

The return journey was started on the 3rd June, *via* Isandhlwana and Rorke's Drift, a halt being made for a day at each of these places. The police visited Fugitives' Drift, where a number of the slain were found and buried.

The shortage of tent-pegs became a nightmare to Sergeant Faddy towards the close of the trip. The tent of the Empress always had its full number, but General Wood expressed his opinion of the situation freely when he found his own bell tent only had one peg to each two ropes. The troopers' tents, meanwhile, were so insecurely fastened down that a good breeze would have blown the lot away. Any man who through carelessness broke a peg at that stage was as likely as not to be hit on the head by his colleagues with a mallet.

After the journey the Empress sent a gold watch and chain for the sergeant and £100 to be shared by the men who had accompanied her; and General Wood wrote the following letter to the commandant:

My Dear Major,—I am anxious to express to you my great satisfaction with the manner in which the escort of Her Imperial Majesty performed their duties. They evinced on every occasion a cheerful willingness to carry out all my wishes. This spirit tended greatly to overcome the difficulties inseparable from such an expedition, and did much to secure the comfort of all.

Chapter 7

In Snow and Sleet

When the Basuto War broke out in 1880 the colonists living near the Drakensberg passes feared that they would be attacked by raiding parties crossing the border, and to allay this anxiety the police were called out. Under Sergeant-Major Stean, the headquarters detachment left Pietermaritzburg on the 27th July, and two days later camped on the left bank of the Bushman's River, where they were joined by the Estcourt division, under Sub-Inspector Jackson. A few days afterwards the Greytown detachment arrived, under Inspector Mansel, and then came the men from Fort Pine under Sub-Inspector Phillips; the whole force being under the command of Major Dartnell.

On the morning of the 10th August the troops marched to the Blauw Krantz River, and as the transport wagons got into difficulties they did not reach camp until after dark, so no tents were pitched. This was unfortunate, for at midnight rain began to fall heavily, gradually turning to snow; and during the whole of the two days following the men were made intensely uncomfortable by a bitterly cold wind which swept off the snow-clad berg.

Driving sleet cut into the men's faces next morning when a move was made, and to give the troopers some degree of warmth Major Dartnell ordered them to walk and lead their horses. After they had covered about five miles in this way, a halt was called near Loskop, when it was found that the wagons on which the all-important cooks and cooking pots were carried had taken the wrong road, so it was late in the day before the half-frozen men were able to get a hot meal, of which they were badly in need. There was joy in the camp when it was discovered that one wagon that had followed the men contained a keg of rum, and a ration was issued "to keep out the cold."

That night the severity of the weather necessitated turning the horses loose knee-haltered, instead of their being picketed. The men had a terribly miserable time, being wet to the skin, with no hope of getting dry. The incessant rain turned the ground into a swamp, and when the march was resumed they were up to their knees in mud half the time; and there was sore trouble also on account of the wagons sticking fast in every *spruit*. On the 12th August the force crossed the Little Tugela, where they remained until the 8th October, patrols covering the Oliver's Hoek Pass and the Bushman's Pass.

When the weather improved the troopers had a much better time at the camp, although the greatest difficulty was experienced in procuring fodder for the horses. The men had daily drills, mounted and dismounted. A simple system of mounted infantry drill was practised here for the first time, and it was afterwards adopted for the whole of the colonial forces, in lieu of the cavalry drill in squadrons, which was too complex for men only called out for a few days' training each year.

A memorable march was started when the camp broke up. While half the men were left at Estcourt, the Commandant, with Sub-Inspector Jackson, left for Ixopo, the detachment consisting of sixty-five men. After a long spell of fine weather the rain began to pour down the day the movement started. It being impossible to take a wagon, several days' supplies, tents, and other impedimenta were placed on a dozen pack-horses. The annals of the corps show that they have had some rough times, but they have never had such a melancholy trek before nor since. The rain fell almost without a break from start to finish. In those days mackintosh coats and waterproof sheets were unheard-of luxuries. Field boots had not been adopted, and the troopers were afraid to take off their wet regulation boots lest they should not be able to get them on again.

When the march was started a wicked pack-horse named Mazeppa was told off to carry the kitchen utensils, and was accordingly loaded up with pots, pans, camp kettles, and similar articles. This was done under the personal supervision of a sergeant, who took infinite trouble to show how a pack-horse should be loaded with such articles. Mazeppa patiently submitted to the operation, which, when finished, made him look very much like a perambulating tinker's shop. Trouble began when the party moved off. Mazeppa resented the indignity of having to carry pots and kettles. He pranced and danced and plunged until he had cleared all the things off his back, and then he was peaceful again. The sight of the wreck nearly made the cook weep.

It was decided not to use the tents, because the water would have increased their weight to such an extent that the pack-ponies could not have carried them, so the first night the men were glad enough to get sleeping accommodation in a couple of gaol cells and a stable at Ulundi.

With their clothing saturated, they resumed the trek next day, and the second night was spent in a stable on the Mooi River bank. It was a very bedraggled and dispirited band when it reached Fort Nottingham. Even the biscuits were sodden and much of the bully beef had become uneatable. Hopelessly, the men looked round for shelter; and all they could find was an old cowshed, open at every side. There was no chance of finding anything better, so they turned in there; and all night the heavy, driving rain beat pitilessly down on them. Sleep was out of the question, except in snatches, and even that was disturbed by a number of pigs that wandered into the place. They were cursed and kicked and spurred, but those pigs had made up their minds not to move away, and they remained amongst the troopers all night, though kept continually on the move.

The next day brought the detachment to the Umgeni River, which proved to be a serious obstacle, for it was in flood. The fact of going into the water did not worry the men, excepting those who could not swim, for they were as wet as ever they could be, but there were the rations to consider. The men's luck, however, was completely out, for in the crossing all the sugar, tea, coffee, and biscuits were destroyed.

At Boston Mills Mr. C. R. Glynn acted the part of the Good Samaritan, providing the troopers and their animals with ample supplies of food; and again on the following day they fell into kindly hands, the residents at Byrnetown supplying them with rations. On the way to the Umkomaas the rain fell more heavily than ever, and the men were never more pleased in their lives than when they came in sight of Ixopo. The first night they bivouacked under a hedge, and afterwards moved to the ground on which the trees of the Residency now stand.

Considering the state of their things, the troopers were somewhat appalled, within a few hours of their arrival, to hear that a kit inspection was ordered. All their steel bits, steel stirrups, and steel scabbards were, naturally, in a state of rust; but the men did the best they could in the circumstances, and the inspection was made in a heavy downpour of rain.

Passing through Ixopo, on his way from Harding, on the following morning, the Governor, General Sir George Colley, held an inspection of the police. They marched past in column of troops and did some skirmishing drill, and the Governor paid them a high compliment, saying they were a body of men which would do credit to any colony, and which any General would feel proud to command.

In the middle of November Major Dartnell's detachment was moved in the direction of Dronk Vlei—and the rain began as usual when they left camp. This time they had the additional worry of wagons. The troopers were all wet through when they reached Mabedhlane, and there they heard, sadly enough, that the wagons were stuck fast, some distance back. The only thing to do was to go back and pull the vehicles out. By sundown the weather had cleared up, and as there was no prospect of meeting any one, the men stripped their wet things off and marched back along the road naked. They found the wagons badly bogged, and after they had struggled for a while to get them out the task had to be abandoned. The tents, blankets, and food were taken off and put on to pack-ponies, which carried them to the camp.

The state of things at Dronk Vlei was no better. There, on the banks of the Umzimkulu River, the ground was so swampy that picket pins would not hold, so the horses had to be turned loose at night. The water became a sort of nightmare. When the men dug trenches round the tents they started springs. All the biscuits went mouldy, and there was no opportunity of getting fresh supplies.

The next move was to the Upper Umzimkulu, *via* Ipolela—a wild, unpopulated district in those days. For six weeks the camp was pitched at Christison's Drift, and from there the narrow passes over the *berg* were kept under observation by patrols.

The Basutos made one raid into Natal, and the police executed a hasty night march to intercept them. A man named Kennedy and some native scouts had been surprised by the Basutos and murdered, but the raiders retired quickly on hearing of the movement of the police, and did not cross the border again at that time.

Trouble was brewing, meanwhile, with the Boers. They had never agreed to the annexation of the Transvaal, and now refused to pay taxes. In the November of 1880 Inspector Mansel and Sub-Inspector Phillips, with the troops from Estcourt, were rapidly marched to Newcastle, and were employed for some time patrolling along the northern border of the colony, constantly watching the Buffalo River drifts, the passes of the *berg*, and the main road over Laing's Nek, with strict orders to avoid any open conflict with the Boers. These instructions resulted in Sub-Inspector Phillips losing two men. At Laing's Nek the Boers took Troopers Taylor and Swain as prisoners, deprived them of their horses and equipment, and sent them to Heidelberg, where they remained until the end of that war.

On one occasion the police were turned out towards midnight and marched to the Ingangane with sealed orders. There it was found that they were to meet General Colley at the Biggarsberg and escort him to Newcastle. In order to avoid capture by the Boers one troop went on to the Biggarsberg Nek to await the arrival of the post-cart from which the general and his staff descended, their places being filled by men of the police. The general and his officers then mounted the spare horses, and rode in the ranks to Newcastle, being joined at the Ingangane by the troopers who had been left there.

Another important duty performed by the police was that of acting as escort to Major Poole, R.A., who had been ordered to make a night reconnaissance to Laing's Nek. About sixty miles were covered that night, sufficient time being spent on the hill to enable the officer to make a sketch in the moonlight.

The Administrator of the Transvaal wrote to General Colley:

The Boers are incapable of any united action, and they are mortal cowards, so anything they may do will be but a flash in the pan.

Right on the top of this followed the disaster to the 94th Regiment at Bronkhurst Spruit, near Pretoria, when 120 men were killed and wounded and the remainder taken prisoners. The garrisons in the Transvaal at Pretoria, Standerton, Marabastadt, Leydenburg, and Potchefstroom were at once besieged.

To relieve the garrisons in the Transvaal became the first duty of General Colley, who had a very small force at his disposal, especially of mounted men. Including the police these only numbered 120, a few of them being volunteers from infantry regiments who could scarcely ride. There were also six 7-pounder field-guns, a naval brigade, with Gatling guns and rocket tubes, a portion of the 3rd Battalion of the 60th Rifles, a portion of the 58th Regiment, and two companies of the 21st Fusiliers. The infantry numbered 870 all told. Thus, in the early stages, prior to the arrival of reinforcements, the police formed almost the whole of the mounted troops that the general had to make use of, and he issued the following instructions:—

The special uses of mounted troops are first and principally for scouting purposes, to feel the enemy, and guard the column against surprise. Considering the small number we have, and the large number opposed to us, our mounted troops will have to be most carefully used and nursed. Ordinarily, one-half will be with the advance-guard on the march and do the actual scouting, the other half being with the rear.

The mounted troops must act as cavalry in action, supporting and covering the flank of an infantry attack, charging and pursuing when opportunity offers, and especially threatening the horses of the Boers when the latter are dismounted to hold a position. A Boer is nervously afraid of being left dismounted; and a demonstration against the horses, when these have been left under cover in order to hold a position, may often result in the position being abandoned.

In all encounters between our mounted troops and Boers it should be remembered that a prolonged skirmish with firearms is almost sure to end in favour of the Boers, who are better shots, and train to mount and dismount rapidly, and shoot from horse-back. Unless, therefore, the superiority in numbers on the side of the Boers be so great as to forbid such a course, the best chance of bringing matters to a favourable issue will generally be to charge. The Boers are not good at hand-to-hand fighting, nor armed for it. It is for this reason I have armed the mounted men with swords, which against another enemy I should not have given them.

With such a small force, it was impossible to detach men for lines of communication, and all supplies had to be conveyed by ox-wagon from Pietermaritzburg without escort. The besieged garrisons in the Transvaal were ill-supplied with food, so the general was compelled to advance without waiting for reinforcements.

The column left Newcastle on the 24th January 1881, about 1200 strong, the general intending to relieve Standerton and wait there for reinforcements. The force was exceedingly small to attempt the invasion of the Transvaal, but the general appealed to the courage, spirit, and discipline of his men to enable him promptly to retrieve the misfortune at Bronkhurst.

The police paraded at 3 a.m. on the morning the advance was started, forming the rear-guard and supplying skirmishers on either flank. The rear-guard had a very tedious time, as the large convoy of wagons delayed the march to such an extent that only four miles were covered in a dozen hours.

The road to the north at that time passed over the ridge near Signal Hill, to the east of the present main road. It was in a very bad state, and the wagons stuck fast every few yards. On the morning of the following day the police had to form the advance-guard. There was something wrong with the commissariat arrangements, and this unfortunately led to the troopers drawing no rations before starting. They were sent out to scour the country, and found no signs of the enemy for a distance of six miles in all directions. At night the camp was pitched at Ingogo Drift, where information was received that Inspector Phillips and a patrol had been captured in the direction of Coetzee's Drift. A force went off at once, but the rumour was found to be false. When they reached Inspector Phillips, he was watching a small party of Boers on the opposite side of the river.

Before the police were able to obtain their first meal that day, "Lights out" was sounded. Immediately afterwards fresh beef was served out to the men, but a Staff officer insisted on the fires being put out. The irregular troops frequently had to submit to treatment like this, but in the end, on this occasion, tinned meat and biscuits were served out to the famished troopers. Although they had been up since 3 a.m., Major Dartnell, with one troop, was turned out just before midnight, to go to the double drift at the Ingogo. It had been feared that the Boers might attempt to cross at this point under cover of darkness, and the police spent the rest of the night there without seeing anything of the enemy.

Very weary, they were put on duty as rear-guard at 7 a.m. the following day. The wagons were dragged painfully up the Ingogo Hill, it being several hours before the top was gained. The force reached Mount Prospect camp at noon, just as a violent thunderstorm broke. The rear-guard had a narrow escape from lightning, a telegraph pole being shattered as they passed it. A laager was formed with the wagons, the horses being picketed inside. Orders were given that no man must remove his accoutrements at night, and that the signal of alarm would be two shots fired in quick succession.

Just before midnight there was a scare. The outlying pickets came into the laager at the double, and all the troops stood to arms for half the night. Nothing alarming happened, however, and it was afterwards rumoured that a sentry, finding his duty monotonous, had fired two shots to liven things up.

No movement could be made the next day, the 21st January, owing to a drizzling rain and thick mist which covered Laing's Nek. A score of the police were warned for special duty. They saddled up and waited in the rain for five hours. The intention, apparently, was to make a reconnaissance across the Buffalo to see if there was a possible route to Laing's Nek from the Transvaal side; but eventually the expedition was abandoned.

The Battle of Laing's Nek was fought early the following day. Breakfast was eaten at 6 a.m., and an hour later the troops moved off, the police being sent as advance-guard. The coming fight was looked forward to with the keenest interest; and the artillery officers, relying on their 7-pounder guns, were betting that they would clear the *nek* in a quarter of an hour. This everybody believed, with the greatest of confidence, would be the case. A detachment of the 21st Regiment was left behind to hold the laager. With the supports to the advance-guard were four guns of the Royal Artillery. Then came the Naval Brigade, with rocket tubes, followed by the 58th, and 3rd 60th Regiments, the mounted infantry forming the rear-guard. Altogether the attacking force comprised 870 infantry, 180 mounted men, six guns, and three rocket tubes.

Very few Boers were seen as the force came near the *nek*, and the general belief was that the imposing British array had had its effect. The police were kept in reserve, together with the 3rd 60th Rifles to guard the left flank, and place *vedettes* along the ridge running up to the Majuba.

The attack was made by the mounted infantry and 58th Regiment, which dashed up the hill unchecked for some distance. When the artillery opened fire three or four Boers were observed galloping over the skyline, and everybody cheered madly, thinking the enemy were on the run.

The police had even mounted their horses in readiness for pursuit, and the mounted infantry were half-way up the hill, when the enemy opened a heavy fire. Both men and horses began to drop, but the British force pushed its way to the summit. Then they turned back, coming down the hill much faster than they had gone up, leaving four dead and thirteen wounded behind.

The 58th Regiment was now moving up the hill on the left of the ridge, their red tunics and white helmets offering a splendid target to the Boers, who were hiding behind rocks on the summit. Colonel Deane took them up as fast as they could cover the ground, and soon the face of the hill was covered with red dots showing where the Boer bullets had found their mark. The attackers and attacked were very close together when the artillery's shooting suddenly ceased, and the front line wavered. The withering fire had thinned the British ranks terribly. All the mounted officers had been killed, and there was only a subaltern left to give the order to retire. As the men came down the hill the Boers left their cover and picked out the running figures with deadly accuracy.

The police *vedettes* were under fire at this time, shots coming from the bush, and the skirmishers had to be withdrawn. Inspector Mansel gave his men the order to draw swords, preparatory to a charge, but this did not prove to be necessary, although the police sat on their horses for some time, presenting a very good target to the enemy.

As soon as the retirement had taken place, Troopers Purser and Ravenscroft, of the police, were sent with Captain M'Gregor, a Staff officer, up the *nek* under a flag of truce, with a message asking that hostilities should cease until the wounded had been brought down from the hill. The Boers agreed to this, and on returning, Purser and Ravenscroft passed along the battlefield telling the wounded to lie still.

As soon as the firing ceased a large party of Boers appeared on one of the spurs of Majuba, and the General gave orders for a retirement, the police forming the rear-guard, but the Majuba party did not fire on them, and the dead and wounded were placed on ambulances. The 58th Regiment had lost about 160 out of 480 men.

The *laager* was reached at 4 p.m. and, after the men had had a hurried meal, General Colley ordered a parade of troops, to which he delivered a short address. He said he had been bound to make the attempt to relieve the beleaguered garrisons in the Transvaal. The attack on the *nek* had failed, but the blame must rest entirely with him .

He complimented all ranks on their steadiness, and regretted that owing to scarcity of supplies, the defenceless state of Newcastle, and the importance of keeping his communications open, it would be necessary to send the Natal Police back to Newcastle with all speed, though he hoped to have them back with him when he made his next advance.

At dusk Inspector Mansel left Mount Prospect with one mule wagon—which rolled into a *donga* while they were descending the Ingogo Hill. They were compelled to remain there until daylight, and, finding a store near, had a glorious banquet of tinned salmon, tinned pears, and bottled beer. It was a difficult task to set the wrecked wagon right in the darkness, but they were able to resume their journey at dawn, and reached Newcastle safely. Here preparations were made for defending the town, and small forts were built to guard the approaches, being manned at night by the police, who also furnished pickets during the daytime. Heavy rains fell, and the water, pouring through the patrol tents, drenched everything belonging to the men.

The police were sent out on the 2nd February to meet a convoy of wagons and wounded men returning from Mount Prospect, and on the same day a party of the police escorted Commodore Richards of the Royal Navy, to Newcastle, from General Colley's camp.

A number of recruits arrived from Estcourt on the 3rd February, and they, with six other men, were left in Newcastle, while Major Dartnell, with under fifty men, went out to hold the Biggarsberg Nek, where it was feared the Boers might attempt to hold back reinforcements who were to arrive under General Wood.

False alarms were continually occurring in Newcastle in these days, and many of the residents took refuge in the *laager* at night. Mr. Rider Haggard, who was in Newcastle, afterwards wrote on the subject:

One night I was sitting in the drawing-room reading, at about eleven o'clock, with the door leading on to the verandah slightly ajar, for the night was warm, when suddenly I heard myself called by name in a muffled voice, and was asked if the place was in possession of the Boers.

Looking towards the door I saw a full-cocked revolver coming round the corner, and on opening it in some alarm, I could distinctly discern a line of armed figures in a crouching attitude stretched along the verandah into the garden beyond.

It turned out to be a patrol of the Mounted Police, who had received information that a large number of Boers had seized the place, and had come to ascertain the truth of the report.

The commissariat supply in Newcastle, as indeed during the whole campaign, was most unsatisfactory so far as the police were concerned. Rations were supplied by the Government, the men being charged 3s. per day each, but these supplies were very inadequate. The police were put to much expense for extras, everything, of course, being sold at war prices. The difficulty of obtaining firewood was a particularly sore point with the men.

On the 8th February three members of the force were sent from Newcastle by Major Terry of the 60th Rifles, with important dispatches for General Colley, receiving strict orders to avoid capture by the Boers, who had for some days stopped all communication with Mount Prospect. Mr. Cameron, a London war correspondent, who wished to get through to the general, accompanied the party. They made a long detour with the object of crossing the Ingogo high up, but very soon found the enemy occupying all the high ground that commanded a view of the country, so they turned east with the intention of passing along the Schuyn's Hoogte Valley, in order to outflank the Boer parties. On reaching the top of a hill they were startled by a sudden outburst of firing. Not knowing whether the enemy had discovered them or not, they hurried on to the highest point, and from there obtained a view of the battle that was being fought near the Ingogo River.

The dispatch riders were spotted by the Boers, who sent a number of men to intercept them, so they had to retire with all speed. The trio found no difficulty in getting away, but it was utterly impossible for them to get through to the general, so they returned and reported to Major Terry. He complimented them on their discretion, saying it would have been most unwise to attempt to get the dispatches through. At four o'clock on the following morning the police were ordered out, unarmed, to take wagons to the scene of the previous day's fighting, and bring in the wounded, who had been left all night on the battlefield.

The injured men were put on the wagons, and were taken back to Newcastle, where the police were hastily ordered out again to Signal Hill, it being expected that the enemy were about to make an attack on Newcastle. They were called in again at 8 p.m., having gone twenty-six hours without food, to find the residents were suffering from a bad attack of "nerves." They clamoured to take refuge in the laager, and were very wrathful when informed that they could not do so until the occasion warranted it.

Several very miserable days were spent after this by the police, who had the task of escorting the heliograph party of the 60th Rifles to Signal Hill. Rain poured down incessantly, and they often sat from 4 a.m. until 7 p.m. wet to the skin, only finding on returning to the laager that they had to spend the night occupying one of the forts.

As it was believed that the British were in conflict only with the Transvaal Boers, and that the Orange Free State was remaining neutral, it came as a shock to the men at Newcastle when a party of Boers descended Muller's Pass, and looted and burnt a convoy of wagons near the Horn River, between the *laager* and the Ingangane. The enemy had made a wagon *laager*, and sent a strong patrol each day to the Ingangane. These patrols were observed by the scouts, but General Wood ridiculed the idea, and narrowly escaped capture on the afternoon of the 15th February, when he made a reconnaissance to the Ingangane, accompanied by Major Dartnell and an escort. The party arrived at the river only fifteen minutes after the Boers had retired. The Natal Police were sent to occupy the heights commanding the Ingangane Drift before dawn, and anticipate the arrival of the Boer patrol. When the enemy did return they found the troops holding the ground, and were compelled to retire.

Sub-Inspector Phillips was sent through with dispatches to Newcastle fifteen miles away, that evening, being ordered to take as escort twenty police. He told Major Dartnell he would prefer to go alone, as he had to cut across country and would probably be noticed if he had a lot of men with him. It was then arranged that he should take half a dozen troopers with him, and he started off at about 6 p.m. The Hussar *vedettes* had seen a large number of Boers, and a subaltern warned the dispatch rider that he was going straight towards them, so he left the road just before darkness set in.

Mr. Phillips was riding at the head of the party, and a couple of hours after the start he stopped suddenly, having nearly walked into a detachment of the enemy who were lying down and holding their horses. It was an exciting moment, and at first it was feared the Boers had seen them, but the police turned aside hastily and were not fired on. Sub-Inspector Phillips handed his dispatches over in Newcastle at 9.30 p.m.

On the 19th February the police joined the party which accompanied General Wood on a reconnaissance towards Wakkerstroom. There was a lot of hard riding on the expedition, nearly sixty miles being covered just under thirty hours, and the Buffalo River, which was in flood, was crossed twice. The police and the 15th Hussars took turns in forming the advance-guard. Although a very large area was scoured that day, no trace of the enemy could be found.

General Wood left a few days later for Pietermaritzburg, to hurry up the remainder of the reinforcements, which were already on the move from Durban. These consisted of the 15th Hussars, 2nd 60th Rifles, and 92nd Highlanders, who had been sent over from India, where they had been recently engaged in the Afghanistan campaign, the two infantry regiments having taken part in Lord Roberts' historic march from Cabul to Kandahar.

Just after midnight on the 23rd February a non-commissioned officer of the Natal Police with a party of eighteen men was sent to search a farmer's house at Schuyn's Hoogte, where Boers' arms and ammunition were supposed to be stored. A thorough search of the building was made, and the police, having found only one rifle, left the place. The reinforcements from India had left Newcastle, and as daylight broke the Hussars entered the house, looting everything worth taking. The column shortly afterwards piled arms near the house, and then about 1500 men, the Naval Brigade, Highlanders, rifles, native wagon-drivers, and others, swooped down to share in the plunder. The small party of police were unable to prevent the looting, and the naval men finished up by applying a burning bundle of forage to the thatch, the place being very soon reduced to ashes.

General Colley sent for the search-party of police, and demanded to know why the destruction had been permitted, but they had only to point to the hundreds of men in the vicinity to explain the situation. A number of geese were hanging incriminatingly from the saddles of the police, and these created a little suspicion until it was shown that the birds were those on which the Hussars had been practising sword exercise.

The farmer claimed £1500 compensation, and a court of inquiry was held. The farmer was paid an adequate sum in consideration of his loss, and the court exonerated the police.

While the troops remained in the valley, Major Dartnell was sent with all available police to protect the left flank of the column, and to watch the Botha's Pass road until the reinforcements had safely crossed the Ingogo River. Afterwards the majority of the police were sent back to Newcastle, where they remained employed in patrolling, escorts, and *vedette* duties until the close of the war.

In the meanwhile, Sergeant Faddy and twenty men of the police were stationed at Schuyn's Hoogte to garrison a small fort, together with a few men of the Highlanders, under Major Napier. A small earthwork had been put up, and the police were kept busily employed in patrolling, and engaged in the thrilling occupation of rounding up poultry at the neighbouring farms, all of which were unoccupied. The police patrol had just left Schuyn's Hoogte early on the morning of the 27th February, and was passing along the road in the direction of the Ingogo Drift, when it was overtaken by Major Napier, who directed the men to go as quickly as possible towards Mount Prospect and ascertain why firing could be heard near there. On arrival at the camp they reported to Major Essex, who kept them all there, excepting one man. He was sent back with a message to Schuyn's Hoogte stating that General Colley had successfully occupied the Majuba Hill, the key to Laing's Nek.

The police watched the figures in the distance on the summit of Majuba Hill. Firing was almost continuous, but it was on the farther side of the mountain. Just after midday they were ordered out to O'Neill's Farm, and as they rode along, the British troops began to retire from the top, the Boers coming over and firing downwards. The fugitives were scattered considerably, many of them having lost their rifles. The police were directed to pick up fugitives, and they did so, carrying them into camp on their horses.

There was much heartburning that night amongst the troops, for each regiment accused the other of having been the first to run.

The only other duty that fell to the police during this campaign was that of escorting President Brand, of the Orange Free State, from Muller's Pass to Laing's Nek, where he acted as arbitrator between the British and the Boers. After a convention with the enemy had been signed, the Natal Government asked that the police might be returned, and on the 30th March they received orders to get ready to go back to their different stations. They were inspected by General Sir Evelyn Wood before they left the camp, and, for a body of Natal Police, their garments were certainly extraordinary on that occasion. Their clothes were so dilapidated that scarcely two men were dressed alike. One-half of them wore helmets, and the other half were adorned with either forage caps or smasher hats. But General Wood did not judge them by their clothing. He said:

> I feel it is only just that your services for the present should be dispensed with, as you have already spent eight months under canvas and done excellent work. I am aware that the late General Colley spoke in the very highest terms of the valuable services rendered by the Natal Police, and in the event of hostilities being resumed, I shall be only too glad to give you an opportunity to add to your very high reputation.

Next morning the police started their homeward journey, the residents of Newcastle distributing cigars to them as they passed through the town. The first evening they were joined by Sub-Inspector Phillips, with his detachment, and they all spent a memorable evening in a cloud of mosquitoes. In order to give the horses some protection, fires were kept burning on the weather-side of the picket ropes, and the men themselves spent the whole night standing or sitting in the smoke. The different detachments turned off to Estcourt, Fort Pine, and Greytown, so that only eight men remained to continue the journey to Pietermaritzburg.

Very little credit fell to the lot of the Natal Police after all they had done during this arduous campaign. The brunt of the work had fallen on the mounted men, of which there were very few other than the police.

At the opening of the Legislative Council in the following October, the Administrator of the Government, Sir Evelyn Wood, said:

> While the forces were in the field, nearly two-thirds of our mounted police were employed watching the frontier. I take this opportunity of recording the fact that the late General Colley appreciated very highly the services of Major Dartnell, and the efficient force under his command.

CHAPTER 8

Disconcerting Discussions

The police had now been almost continually on active service for three years, and were somewhat upset at the tone of certain discussions in the Legislative Council concerning their utility.

Complaints were made that a sufficient number of the police had not been kept on patrols in the rural districts, both for the prevention of crime and the protection of the residents, especially in view of the fact that the force had cost £34,000 during the year. The reply of the Colonial Secretary was:

> I think it is not want of will on the part of the Government that prevents the police from patrolling more than they do. We have had wars lately all round, in Pondoland, in Basutoland, in Zululand, and in the Transvaal, and the police have been more or less actively engaged throughout. It is not a fact that patrols have not been sent out. There are only five detachments of the police besides those in Pietermaritzburg.
>
> Ten thousand men are not considered too many to form the police of Ireland, a country not much larger than Natal, and, that being so, how can it be expected that with our small force we can do all that has been asked? Twenty detachments would not suffice to do the work some people demand. Assuming that 50 detachments would do for all the colony, and that 150 is the number available, we should have three men in each detachment. Then there is the question of food and stabling. That is a very difficult problem, and one not very easily disposed of.
>
> I must also draw attention to the insufficiency of pay to the police to enable them to keep up patrols. The men at Estcourt at the present time pay 4s. 10d. per day for the upkeep of their

horses and themselves, out of their pay of 6s. per day. Then when we consider that a man has to purchase his horse, and keep up his clothing, we, must come to the conclusion that he really cannot keep things going. He gets no extra pay on patrol. When the grass is bad up-country, he has to pay 2s. 6d. per feed for his horse.

Taking everything into consideration, the wars there have been, and the fact that fifty-six patrols have been made during the year (apart from those in Umvoti County, where they are reputed to have been numerous), I think the Government does not lie under such a heavy indictment as some members would lead us to suppose.

It is only a few days since I had a serious conversation with Major Dartnell, and he expressed himself not only willing but desirous of making the force as useful as possible. But if this chronic state of war keeps up, we cannot expect that they can remain both police and military.

There is no doubt that a wholesome impression was caused in those days by the passage through a district of a body of police. In some places the presence of a couple of policemen had the effect of stopping stock thefts for months. In accordance with the wish expressed by the Legislative Council that the police should be distributed throughout the country districts, a number of small out-stations were formed towards the close of 1881.

The first was at Zaaifontein on the Drakensberg, and six men and a corporal, who were dispatched there from Fort Pine, had an unhappy experience. They had only one pack-horse to carry the kits of the seven men, and the house which was to be their headquarters "rent free" was merely a shed of one room on the slopes of the Drakensberg, where for seven months the men lived in the greatest discomfort.

There was no store within thirty miles, there was no stable nor kitchen, and their cooking utensils consisted of one pot. Moreover, they practically got nothing but buck and pumpkins to cook.

Other out-stations formed during that year were at Newcastle, Fort Nottingham, Boston, York, and Polela, being followed shortly afterwards by those at Ixopo, Noodsberg, Umsinga, Lion's River, and Ladysmith.

After a while it was decided to make life a little less unbearable for the benighted troopers in these outlandish places, by conferring on them such luxuries as bedsteads, tables, forms, stoves, a chair or two, and a few other necessary articles of furniture.

There was a pest of wild dogs in the Estcourt district early in 1882. These savage animals had created havoc amongst the sheep along the banks of the Upper Mooi River, and although the farmers complained bitterly of their loss, they gave the police a very frigid welcome when they went to hunt the dogs down, and offered no assistance whatever.

The question of increasing the numerical strength of the corps was debated at considerable length in the Legislative Council, and during the year provision was made altogether for 8 officers, 28 non-commissioned officers, and 264 troopers.

There was some uneasiness amongst the men, for although the force was organized originally for defence as well as a police force, the authorities were continually at loggerheads when discussing the problem as to whether the Natal Police were to be soldiers or policemen, or both. It is not difficult to understand that as the men's services had been spoken of very highly by some of the most distinguished officers of the British Army, including Generals Lord Wolseley, Sir Evelyn Wood, Sir Baker Russell, Sir George Colley, and Sir H. Clifford, they were very anxious to maintain their reputation as a military force.

The commandant, knowing how frequently they had been called upon for military service, stated at this time, that a high state of efficiency or discipline could not be maintained when men were scattered throughout the colony, under the control of non-commissioned officers only, a certain amount of drill being necessary to instil discipline and ready obedience to orders, without which anybody of men becomes a mere demoralized rabble in the presence of an enemy.

It was pointed out then that it was possible to employ the police in a dual capacity by forming troop stations in different places, under the command of an officer, each detachment having enough men to drill and keep in training. This system was subsequently carried into effect, and is maintained today. In the event of trouble with the natives, troops from the various outlying stations are called into their district headquarters. This is very effectual in checking native risings, as a united body of police under the present system can get to the scene of a disturbance within a few hours of the order being given.

When the present Adjutant, Major O. Dimmick, joined the corps in April 1883, the headquarters were still at a queer little shanty in Church Street. There were about a hundred men stationed at the building, which had not adequate accommodation for a score of them.

INSPECTOR DIMMICK, ADJUTANT OF NATAL POLICE.

Most of the troopers slept under canvas in the small yard, where there were also about eighty horses picketed. Even in those days, nearly a decade after the corps had started, the men were having a hard time, and the recruits, who were still of a rougher class than those who constituted the force in later days, were dispatched to out-stations as quickly as possible after they had been drilled at headquarters. The uniform was then a black one, and the men carried a carbine at the side of the saddle, its muzzle resting in a bucket.

A fresh disturbance arose in Zululand in 1884. Although Cetewayo was living as a refugee near Eshowe, he incited his adherent to attack Sibepu's tribe, the Mandhlagagi, which had given the king's followers a severe beating at Undini in the July of the previous year, and had driven Cetewayo himself from his *kraal*. In January 1884 the Usutu party [1] met with another defeat, and not long after that Cetewayo died. The loyal natives in the reserve were subjected to much annoyance by the Usutu party, which assumed a defiant attitude towards the Resident Commissioner.

A force of 3000 loyal natives, including 50 of the Zululand Police, were sent to Nkandhla, where the Commissioner's camp was attacked by the late king's people, who were repulsed with heavy loss. This fight took place close to Fanifili's store, which was the scene of considerable unrest during a more recent period.

The brothers of the late king endeavoured to persuade the Transvaal Boers to help them to establish the strength of the Usutu party. This they agreed to do, and the Boers, who were already in force in Zululand, proclaimed Dinuzulu as king in May 1884. A few days later the Usutus were pounced upon by the chief Hlubi, with his Basutos and loyal natives, and the Usutus had 200 men killed, and more than 1000 head of cattle captured.

The Boers joined issue with Dinuzulu, and, attacking Sibepu, drove him out of his territory. The Boers promptly claimed in return for their services 8000 farms occupying nearly three million acres of land, and proclaimed the territory a Boer Republic, under the Protectorate of the Transvaal. It was in this way that the best part of Zululand was lost to the Zulus, and to the British Government which had spent millions of pounds in conquering it.

While these disturbances were in progress, a strong body of Natal Police, under Inspector Fairlie, were sent to the border. For about four months they were encamped at Fort Buckingham, an outpost being

1. The Zulu king's adherents.

formed at Middle Drift with one non-commissioned officer and six men, these being relieved every week.

Patrols were constantly sent out along the Tugela River from May until October, and the men suffered severely from intense cold and exposure. The horses died rapidly, very few of them surviving the expedition. Many of them died afterwards from a form of pneumonia brought on by the cold weather. The detachment from Estcourt lost every horse they had before the year closed. The Umhlali detachment patrolled the lower portions of the Tugela from Thring's Post to the mouth of the river, watching the drifts and preventing filibusters from leaving Natal to join Sibepu's party in Zululand.

While these detachments were employed on what was practically military duty, the Fort Pine and Newcastle men were stationed at the Orange Free State passes to the Drakensberg, preventing natives from entering Natal, as smallpox had broken out at Kimberley.

There was a good deal of gun running into Pondoland at this time, and the men of the Harding detachment had some exciting adventures while putting a stop to this practice at the drifts to the Umtamvuna River, but there was a serious outbreak of glanders amongst their horses, which disabled them for a long time shortly afterwards. The colonial veterinary surgeon ordered the destruction of every animal in the place, the stable, and all the stable utensils. After this the detachment was withdrawn from Harding for a year.

Towards the end of 1884, detachments of the Natal Police were placed at Ladysmith, Umsinga, Thring's Post, Dundee, and Van Reenen's Pass, the men at the last-named place carrying out the duties in connection with the Customs, Excise, and Telegraph Department.

When the year 1885 opened, the force consisted of 300 Europeans and 25 natives, but a wave of retrenchment passed over the colony, and the threat, often repeated, to reduce the number of the Natal Police was carried out to some extent. But the following year a much more serious step was taken in this direction, the Europeans being reduced to 180 all told, and the whole of the native policemen were wiped out.

This made it exceedingly awkward for the Europeans at work on the back-stations, they being deprived of one of their most useful sources of information. Most of the Europeans who left on this occasion joined in the rush that was then taking place to the gold mines.

In 1887 the inspection of hut tax licences by the police was started, and new stations were established at Acton Homes, Impendhle, Oliver's Hoek, and Umlazi. The detachment at Van Reenen's Pass were having a very busy time, there being an enormous amount of traffic going through to Johannesburg. That year over 29,000 wagons passed the place both ways, and the licence for each one had to be inspected. In addition to this, the police, acting as Customs officers, examined nearly 50,000 packages.

The wave of economy that spread over the colony resulted in the officers' pay being reduced by 5 *per cent.*, and all other ranks had 6d. per day knocked off; but, a year later, when a reign of prosperity had set in once more, the whole of this was returned to the men in the form of a bonus.

There was considerable alarm amongst the residents of Alfred County, on account of the attitude of the Amanyuswa tribe, which had assembled for the purpose of "doctoring." The report was received that they appeared to be on the warpath, so a detachment of the police was hastily dispatched from Harding to check any disturbance. The tribe soon settled down and dispersed.

When the prosperity of Natal increased in 1889, the strength of the force was raised by fifty men, but, such were the vicissitudes of Natal's chief defensive body in those days, these fifty men were taken away again a twelvemonth later. The force was spoken of, in consequence, as the "financial barometer of the colony," rising and falling, as it did, with the revenue.

Again there was anxiety amongst the white settlers in Alfred County owing to unrest in Pondoland, and amongst the natives on the southern border. Every available man, with three officers, was sent to Harding towards the close of the year, and strong patrols were kept continually on the move while Sigcau, the paramount chief of Pondoland, was engaged in a bitter battle with his uncle, Umhlangaso, who was compelled to take refuge in Natal on one occasion when hotly chased by Sigcau at the head of an *impi* of 10,000 men. Such is the respect that the native has for the white police, that the *impi* refrained from crossing the border as a result of their presence.

Detachments of police were sent this year to Port Shepstone, Coldstream (afterwards known as Charlestown), and New Guelderland, near Stanger.

Although the conditions at the old barracks had always been both unpleasant and insanitary, it was not until an outbreak of enteric fever laid a large number of the men out, and killed five of them, that new premises were obtained. Recruits were moved to the site of the present barracks on a hill overlooking Pietermaritzburg, where a camp was pitched, and the handsome building, which is at present used as headquarters, was soon afterwards erected.

CHAPTER 9

Disturbances in Pondoland

It was in 1889 that the Natal Police for the first time met Dinuzulu, whose name has been before the public a great deal in recent years. In this year he was taken prisoner as a rebel against the Imperial Government, and the police received him at the Lower Tugela, escorting him to Pietermaritzburg before he embarked to undergo part of his sentence at St. Helena.

At about this time several years' continuous anarchy in Pondoland began. Umhlangaso and his followers, who lived on the border of Natal, absolutely refused to submit to Sigcau, the paramount chief. A message was sent to Pietermaritzburg stating that the natives on the Natal side of the border were getting troublesome, and that the chiefs Umbono and Umpikwa appeared likely to come to blows. Some of the bitter enemies of the police in the Legislative Council had stated that a sufficient number of police to be useful could not be assembled in less than a fortnight. This statement was, of course, absurd, and on this particular occasion, 110 men were gathered from stations in all parts of the colony.

The majority of these were on the extreme southern border within forty-eight hours, and those from the most distant stations had arrived on the morning of the fifth day from the time the orders were dispatched from headquarters. Newcastle was then the terminus of the main railway line, and there were no branch lines, so most of the men had to do the greater part of their journey on horseback. In every instance the troopers who went from Pietermaritzburg to the border travelled by road, which journey today is in itself considered a good five days' trek. Harding, which was the point where they assembled, was nearly the most distant point in the colony from the railway, and these forced marches had all to be conducted in terribly bad weather.

The first detachment of police arrived in time to prevent bloodshed between the two tribes; but there was some fighting, and armed natives from Pondoland, having crossed the Umtamvuna River, joined gaily in it. The arrival of the police was so unexpected that a large number of prisoners were taken, and many of the natives were disarmed.

Early in 1891 the camp was moved from Harding to a point overlooking the Umtamvuna, near the drift, patrols moving up and down the river daily.

When taken to Pietermaritzburg, Umbono was ordered to pay a fine of £650, and as he showed no inclination to hand over the money, the police marched to his kraal and surrounded it. This demonstration altered the chief's mind, and he was not long in paying the fine.

The fighting was resumed in Pondoland not long afterwards, and it took place so close to the border that Sigcau's *impi*, numbering 10,000 warriors, drove its enemy through the river into Natal. The two forces remained on opposite sides of the water, sniping at one another, until Colonel Dartnell crossed with a small escort and directed the paramount chief to retire. The firm attitude he adopted had the desired effect and, there is no doubt, averted a great deal of bloodshed, for had the pursuers once crossed the river there would have been a massacre not only of the fugitives from Pondoland, but also of the Natal natives.

The police, in the absence of rapid transport for supplies, were having a rather trying experience, and while they were doing most useful work in the south of the colony, abuse was being hurled at them very freely in the Legislative Council.

"As a police force they are utterly useless in the prevention or detection of crime," said one speaker. "The organization is on a wrong basis altogether. When you travel about Natal you will find people in every district say that the police are an utter failure in many respects."

"As a military force," said another speaker, "the Natal Police are really very contemptible. If one looks to them for defence it will be a very miserable defence indeed."

The Colonial Secretary pointed out that these were intemperate remarks. "It is an exceedingly useful force," he said, "a singularly fine corps, and at this moment it affords a nucleus for a defensive force such as probably no other colony in the world ever possessed on the eve of adopting Responsible Government."

In spite of a spirited defence which was made on behalf of the Natal Police, their numbers, which a little while previously had been added to, were again reduced by fifty men. Fortunately this reduction did not involve hardships on the men dismissed, because the other South African police forces took them over.

The scene of trouble was moved from the borders of Pondoland to the Bulwer Division, where a number of natives assumed a defiant attitude towards a magistrate. Some native police were sent out to make arrests, but these men were driven back, whereupon Corporal Strutt took out a detachment of six European troopers, and these were joined by some of the white residents. They marched out in the direction of the rebels, whom they found armed and still defiant. The white force opened fire on them, and those who refused to lay down their arms were killed. From the summit of a hill not far away another body of armed natives watched this skirmish. Doubtless their intention was to assist their friends until they saw what happened, and then they disappeared discreetly into the bush, and created no more trouble.

Up to this time the position of the police as a police force had been a somewhat curious one. The magistrates in the various divisions had worked independently, no central authority existing for dealing with cases. No intelligence regarding crimes was ever sent to headquarters by the magistrates, and a warrant, if not executed at the first attempt, was filed. The depositions were lost, and of course no record of the doings of criminals was kept. The clerk of the court prosecuted in criminal cases. The magistrate had charge of the gaols, and outside the central gaols there was no separate accommodation for women prisoners.

A Magistrates' Commission, which had taken evidence in all parts of the colony, presented its report in June 1892, and in this made the very recommendations which the Commandant of police had been urging year after year. Up to now there had been several distinct bodies of police in the colony—the Mounted Police, Borough Police, and Local Board Police Forces, the Magisterial Native Police, Messengers and Convict Guards, the Magisterial Patrol Police, and the Water Police. In its report the Commission said:—

> The police in the country districts, almost entirely natives, are under the direct control of the magistrate. They are employed in various ways, but only to a limited extent in police work. Under this system the magistrate is practically the chief detective in his division. He works up evidence in important cases, and

then has to sit in judgment. A small number of patrol police are employed, and under proper control and supervision they may be very useful. The magistrates have, however, neither time nor the opportunity to supervise such a force properly. The Commission have come to the conclusion that the scattered forces now in existence are not suited to the present circumstances of the colony, and that the amount of money now expended over them may, by means of different organization, be utilized so as to bring about much better and larger results. We consider that the time has arrived when a police department should be established under a Chief Commissioner.

In spite of this, no change was made until two years after the report was issued.

In the meantime, the main body of the Natal Police were very actively engaged in the south of the colony. Frequent scares occurred on the border, and fighting took place continually in Pondoland until September 1893, and then the paramount chief prepared to make a very serious attack on the neighbouring natives. The police with a Maxim gun moved along the rugged country, overlooking the Umtamvuna River, to a site near Luji's Drift. They had just off-saddled when a large *impi* appeared. It was that of Sigcau.

He was marching upon Maqutu and his men, who had spoken bravely of opposing the paramount chief at a narrow *nek* of land leading to a hill, but the moment the *impi* put in an appearance Maqutu and his valiant men disappeared. The victorious *impi* swept through the *kraals* of Maqutu, burning the huts as they passed. There was a dense bush not far away, and shots were fired from this by Maqutu's followers; in a very short time Sigcau's *impi* was retiring, and fifty of his men were killed.

Thousands of Pondo women and children with their cattle had crossed to the side of the river where the police were stationed, and remained in full view of Sigcau and his men, who, as usual on such occasions, were anxious to capture the animals. An impi of 10,000 men advanced in four columns to Luji's Drift, which they would in all probability have crossed with the object of securing the cattle had the police not lined up and made a demonstration.

When Sub-Inspector Clarke crossed into Pondoland and joined Sigcau's *impi* with the object of interviewing the paramount chief, the latter's followers had increased to 15,000 men. The chief himself was surrounded by an escort of Europeans and half-castes, who had been compelled to turn out. At the head of his column there were about 2000 mounted men, whose horses were jaded and in a sorry state, for they did not appear to have been off-saddled, fed, or watered for some time. Hundreds of breech-loading guns were held by men in the ranks, but the *impi* appeared to be somewhat short of ammunition . The men on foot marched in companies, each warrior being supplied with two large lumps of *mealie* bread, packed in grass rope, and carried over the shoulder. They had only one small beast with them for slaughtering purposes, it being evident that they expected to feed on the cattle of their enemies.

In November 1893, the unrest was as bad as ever in Pondoland, and the paramount chief, who was then very depressed, informed representatives of the police that his men were unwilling to do his bidding in making battle against Umhlangaso. The latter chief was very proud of his arrangements for meeting the enemy—if they cared to come. These preparations consisted of a small structure, which he called a "fort." This at the most would have held about twenty men. It was strengthened by a fence of barbed wire, and a most ridiculous site had been chosen for it, because it only commanded a space of about fifty yards. Sigcau had, however, heard of this wonderful structure, and the tales told about it to his men were so exaggerated that they declined to attack it.

On the 9th January Umhlangaso got into a fright as great as that of his opponent, and sent a message to Colonel Dartnell stating that if the police would only assist him he would in return hand over the whole country to Natal!

The two chiefs came to blows on the 11th January, and the police turned out to watch the battle, which proved to be a severe one. Sigcau's brother led the first attack, but it was feeble. Umhlangaso's men, the Umsizis, executed a clever manoeuvre. They retired slowly until the attackers were wedged in between two lines of bushy country. Then the Umsizis poured out in dense masses from the bush on either side, stabbed the men as they sat on their horses, and drove the *impi* back.

The following day while the police were at Middle Drift Sigcau's mounted men again came down to the river and opened fire on their enemy on the Natal side of the water. Whether the police were mistaken for the enemy or not, it is difficult to say, but many of the bullets fell close to them. As there appeared to be every prospect of the Pondos crossing over into Natal, the Maxim gun was trained on the drift, and the Pondos retired.

Some of the police paid a visit to the scene of the battle the following day and found scores of bodies lying about mutilated. There were more than a hundred dead natives outside the bush and many more amongst the trees.

CHAPTER 10

Important Changes

The year 1894 was a momentous one in the history of the Natal Police, for as a sequel to the inquiries made by the Commission all the police forces in the colony were amalgamated, under Colonel Dartnell as Chief Commissioner.

The Attorney-General, the Rt. Hon. H. Escombe, in moving the second reading of the Police Bill, pointed out that Natal was essentially a country to be governed by police, especially by police as distinguished from soldiers.

"There is at present a police force," he said:

...... which is weakened by disconnection. It consists of various bodies distributed through the land, under different heads, subject to no central power; and as a consequence, it is not properly in hand. The present measure will bring the whole of the separated police forces of the colony into one police unit.
A difficulty would have arisen in the matter of a Chief Commissioner of police if it had not been for the loyalty to the public service of Colonel Dartnell. He was told what the wishes of the Government were as regards the consolidation of the different forces. He was addressed in the capacity he is known so well to fill, that of a dashing soldier, and he was asked whether, having regard to the necessities of the case, he would accept the position of Chief Commissioner. We knew perfectly well that if that distinguished officer said he would, we might rely absolutely on his exact fulfilment of the duties of the office.
I am glad to say that without the least reserve or hesitation, he stated that he would comply with the wish of the Government. We found a most complete accord between General Dartnell

and ourselves, as regards the general control of the force. He knew, as we all know, that the peculiar character of the population here requires a police force which can move about in a strong body when necessity arises.

Under the Act the magistrates will be relieved from a duty which does not belong to magistrates. Hitherto they have, to a large extent, had their time occupied in acting the part of detectives, and because the duty is not consistent with that of a magistrate the work has not been done to the satisfaction either of the officers concerned or the public at large. Nothing can be more wrong in principle than for a magistrate to have to unearth crime, and then to try the criminal.

Colonel Dartnell and Sub-Inspector Clarke put their heads together and prepared this scheme of reorganization, which worked so successfully that it was subsequently adopted by every other colony in South Africa. To put it into working order in Natal was no light undertaking, especially in view of the fact that there was only a week in which to draw up the rules and regulations. From the date when the force was first started it had been known as the Natal Mounted Police. This body ceased to exist on the 30th June 1894, on which day there was a gathering of the officers of the old force, who were:

Colonel Dartnell, Commandant; Inspector W. F. Fairlie; Inspector F. A. Campbell; Inspector Phillips; Inspector Sewell, Paymaster; Inspector Masson; Sub-Inspector Stean, Adjutant; Sub-Inspector Dorehill; Sub-Inspector Clarke.

The new force, known as the Natal Police, was increased from 200 to 300 Europeans, and 100 natives were added to the ranks. Eleven police districts were established, and the out-stations were increased in number from twenty-six to sixty. It was hoped that the municipalities in the colony would come under the Act, but Pietermaritzburg, Durban, and Newcastle declined the offers made to them.

In some instances the magistrates submitted with ill-grace to the new regime, and one or two of them even today would be glad to have control of the native police. On the whole, however, the annual reports showed that the new system was a considerable improvement on that which it had superseded. The number of arrests in the first year rose from 2564 to 16,568, this showing that there must have been a lot of undetected crime prior to the change.

Before the force was reorganized, complaints were made that, owing to the inefficiency of the police, there was an annual loss of sheep by theft to the extent of 100,000. During the first twelve months of the working of the new system 2170 sheep were reported lost, and out of that number 893 were recovered. If a certain percentage of deaths be allowed, it will be seen how great was the miscalculation, or else how great was the improvement in the police. The average number of sheep reported missing annually has never since then exceeded 1000.

When the Natal Police took over the gaols they found them in a chaotic state. There was no system whatever, each establishment working independently of any other.

As soon as the change took place, applications were made in all parts of the colony for police stations, and the additional men enlisted were soon absorbed. As a result, a further increase of 200 troopers became necessary early in 1896, but as good men were not readily picked up in Natal, recruiting was started in England, and 100 men were enlisted there.

Shortly afterwards there was a plague of *rinder*-pest in the colony, and in order to place a strong guard on the borders of the Transvaal and the Orange Free State, to prevent cattle from being driven into Natal, the police had to be withdrawn from all the stations in the northern part of the colony.

Early in 1897 there was a panic in East Griqualand, where a native named Le Fleur was organizing a rebellion. Alarming rumours were flying about. Many of the inhabitants formed laagers, and a large number fled to Natal for refuge. There was no force in Cape Colony available to suppress the trouble, and the Natal Police were hurried down to the border to protect the fugitives. A body of 170 men was mustered, and as many of these were recruits fresh from England, and without uniform, they had a very uncomfortable experience while marching through heavy rain to Ixopo, where the residents were found to be in a state of great excitement.

A small body of the police went as far as the Umzimkulu River to find out exactly what was happening. They met large numbers of men, women, and children tramping wearily through liquid mud, the women and children driving cattle or *voor*-looping, and the men driving wagons and horses. Not one of them seemed to have any clear idea what the danger was from which they were fleeing, though they all stated that they had been warned by natives to "clear out."

Native spies that had been sent out reported that Msingapanzi's people intended to make an attack upon the magazine and secure the arms and ammunition it contained, but soon after the arrival of the

Natal police Field Force with Maxim guns in 1879

police the spies reported that this attack had been postponed.

Higher up the Umzimkulu a *laager* had been established at Graf ton's Farm, and early on the morning of the 24th January 70 men of the police were sent off to protect the refugees there.

There was great indignation at Ixopo on account of the inaction of the Cape Colony authorities. It was felt that the Cape Mounted Rifles should have been sent to their assistance, and at a meeting of residents a vote of thanks to Natal for saving the situation was passed.

As the unrest amongst the natives extended to Alfred County and the much-troubled Pondoland, a force of 60 men was sent to patrol the southern border. Later on they marched from Ixopo, joining the detachment at the Upper Umzimkulu, and patrols were sent to the Drakensberg. Towards the close of the march the police arrived at Bulwer, after having experienced ten days' incessant rain.

As the Natal winter approached they were ordered to the coast, but were delayed for three days at the Lorana River by a snowstorm which had a disastrous effect on the horses. A fortnight later the force got to Ixopo, having entirely run out of supplies, and these had to be ordered from Pietermaritzburg by wire. It was nearly a week before they were able to resume the march, and they got to Port Shepstone early in July, spending three months at that place. While they were there, fifty of the horses had to be destroyed owing to an outbreak of glanders. Before the force got back to Pietermaritzburg at the close of the year, glanders again appeared, and many more of the animals had to be shot, the total loss during the twelve months being 103, equal to 20 *per cent,* of the total strength.

When this field force had been at headquarters just three days, orders came for a detachment to march up into Zululand, which province had just been taken over by the Natal Government. Within an hour they were ready, and left under Inspector Dimmick for Eshowe and Nongoma, the march being accomplished over very bad roads, in constant rain-storms, and during excessively hot weather. For five weeks the rain continued, and horse-sickness was rampant. On the top of this, neither supplies nor letters could be got from Eshowe.

Early in February the police were ordered to Emtonjaneni, to meet Dinuzulu,[1] who had returned from exile at St. Helena, and on the way there they had difficulty in crossing the flooded Black and White Umfolosi Rivers. The party which the police took back with them consisted of Dinuzulu, his two wives, and five children, Dinuzu-

---

1. Generally spelt incorrectly "Dinizulu."

lu's uncle, with his wives and children, Tshingana and his family, Miss Colenso, who was one of Dinuzulu's chief supporters, several women, numerous servants, and a following of about five hundred Zulus. All these people struggled along the road for a couple of miles, when the Commissioner of Native Affairs sent a message to state that such a large following was unnecessary and must be dispensed with. On the Ulundi flats, however, nearly a thousand additional Zulus assembled to welcome the returned chief, and they proved very useful at the Emfabeni, where the road was impassable. The Zulus soon made the drifts fordable, and on the 23rd February the hill where the Usutu *kraal* was afterwards built was reached, and the police remained with Dinuzulu for a few days until he and his followers settled down.

Nearly all their horses had died during this trip, and out of three spans of mules, only five remained alive.

Inspector Fairlie took charge of the detachment at Nongoma, which remained there until Dinuzulu was again imprisoned, nearly twelve years afterwards.

The Zululand Native Police force was merged into the Natal Police in 1898, the latter body taking over all the European officers. Mr. Mansel, who had raised' the Zululand Native Police, now became second in charge of the European body. Ten police stations were established in Zululand, which was divided at first into five districts. The horses died rapidly, until the remount fund became entirely exhausted, and a supplementary vote had to be placed on the estimates.

An expedition left headquarters in Pietermaritzburg in April 1899 to locate the wreck of the *barque Dorothea*, which was stated to have a huge quantity of gold on board. Two trips were made to Cape Vidal with a diver and diving apparatus, and though some weeks were spent at the scene of the wreck, bad weather prevented anything being done at that time. The *Dorothea* has since become famous, for many syndicates have worked at the place—without success. Each party has been accompanied by a member of the Natal Police, acting on behalf of the Government.

CHAPTER 11

The Last Boer War

The Natal Police took a very active part in the Boer War of 1899-1902, but they won little distinction as a body, for, from the very beginning, they were split up into small detachments, although it was hoped when hostilities began that they would be formed into a field force about 400 strong.

The order to prepare for service was given at headquarters in August 1899, and it was decided to use pack-horses as a first line of transport. Pack-ponies were properly fitted with saddles which bore numbers corresponding with the animals. All loads were weighed and balanced, and every man knew exactly what his pack would contain, and where it was to be carried. Mounted natives were to lead the pack animals, thus relieving the Europeans for fighting purposes.

Colonel Dartnell was invited to join the Staff of the General Officer Commanding, and the first body of men called out for service in Natal consisted of 25 police, under Sergeant Woon. They were dispatched to the Upper Tugela magistracy on the 1st September to patrol the passes on the *berg*, and watch any movement of Boers in the direction of the Orange Free State ,

A curious point arose when the resident magistrate desired to take command of the police in the field, Sergeant Woon having been ordered to take his instructions from the magistrate as to the direction of patrols.

The enemy moved into Natal, and the question of the command of the police was referred to the General Officer Commanding. It was ruled that in all military operations the non-commissioned officer or even the senior trooper of a party would take charge of his men, because a magistrate might lead them into a tight corner, and not know how to get them out of it. This detachment was subsequently joined by the Natal Volunteers, and retired with them to Ladysmith, taking part in the defence of the town.

A hundred men remained at headquarters, and there were constant drill and target practice. They were inspected by many distinguished officers, including Generals Sir George White, Sir Archibald Hunter, Penn-Symons, and Yule, every one speaking highly of the first line transport and the celerity with which the men were able to turn out in marching order.

Orders were received by the men at headquarters, on the 29th September, to go to Dundee and await General Penn-Symons, and just as they were ready to march out, the Prime Minister telephoned to say that there was considerable trouble with the natives in Alfred County. When the men heard of this they were, naturally, keenly disappointed, for they had had quite sufficient of scares on the southern border, and General Penn-Symons gave the order that some of the recently raised irregular forces could be sent down to the troubled area if necessary. Even then, however, the detachment was prevented from joining the General.

On the 17th October a party of Boers were making their way through Umvoti County to destroy the Inchanga Tunnel on the railway, and thus prevent the passage of troops from Durban to Ladysmith. A special train left Pietermaritzburg at once with every available member of the Natal Police. They encamped at Botha's Hill, sentries being placed at the entrance to the tunnel, and a special engine being kept in readiness to move the men rapidly if necessary.

Just before midnight furious firing was heard, and supports rushed down to the engine. It was found that the sentries had shot at some figures near the line who failed to respond to a challenge. Later it was discovered that a European platelayer had had his hat shot through, and he also demanded a new pair of trousers; and a *coolie* had been shot in the leg. The platelayer had been told to patrol the line, and as he had not been told of the arrival of the police, he thought, when challenged, that the Boers were in possession of the place, so he threw away his lantern and bolted.

This detachment, which was recalled to Pietermaritzburg late in October, was subsequently broken up, some of the men joining Colonel Leuchars' column on the Greytown-Helpmakaar road, and others forming General Buller's bodyguard.

Orders were issued to all police in the Newcastle and Dundee districts to hold themselves in readiness to retire on Dundee, and this mobilization took place on the 14th October, although the detachment at De Jager's Drift was left to watch the movements of the enemy on the opposite side of the Buffalo.

At this station there were Sergeant Mann and Troopers Askland and Alexander, who were kept busy patrolling the Transvaal border. When the situation became more strained they were strengthened by the addition of Troopers Ferguson, Kenny, Harris, and Atwood. They had instructions to retire towards Botha's Nek if their position became untenable, and they were ordered to ring up Dundee on the telephone every two hours, day and night. Small parties of the Boers were constantly seen on the other side of the drift. On the 14th October Trooper Harris was captured while patrolling at the Emjanyadu Hill, and a couple of hours later eighteen Boers crossed the river and captured the police horses, which were out grazing. Not a shot was fired, and the animals were driven straight across into the Transvaal. From their position the Boers could see a party of mounted troops some distance away on the main road, and, having observed these, evidently thought they would secure the horses while there was an opportunity.

Sergeant Mann received instructions to remain at his post, and to secrete all arms and ammunition. He was told that a party would be sent to their relief, and while these orders were being sent the wire was cut. Not long afterwards a score of Boers crossed the river at the drift, and, galloping up to the camp, surrounded it and made its occupants prisoners.

Trooper Ferguson managed to hide himself away and escaped capture, subsequently walking off wearing a *kafir* blanket. The prisoners were sent to Vryheid by mule wagon.

When the Battle of Talana was fought, the police joined the 67th Battery and the Leicestershire Regiment. Colonel Dartnell, with Sergeant Good and Trooper Wright, of the police, accompanied General Penn-Symons in the fight. Sergeant Good's horse was shot, and Trooper Wright was wounded, being shot through the head. He died nearly twelve years afterwards from the effects of the wound. General Yule, who had succeeded to the command when General Penn-Symons was wounded, feared that an attack would be made by the Boer commando at the Impati Mountain. The mounted men reconnoitred, and reported that the enemy were there in strong force. Tents were struck, it being decided to form another camp and make a stand on one of the spurs of the Indumeni, where trenches were dug, only to be filled by rain-water.

Shells from the Boer commando fell unpleasantly near. The British batteries attempted to reply, but were out of range, and General Yule received the disconcerting news that reinforcements could not be sent to him because the troops at Ladysmith were engaged. The rain continued to fall, causing the greatest discomfort to the men, who had no tents or blankets, and were short of food.

When the news of the Boer defeat at Eland's Laagte reached General Yule on the 22nd he made a move in the direction of Glencoe to intercept the retreat of the enemy, but the Boers were too strong, and the General had to retire. That night, upon Colonel Dartnell's suggestion, concurred in by the Officers Commanding Regiments, he decided to make for Ladysmith, travelling *via* the Helpmakaar road, and the march began at 9 p.m. It was pitch dark, and Mr. C. F. Dodd, an ex-trooper of the Natal Police, guided the column out of Dundee. Orders were given for strict silence, but the guns and transport wagons made quite enough noise to let any Boers who might have been in the vicinity know what was happening.

Without a break, the troops marched all night, and at dawn had five hours' much-needed rest and a good meal. At midday the general decided to wait at the head of Van Tender's Pass for darkness, before making a further move, and that night the column was guided down the path to the Waschbank River by Trooper Jock Grey of the police. Again the column marched all night, and when the Waschbank was reached, soon after daylight, many of the troops were thoroughly worn out. They slept there for some hours, but a heavy thunderstorm caused much misery in the afternoon, the river rising twelve feet and turning the country into an ocean of mud.

The retirement was continued at 4 a.m. the following day, and as there was no sign of pursuit the march was conducted in a more leisurely fashion. At Sunday's River another halt was made, and the horses were given an opportunity of grazing. Some of the men on this occasion were able to strip for the first time for five days. That evening troops arrived from Ladysmith to assist the column over the last stage of the journey, and as Boers were reported to be in the vicinity, General Yule decided to undertake another night march, again in pouring rain.

It was a long and painful night for all concerned. Mules, horses, and men were knocked up, and the column was broken every few minutes. Once the wagons stuck fast for two hours, and the advance-guard, knowing nothing of this, went right away and left them. Nobody was sorry when Ladysmith was reached at breakfast-time.

While this retirement from Dundee was in progress, General Sir George White feared that the Free State commando, which was said to have reached Bester's Station, would intercept the column, so, with the object of engaging the attention of the enemy, he moved out of Ladysmith in the direction of Eland's Laagte.

He had with him a troop of police, who paraded with the other troops at 3 a.m. on the 24th October, and, with the volunteers, formed the rear-guard until, about six miles out of the town, the 5th Lancers, at the head of the column, came under fire. The police and other mounted men were then sent to form the advance-guard.

As soon as the infantry were in position facing the Intintanyoni Mountain, the police and volunteers were moved to a ridge on the right flank of the enemy, who held a very strong position overlooking a valley, and were about six thousand strong. From where the Boers were they could watch every movement of the British troops, who, on the other hand, found it most difficult to pick out a target, the enemy having excellent cover.

There was a kopje in the valley which dominated the whole position. It was seen that a number of Boers were making for it, and had they reached the place they could have enfiladed the troops. Major Bru de Wold, Chief Staff Officer of the Volunteer Brigade, pointed out to the police (who numbered about thirty) what was happening, and ordered them to take the kopje. Hastily dismounting, they ran down the slope and started to cover the clear space, about two hundred yards in width, to the *kopje*.

The moment they left the ridge the police were fully exposed to the raking fire of the enemy, who had got the range nicely and were taking careful aim from a distance of some six hundred yards. Halfway across this space there was a farmer's barbed-wire fence, about five feet high, and constructed of eight tight strands. The troopers scrambled through this formidable obstacle, not without receiving many a nasty scratch, and in scattered order straggled to the coveted *kopje*.

When they had taken possession of it the rest of the brigade began to follow. Foreseeing disaster as the men got to the fence, where they would have been ploughed down while clustered there, Trooper Dick Seed, of the Natal Police, raced back from the *kopje* across the open space, where bullets were flying thick and fast. With a pair of wire cutters he made an opening in the fence so that the brigade, which consisted of about four hundred men, could get through quickly. He did this at the risk of his life, for while cutting the fence he made an excellent target for the Boers, who were uncomfortably close.

When the general considered that his object in saving the Dundee column from attack had been achieved, he moved off with the main body, and the brigade on the isolated *kopje* was left, the whole of the enemy's fire now being concentrated on it. It was obvious that they were going to have a hot time as soon as they left shelter and started to cross the open space again, so Seed gallantly hurried to the fence and hacked a larger opening in it; and the brigade was able to retire at the double.

For his bravery Trooper Seed was specially mentioned in dispatches, and as a reward was promoted to be sergeant.

The fight at Eland's Laagte had taken place before this. Although the police took no part in the action, several men were sent out at night to assist the wounded, but this did not entitle them to the Eland's Laagte clasp.

An escort of police under Sub-Inspector Petley took a party of 188 Boer prisoners down to Pietermaritzburg from Eland's Laagte.

The members of the Natal Police in Ladysmith, who numbered at this time about seventy, consisted of the detachment from Newcastle (excepting Sub-Inspector Petley and the escort for the prisoners), and the men from the Dundee and Ladysmith districts. Colonel Dartnell was transferred to the Staff of General White, and Sub-Inspector W. J. Clarke was sent from Pietermaritzburg to take charge of the men, who were attached to the Volunteer Brigade under Colonel Royston.

Most of the Natal Police had their first experience of being under fire on the morning of the 30th October—"Mournful Monday." They paraded at two o'clock, and were ordered to join the volunteers near Lombard's Kop. They moved on to the ridges running north-east from Gun Hill, and had no sooner linked their horses under cover and reached the top of the ridge than they found themselves under a heavy fire. Three cavalry regiments under General French halted near the place where the Natal Police were, and as they offered a good target for the "Long Tom" on Pepworth Hill, the troopers had a good deal of the shell-fire drawn in their direction. There were plenty of stones along the ridge behind which they could obtain cover from the enemy's rifle fire. They were armed with carbines, which, being nearly worn out, were practically useless, and were exchanged in the evening on the return to camp for long rifles.

The firing slackened somewhat near midday, and a staff officer who was passing gave the police and volunteers the order to retire. They returned to their horses, and were just in the act of mounting, when another Staff officer galloped up.

"What the deuce are you doing?" he asked.

They explained what had happened, so he said abruptly:

"Oh, that was a mistake! You must hold the ridge until the infantry have retired."

And so the mounted men returned to their position. There was a great deal of confusion in other parts of the field. Horses without riders were straggling about in every direction. In one instance a horse, with a dead man hanging by the foot in the stirrup, galloped across the rear of the police, and mules drawing ammunition carts, without drivers, were stampeding across the veldt. One of the police, at the risk of being court-martialled, went down the hill towards several cavalry horses that had been terribly cut up by shell-fire, and put them out of their misery.

When the retirement began, the regiments became badly mixed up, and in some instances there was no attempt at formation. Soldiers left their rifles and ammunition on the hills, and Maxim guns were abandoned. The men, after marching all night, had been fighting all day, and suffered badly for want of water. The mounted troopers, whose experiences had not been so trying, retired in good order, being detained for a little while to act as escort to the 53rd Battery. This time the police were subjected to a heavy shell-fire, and one shot cut a trooper's horse in half without injuring its rider. Thinking, even at such a moment, of his clothing and equipment account, the policeman slipped the saddle and bridle off the carcase, and placed it on the limbers of one of the guns.

While this column was engaged outside the town, news was received that the enemy were advancing from the west, and that Ladysmith was being bombarded. The men who were retiring realized that the town was about to be besieged. The Naval Brigade had arrived with their 4.7 guns, and it was stated optimistically that before twenty-four hours had elapsed not one of the Boer guns would be within range of Ladysmith.

It was felt certain that reinforcements would come to the relief of the town, and both Colonel Dartnell and Colonel Royston urged that the colonial cavalry, consisting of the Volunteer Brigade and the Imperial Light Horse, should be sent out to meet them. This was discussed with the General Officer Commanding, but it was not until the 2nd November, the day on which the last train left Ladysmith with General French, that Colonel Dartnell was asked if he could get away, as had been suggested, with the colonial cavalry. The Boers were then all around Ladysmith, and Colonel Dartnell replied that he thought it could be done, but only with heavy loss, so the attempt was not made.

When the Siege of Ladysmith began there were 60 members of the Natal Police at Nongoma, 10 at Nqutu, 84 at Ladysmith, 40 at Tugela Ferry, 40 at Estcourt, and 120 at Pietermaritzburg.

The work of the force was being carried on as usual at nearly all the small out-stations south of the Tugela. A number of men had been specially enlisted for six months' service, many being ex-members of the force.

As fast as reinforcements arrived on the coast, they were hurried on from Durban to Estcourt, where General Hildyard soon had a strong force under his command. Before this the lower part of Natal was practically defenceless, and anxiety was felt for the security of Pietermaritzburg. If the enemy had descended on that town, there would have been only some Town's Guardsmen and some recruits of an irregular force, besides the Natal Police, to defend the place.

In the middle of November 4000 Boers under Commandant General Joubert started south from Colenso. The detachment of police at Estcourt had been augmented by men from headquarters, and these were ordered with other mounted men to patrol the country and watch this raiding party. Eight of the police reported on the 14th November that the enemy were in large numbers to the south of the Tugela, and again on the following day made a similar report to the officer commanding the armoured train. This officer, being sceptical, decided to go and see for himself. The train on which he went ran into an obstruction put there by Boers, and for some time two field-guns, a *pom-pom*, and about three hundred Mausers were blazing away at it. Part of the armoured train, with about one-third of the men, got back to Estcourt, and the police retired along the road.

General Joubert began to retrace his steps to the north of the Tugela on the 25th November, taking with him a large herd of captive cattle and horses. No serious attempt was made to attack him on this march, but the police and mounted men were directed to keep in touch with the enemy.

For some time prior to this, Sub-Inspector Maxwell, with 40

non-commissioned officers and men of the Natal Police, had been constantly patrolling to the north of Greytown, and for the valuable information which they sent in, they were thanked in a special order by the military authorities. This detachment was ordered on the 22nd October to join Major Leuchars, of the Umvoti Mounted Rifles, and was moved to Tugela Ferry, being joined a few days later by 60 of the Natal Police under Sub-Inspector Abraham.

This force fell back to the Manuceni, about five miles from the Tugela, when a large body of the enemy were reported at the Mooi River. The Boers set fire to the police camp and to a store, whereupon the police and mounted rifles promptly moved out and opened fire on the enemy with a Maxim. The Boers kept up a hot fire for a while and then retired. A few days later another skirmish took place, but no damage was done, apparently, on either side. This detachment of police was reinforced from time to time until it rose to 180 men.

General Buller announced his intention early in November of supervising in person the advance of the troops to relieve the besieged garrison of Ladysmith. He arrived in Natal on the 25th November, and joined a strong force of British troops at Frere, his bodyguard consisting of 40 men of the Natal Police, under Inspector Fairlie. The remainder of the police there were attached to a composite regiment under Major Gough, of the 16th Lancers. This formed a portion of the mounted brigade under the command of Colonel the Earl of Dundonald. The troops moved forward to Chieveley on the 12th December, the mounted men being sent scouting in front.

Two days later the plan was announced for the attack on Hlangwane Hill, and while it was still dark on the following morning the police moved out as part of the advance-guard. The mountain was occupied by the enemy, who were shelled by the 7th Battery Field Artillery, the composite regiment accompanying them. The Irish Brigade and Colonel Long's guns met with disaster, and the mounted men, who were under a very heavy fire, were ordered to stand fast. It was an hour after the troops were ordered to retire that the mounted men received similar instructions, and though they were being heavily attacked the movement was well executed. The police had considerable difficulty in bringing away the Maxim gun, which had been hotly engaged.

Several of the police had narrow escapes during the day. A shell went between the legs of one of General Buller's escort while he was resting on an ant-hill.

A section of General Buller's force was withdrawn to Frere, owing to scarcity of water, but the composite regiment stayed at Chieveley, and reconnoitred in the direction of the Tugela.

General Buller started in a westerly direction on the 10th January, and as it had been raining heavily for three days, this was a very arduous undertaking. The infantry, following the transport, had to flounder through a sea of mud, but the mounted men, being in the advance-guard, were better off. The composite regiment had left to hold Springfield, and next day moved on to Potgieter's Drift, where a punt was seized and brought to the south side of the river, under a heavy fire from the Boers.

When darkness had fallen on the 16th January, General Warren's column, to which was attached the composite regiment, marched to Trichard's Drift, where the Royal Engineers made a pontoon bridge. The mounted men, however, were ordered to get across the drift, and many of them had narrow escapes from drowning.

A private of the 14th Hussars was swept down the flooded stream. Trooper Roddy, of the Natal Police, while standing on the bank some distance away, saw what had happened. Without a moment's pause he plunged into the river fully equipped, bearing the weight of his revolver, *bandoliers*, and ammunition. He got to the drowning man and brought him back to shore, but all efforts to resuscitate the hussar failed.

For this act of bravery, which was witnessed by the whole brigade, Roddy was rewarded with the Royal Humane Society medal.

The difficulties encountered in crossing the flooded river may be judged by the fact that without any rest being taken it took twenty-six hours to get the transport over the pontoon bridge.

While this operation was being carried on, patrols of the police were sent out, and in the afternoon a party of about three hundred Boers were seen riding down from Tabanyama towards the store at Venter's Drift. An attempt was made to ambuscade them, and the mounted men, by galloping at full speed, seized two *kopjes* to the west of the store. The Boers had no suspicion of the presence of the enemy, until someone carelessly fired a rifle, and then there was a general fusillade. The majority of the Boers turned and escaped, but some of them sheltered behind neighbouring boulders, and spiritedly replied to the fire. Supports were brought up, and the Boers surrendered, their total of killed, wounded, and captured being about fifty.

The police continued to guard the left flank of the troops until the

20th January, when the force was split up.

On the 12th January a further movement for the relief of Lady smith was announced, and the column started from Chieveley, the mounted brigade covering its flanks. The police took part in the capture of the Cingolo Hill. Lord Dundonald decided to attack it from the rear, and then forced his way up a steep hill covered with boulders, where he surprised a commando of 300 Boers, who were so intent on watching the infantry that they neglected the rear. The police reached the summit first, and after a slight skirmish the whole mountain was in the hands of the British force, the mounted men spending the night on the position they had won.

Early on the 20th February it was discovered that the Boers had abandoned Colenso, and all their positions to the south of the Tugela; and a week later the final operations were started. The Boers retired from a strong position on the north of the Tugela, and General Buller advanced towards Ladysmith.

CHAPTER 12

Besieged

There were 84 members of the Natal Police in Ladysmith when the siege began. Colonel Dartnell was attached to the Staff with General White; Inspector Dorehill acted as District Officer, taking no part in the military operations; and the two officers serving with the Natal Police field force were Inspector Little and Sub-Inspector W. J. Clarke. The force formed a unit in the Volunteer Brigade under Colonel Royston, Commandant of volunteers, but were under canvas in the centre of the town instead of joining the camp of the volunteers.

The Boer gun on Pepworth's Hill came into action on the 30th October, and the military moved to a position as little exposed as possible. The shells from Pepworth's Hill came rather close to the police camp, and on the 3rd November one of their horses was wounded.

In the early days of the siege the police provided pickets on the banks of the river at night, returning to camp at 5 a.m. On the 4th November one of the wounded prisoners sent in by the Boers was Trooper Wright. He had been shot through the head when accompanying Colonel Dartnell, who brought General Penn-Symons out of the action at Talana.

Lieutenant Hooper, of the 5th Lancers, arrived in Ladysmith with dispatches for Sir George White from Pietermaritzburg on the 6th November, having succeeded in evading the Boer pickets. He was guided from Estcourt to Onderbrook Spruit by Trooper S. H. Martin, of the Natal Police.

Shortly after leaving Estcourt, they were caught in a very heavy storm, and in consequence thought it safe to ride along the main road as far as Colenso. Near the railway gates they came across one of the enemy lying in the road dead, and also two horses.

On entering the village, they observed a flash-light in one of the houses, and thought it was a signal to the bridge. They crossed safely, however, but shortly afterwards lost their way while ascending the hill on the opposite bank, the night being pitch dark. Eventually they found the right track, and travelled onwards for five or six miles, passing through the enemy's first camp of about eighty tents on the right-hand side of the track. They went unchallenged and continued the journey, inclining to the left to avoid another laager which was right across their path.

Coming to a *kraal* which they thought was inhabited by natives, on account of the barking of dogs, they were surprised to hear the Dutch language being spoken, so made off hurriedly in another direction.

At dawn, parties of the enemy could be seen all over the *veldt*, and just as they were going to cross a road, a native ran towards them, shouting that there was a very large Boer commando over the brow of a hill, about three hundred yards away. Trooper Martin got off his horse and crept to the top of the ridge, where he looked down on the enemy's camp, fires being scattered over a large area.

This obstacle necessitated their retracing their way for about eight miles. They rode along the side of a hill and descended into a valley, where the enemy's patrols could be seen moving about, and where many tents were pitched.

As they drew near the residence of Canon Troughton, a native approached them cautiously. They went towards him, and asked what chance he thought they had of getting into Ladysmith. He laughed, and replied that all the main roads and drifts were thoroughly guarded. This native had been sent by Mrs. Troughton to warn the dispatch riders. She afterwards told them she had seen in the distance that they were English.

They went up to the house, being met at the gate by Mrs. Troughton, and a few minutes afterwards one of the enemy's patrols arrived, and demanded information concerning the two white men whom they had sighted. They were answered by a white man who was working for the Troughtons, and being satisfied, did not search the house.

Seeing that they had got into a tight corner, and were in imminent risk of being captured, they read the dispatch, which had been written on cigarette papers, and then burnt it, in accordance with orders which they had received before leaving Estcourt.

The patrol remained near the house for some hours before departing, and even when it had gone the two men had to be exceedingly careful, as there were two camps just behind the hill at the back of the house.

Eventually a native guide was found who knew every nook and crevice of the *veldt* round there, having lived in the locality all his life. He would only guarantee to take one of them through, so they tossed for the honour, and the lieutenant won. He and the native left the homestead towards midnight for the shortest but most dangerous part of the journey, it being decided that if the native did not return within two days Trooper Martin was to undertake the trip.

While waiting, Martin ascended some of the hills, and made rough plans of the camps, handing these to General Wolfe Murray on his return to Estcourt.

The native returned at about midnight on the 6th November, and gave the trooper a small note, which stated that Lieutenant Hooper had succeeded in getting into Ladysmith.

Next morning Martin left Canon Troughton's house, leading the lieutenant's horse, but as natives reported that the Boers had recaptured Colenso, he was unable to return by the same route. He pushed on throughout the day, and, making a wide detour along the Tugela River, found a drift and managed to reach some of the British outposts, who promptly arrested him and took him before their officer. The latter, on hearing Martin's story, sent him on to Estcourt with an escort of two privates, and he reached his destination the same evening.

General Wolfe Murray complimented the trooper on what he had done, and sent him to the Prime Minister with the following letter:—

I desire to bring to your notice the services of Trooper Martin, of the Natal Police. He guided Lieutenant Hooper, of the 5th Lancers, carrying dispatches to Sir George White from Estcourt to the vicinity of Ladysmith.

Trooper Martin remained with the horses in hiding, within the enemy's lines, until he received word of the lieutenant's safe arrival in Ladysmith. I wish to record my satisfaction of the way he performed an arduous duty, and trust his name may be noted for advancement when the opportunity offers.

Trooper Martin was promoted to be a sergeant as a reward for his services.

Just as the police in Ladysmith reached camp from their night picket on the morning of the 7th November, a very heavy bombardment of the town began, and until nightfall the troopers remained in the bed of the river, keeping their horses well under cover,

When the firing was resumed two days later, the police were told off to watch the racecourse side of the town, and the horses were kept ready saddled under cover.

Just after that the pickets were changed, the police and volunteers guarding the line from the point of Caesar's Camp to Platelayer's Cottage, and this continued until the end of the siege, the two officers of the police going on duty on alternate nights. As a rule the pickets were formed by about equal numbers of police and volunteers, the sentries being pushed well forward at night, and withdrawn at daytime to the cover of the thorn trees.

The shell fire from the Boers' guns on the surrounding heights was kept up fairly regularly, and the losses from it were surprisingly few. Things became somewhat monotonous when the garrison had grown accustomed to being under fire. Towards the end of November rations were reduced, the stores being denuded of jam, milk, and butter. Trooper Duncanson, of the Natal Police, was killed by a shell fired from Gun Hill, next to Lombard's Kop. He was acting as cook, and while passing through the doorway was struck in the chest by a shell which came through the roof without bursting.

When *mealies* and hay began to get scarce, and the long-expected relief column did not appear, the rations for the horses had to be cut down. The corn was required for the imported cavalry horses, and the animals belonging to the police were allowed two pounds of hay each per day. Wherever the horses were grazed the troops near them complained that the animals drew shell fire, and asked that they should be removed. When the hay gave out altogether, the horses were turned loose on the racecourse, only being mustered occasionally, with the result that at the end of the siege they were in excellent condition, very few of them having died.

On the 2nd December communication was established by means of heliograph with the relief column near Weenen, where the heliograph party had an escort of police. It was estimated that the weapons on Gun Hill fired a ton and a quarter of shell into the town that day, without causing a single casualty. A strong force, consisting of the Imperial Light Horse, volunteers, and the police, moved out at 10 p.m. to destroy the enemy's guns there. It was very dark, and the force made slow progress. The order had been given that strict silence was to be preserved, but as there were over 600 men going over stony ground the noise they made must have been heard at a considerable distance.

It was long after midnight when they reached the base of Gun Hill. The Imperial Light Horse and *carbineers* went off to make an attack on the right, the police being sent to the left to prevent the enemy's reinforcements joining their comrades on the top. The movement was entirely successful, but the police heard no orders to retire, and only began to move back when it was found that the rest of the troops were on their way to Ladysmith. It was afterwards discovered that a bugle had sounded the "retire," which had not been heard owing to a hill that intervened.

Towards the middle of December the police were attached to a mobile column, which was formed with a view to assisting the relief operations. Heavy firing could be heard on the 15th in the direction of Colenso, and on the following day the Boers resumed the bombardment of Ladysmith, one shell landing within a yard of the police officers' tents. Another shell pitched into the police camp a few days afterwards, all the windows of the police offices being broken by the concussion, and an hour or two afterwards a shell struck the foundation of the place where they had their mess. The police refused to adopt the shell-proof shelters, saying they preferred to take their chance in the open rather than be killed in a hole.

Through the thoughtfulness of Colonel Dartnell, and Major Karri-Davis, of the Imperial Light Horse, the children of the besieged town were not deprived of their usual Christmas festivities. All the little ones in the place were invited to a party on the 25th December, and toys from large Christmas trees were distributed, after which the adults held a dance.

Another shell came into the police camp on the 29th December, striking the ground between two bell tents, but fortunately caused no damage, and on the 4th January a shell wrecked Colonel Dartnell's tent, outside which Inspectors Dorehill and Lyttle and Sub-Inspector Clarke were standing. Everything in the tent was smashed, but nobody was hurt.

Sickness began to increase at an alarming rate, there being 1650 patients in the hospital at the beginning of the year. Out of a total strength of 850 men, the volunteers had 240 men down; 30 *per cent*, of the Naval Brigade were on the sick list, as were also 25 *per cent*, of the Imperial Light Horse. The only man of the police in hospital at that time was Trooper Wright, and this was due to the fact that they had alternate days of duty out of the town. Their turn for sickness came later on.

On the night of the 5th January, 45 of the Natal Police, with 24 of the *carbineers*, went out on picket, the police being stationed up the line to the foot of Caesar's Camp, and bullets began to fall in the neighbourhood of their bivouac soon after midnight. These shots came from the direction of Wagon Hill. Thinking the Manchester Regiment were firing on them, some of the police went up the hill to remonstrate, but when they got near the summit they heard words of command in Dutch, and came down the slope at the double. As the day dawned the horses were seen by the enemy, and before they could be removed the Boers killed or wounded every one; though not one man was touched.

The police advanced on foot through the bush under a heavy fire, Sergeant Woon, Trooper Pinto-Leite, and Trooper Rivett being wounded before they reached the base of Caesar's Camp, within two hundred yards of the enemy. Here they were joined by the Natal Mounted Rifles, and the 53rd Battery, which came out from Lady-smith with their big guns, fired 138 shots over their heads, the rattle of musketry at the same time being deafening. The Boers directed a "Long Tom" towards the 53rd Battery, and the bombardment was kept up by both sides all day until 5 p.m., when a heavy thunderstorm came up. The ground on which the police were lying was flooded, and they were relieved by a picket of *carbineers* at 6.30, getting back to camp by a circuitous route, the river being flooded.

The total loss to the British that day was 424 killed and wounded.

Sickness still continued to increase at a terrible rate, there being 2400 patients in the hospital by the middle of January, including six members of the police force, four of whom had been wounded.

On the whole, January was a fairly quiet month, the only excite-ment being caused by the shells, four more of which pitched near the camp of the police without doing any damage. In the distance some Boer tents were seen to disappear, and it was thought that the reliev-ing column had made some progress, but owing to cloudy weather nothing could be done with the heliograph.

The men were now beginning to suffer badly through lack of food; rations were cut down to half a pound of horse flesh and two biscuits per day per man. All units except the police were supplied with canvas troughs and blankets for filtering boiled water, but as there were insufficient to go round, the increase in the number of sick men may be attributed to that. The volunteers, who were not accustomed to this hard life, were in a sorry plight, there being 650 men sick out of a total of 900. As the police comprised the smallest unit of the Volunteer Brigade they always came in last for the rations, and only too frequently their supply of biscuits consisted of broken fragments and crumbs.

As the days wore on painfully, and more of the police became ill, their whole available strength had to be sent out on picket every night, and they could only muster 2 officers, 6 non-commissioned officers, and 16 men. Almost the sole topic of conversation was the lack of food, and on the 27th February rations were reduced to a quarter of pound of biscuits and three ounces of bad *mealie* meal per man.

There was joy in Ladysmith on the last day of February, when Boers could be seen trekking to the north in small bodies, and in the evening cheering in the region of Caesar's Camp announced the arrival of the relief column's advance party, which included Sub-Inspector Abrahams and 15 of the Natal Police. There was great disappointment when it was found that they had not brought any food with them.

On the following day 43 of the police formed the advance-guard, when a reconnaissance was made towards Modder Spruit, where a few Boers opened fire. The police worked round the flank, extending in skirmishing order on foot and leading their horses. As they cleared a ridge they came into the line of their own shrapnel fire, which cost them two horses. From the top of a hill they could see the Boers loading guns on to some trains, and a message was sent back to Colonel Knox for a fifteen-pounder to shell the first engine, which would have resulted in the line being blocked.

The message came back that the Gordon Highlanders were too exhausted to act as escort for the gun. The mounted men moved on in the direction of the trains, and were met by a few shots, three of the Natal Police—Inspector Lyttle, Sub-Inspector Clarke, and Trooper Smith—being wounded. Orders came to retire, as the infantry of the Ladysmith garrison were too exhausted to overtake them.

The siege had lasted one hundred and twenty days, and during that time 10,688 people were admitted to the hospital. Of that number 600 died. None of the Natal Police died of sickness until after the relief column appeared, though there were then 21 of the troopers on the sick list. Of these 7 subsequently died—equal to 8 *per cent*, of their strength.

When the welcome orders to march to Pietermaritzburg were given, the police were addressed by Colonel Royston, who thanked them for their services. He said they had always done their work cheerfully, and without criticism; his only regret was that he had not had a thousand of the police under his command, because in that case he would have been able to make a name for them and for himself.

When they arrived at Colenso they expected to find railway trucks awaiting them, but were disappointed, and completed the journey to Pietermaritzburg by road.

It was a curious fact that the police formed the only unit not mentioned in dispatches, by the General Officer Commanding, in connection with the siege of Ladysmith. It was afterwards explained by General White that though he knew of the valuable services that had been rendered by the police, the Brigade Commander, Colonel Royston, did not speak of the force in his returns, and Colonel Royston died soon after the siege.

Some excerpts from a diary kept by Sergeant Seed, of the Natal Police, during the Ladysmith siege throw an interesting sidelight on the experiences of the corps during that trying period. Nearly every day he began with the word "Shelled." On the 12th November his record states laconically:

"No shelling today—quite a day of rest."

Other entries were:

October 30.—We started out at about 1 a.m., and by a roundabout way got into position under Lombard's Kop, where the fighting started at once. It was a grand sight to see the way the artillery worked, and we had a splendid view of the whole field. The Boers had had a warm time when we were ordered to retire. It was a fearful task to get back, for we had to thread our way through thick bush at a walk while they shelled us with heavy guns, but they did little damage. I do not want this experience again.

December 7.—Shelled. We received an order at 10 p.m. to turn out dismounted, and paraded with the volunteers and Imperial Light Horse. Nobody knew where we were going, or why, but when we were well on the way it was whispered along the line (everybody had been told to be as quiet as possible) that we were to try to capture a 'Long Tom.' We crept along silently, halting now and again to listen whether we had been discovered. At last we were halted. The Light Horse were told to assault the centre of the hill, the police had to guard the left flank, the rest were on the right. We all moved quietly into our positions and waited.

The Light Horse went slowly and silently up the hill in the darkness, which you could almost have cut with a knife. A Boer sentry uttered a hasty challenge, but was promptly 'outed,' and a rush was made for the gun. The guard was so taken by surprise that very little fight was shown, and most of the enemy got away in the darkness . In about twenty-five minutes, though it seemed more like a couple of hours, the order was given to retire. As soon as all the troops were clear of the top of the line, 'Long Tom,' with two of his smaller friends, went up in the air. We all gave three cheers and cleared off—and it was quite time, for beacon fires sprang up all round, for miles, calling reinforcements.

December 8.—General White held a parade to congratulate us on last night's work.

December 17.—Very glad that the river picket has been given to someone else. I have only had my clothes off six times since the siege started. We are all getting very sick of it. No news arrives. There was an auction sale last night of all sorts of goods, put up by anybody. The troops have next to nothing to wear, and all the stores and the shops have been taken over long ago by the authorities. These were some of the prices realised at the auction—

Bottle of whisky	£3	15	0
Tin of Swiss milk	0	5	6
Eggs, per dozen	1	1	0
One pumpkin	0	5	0
Tobacco (common stick) per pound	1	0	0
Twenty potatoes	0	12	6
Cigarettes, per packet of ten	0	4	6

December 21.—A shell fell into the tent of Trooper Barnes of the Natal Police, but hurt nobody, although we were all standing near, and there were some wonderful escapes.

December 31.—Shelled. No news of Buller. Things are getting fairly serious.

January 1.— Heavily shelled. Colonel Dartnell's tent was blown to ribbons.

January 6.—While we were on outpost duty at the foot of Caesar's Camp, sometime after midnight shots came whistling into us like hail. For a few moments we thought our fellows on the hill must have made a mistake, and taken us in the uncertain light for Boers, but our minds were soon at rest on that point. The front portion of the hill was in the possession of the enemy. They were immediately above us, and it was wonderful that we ever escaped, as we had to thread our way over rough ground and thick bushes right under their noses for about a mile, and we could rarely let our horses do anything but walk.

As it was, five of our animals were killed, and about the same number were wounded. Every yard I went I kept wondering how it was that I was not hit. When the horses were under cover we formed and advanced, trying to get back to the positions which we had been forced to desert. We got there, but not before three of the police were shot within a yard or two of me. When the artillery got into action, the tide began to turn. The enemy were driven back bit by bit, but they fought like very devils, their numbers and the rumour that we were half-starved, making them feel certain of success. The fighting went on for thirteen hours, and at nightfall rain began to come down in torrents, streams of water running over our backs as we lay. Everybody was exhausted when we got back to camp—but Ladysmith was still ours.

January 14.—Dined with an old comrade named Buddle, who gave me the first decent meal I have had for a very long time.

January 26.—Sickness is very bad everywhere, and we have next to nothing to give the patients. One hates to ask about one's friends now, because the answer is almost certain to be 'He's in hospital,' or 'He's dead.'

January 31.—Things are just about as bad as they can be; the sick are dying at the rate of fourteen or fifteen a day, partly because we have so little food. We feel first-rate in health, but are terribly weak for want of food.

February 9.—At the auction I saw a three-penny packet of cigarettes sold for twenty-five shillings, and fifty cigars fetched £10. Twenty pounds was offered for a sack of flour, but the flour was not there to be bought. Eight of the police horses have been slaughtered for the invalids' food.

February 12.—We were heavily shelled, and the police had some very narrow escapes. We were out for five hours cutting down thorn and brushwood between our lines and those of the Boers. It was hard work on our present rations. I do not believe that there is a regiment here that could walk ten miles.

February 28.—We have been relieved at last, but I can hardly believe the good news. Rations had been cut down again to a quarter of a pound of biscuits and a quarter of a pound of grain. Late last night the Boers were seen on a small *kopje*, and we were all turned out expecting a general attack. As soon as our gunners found the range, the enemy dispersed, and we got back to bed just before dawn.

March 1.—We had a short, sharp fight about a dozen miles away with a large retreating mob. We were in a very tight corner once. The advance party, which consisted of about twenty of us, were in a small drain that did not really give us cover, and we were lying down holding our horses by the reins for over an hour. Nobody came to our assistance, so in the end we had to make a rush for it. When we got under cover, we found that the whole British force was retreating, the men being knocked up; and some idiot had reported that we had already returned, so they left us to ourselves. During the day a shell from our own guns struck the ground about fifteen yards behind me. It drove a piece of stone into my back, knocking me out of my saddle. I was pretty badly shaken up, but no bones were broken.

March 5.—We have started for Maritzburg. Both men and horses are extremely weak, and only covered about three miles before outspanning for the night.

March 7.—We reached Estcourt today, and as soon as the tents had been pitched, a terrible thunder-storm came on, water rushing through the tents several inches deep.

March 8.—We are still at Estcourt, and 22 men were added to the sick list, some of them having tried to tackle solid food too early. The rest of us will have to drag our weary bones and starved horses on by road tomorrow.

March 12.—We are at Maritzburg. I was fairly done up when we got in, and the poor old nag could scarcely drag one foot after the other. If I had dismounted to ease him I could never have got into the saddle again. Thank God the whole thing is over, although I would not have missed it for worlds. "

CHAPTER 13

After Ladysmith

After the relief of Ladysmith, the various detachments of the Natal Police were very much scattered, and it is impossible to give a connected account of their doings during the rest of that war.

There were about 60 men at Nongoma, with two Maxim guns, defending the laager that had been formed round the court-house, and still farther north there were small detachments at Ubombo, Gwaliweni, and Ingwavuma.

The force at Gwaliweni consisted of 17 men of the Zululand Police under a sergeant and two European police. The Boers had established a post within half a mile of this station, close to the Swaziland Border. Instructions had been issued to the Zululand officials that no offensive measures were to be taken against the Boers, and the natives were told to take no part in the operations, as this was entirely a quarrel between the white men.

In October 1889, the Swaziland commando, numbering 200 men, ascended the Lebombo Mountains at Gwaliweni. Having anticipated this invasion, the police had retired to Ingwavuma to defend the magistracy, where there were 10 Europeans and 25 of the Zululand Police. Acting on instructions from the Natal Government, the force evacuated their position, and retired to Nongoma to join the field force detachment under Inspector Marshall. The Ingwavuma men returned to their station the following May, reoccupying it without opposition; but while the magistrate was absent, a small party of Boers attacked the court-house. They were driven off with the loss of one man and two horses.

As soon as the war was declared the detachment at Nondweni moved to Nqutu, where the magistrate, Mr. C. F. Hignett, had under him 9 of the Natal Police, 50 Zululand Police, and about 8 civilians.

There was a Boer commando near Nqutu, and on the 30th January 1900 Trooper Wevell was sent with a letter to the Commandant stating that the magistrate would not hold himself responsible for the natives if the Boers entered the district. The commando appeared on the following morning, being about 400 strong, and sent a messenger, under the protection of the white flag, calling upon the garrison to surrender. The magistrate refused, and the cash in his safe was buried in a garden, where it remained until the officials returned some months later.

As soon as the firing started it was seen that the position was hopeless. The enemy soon got the range with their *pom-pom*, and a shell came flying into the court-room. The Government had instructed the magistrate not to defend the post against a strong force, and so a white flag was hoisted. The native police, always keen for a fight, were very much annoyed at this. Some of them refused to lay down their arms and escaped into a plantation not far away.

The police and other officials spent that night as prisoners in their own gaol cells, and on the following morning were mounted on broken-down steeds which took a dozen hours to get to Helpmakaar. From there, the prisoners were sent by ox-wagons to Dundee, and they completed their journey to Pretoria in a sealed meat truck, in which there was very little ventilation. They were taken in horse-boxes to Waterfall, where Trooper Collins contracted enteric fever and died. These prisoners were released the following June by General French's column, and the police remained in Pretoria on duty until railway communication with Natal was re-established.

Three troopers of the Natal Police, named Williams, G. B. Moor, and A. Date, took part in a daring encounter near Nqutu in 1901. They decided to seize some of the Boers' cattle, after hearing that it was the intention of the enemy to cross from Babanango Hill to Isandhlwana to loot cattle belonging to an Englishman who lived near there. Having been joined by three other men, the trio of police set out at night on their horses, but when they got to Salutshana Hill a *kafir* stopped them and said there was a Boer commando numbering 50 men just beyond the top of the hill.

Making a detour, they got to the summit, and saw the Dutchmen not far away, saddling up and moving slowly along the side of Salutshana, in half sections. There were only half a dozen men on the top of the hill, but they could not resist the temptation to have a shot. Taking steady aim, they emptied their magazines, and demoralized the

146

enemy for a time, killing six of them. As soon as the magazines of the attacking party were empty the Boers realized that there were very few Britishers there, and they charged up the hill. The police and their comrades leaped on their horses and galloped for their lives. Williams had a narrow escape, falling with his horse into a deep donga, but in some extraordinary way both he and his mount avoided injury, and, climbing out of the hole, got away.

The only colonial mounted troops remaining in the vicinity of Dundee after the disbandment of the Natal Volunteer Brigade were the Natal Police, under Inspector Marshall, and the volunteer composite regiment. On the 13th December 1900 a convoy of 60 wagons was sent out in the direction of Vryheid, under a strong escort, which included 64 Natal Police with two Maxim guns. When they were approaching Scheeper's Nek, Inspector Marshall noticed some one taking cover in the distance, and immediately gave the men under him the order to gallop to a depression.

They had just time to dismount and lie down when a heavy fire was opened on them at a range of about six hundred yards, but only three horses were shot. The fire was returned, and Trooper Aldwinkle went back, through a hail of bullets, with a message to Major Wing of the Royal Field Artillery to shell the position. This was done, and the enemy's fire slackened, whereupon the police advanced in successive rushes to a stony *kopje*. The enemy retreated in two bodies, one making towards Nondweni and the other towards Blood River Poort. Sub-Inspector Ottley's police Maxim section came in contact with the rear-guard of the enemy, and the Boers, firing as they rode away, killed several horses.

After Colonel Dartnell and his men got away from Ladysmith, that officer took command of the Volunteer Brigade, he still being commandant of volunteers. They took part in the capture of Helpmakaar, but saw no more fighting during the war.

General Buller reorganized his columns for his advance northwards, and the command of his body-guard of police was now undertaken by Sub-Inspector Abraham. This escort was in action at Alleman's Nek on the 11th June, the fight leading to the evacuation of Laing's Nek by the Boers, and enabling Colonel Dartnell, with the Volunteer Brigade, to enter Charlestown without opposition. A diary was kept by the police during General Buller's advance, but this unfortunately has been lost. The men, however, were with the General at all the actions in which he participated, including Amersfort, Geluk,

Bergendaal (where Sub-Inspector Abraham acted as A.D.C. to General Duller), Machadosdorp, Witcliffe, Lydenburg, Mauchberg, Devil's Knuckles, and Kruger's Post, and remained with him until he returned to Natal.

Early in January one of the columns formed for operations in the eastern Transvaal, consisting of 2600 men and nine guns, was commanded by Brigadier-General Dartnell. Several non-commissioned officers and men of the police were attached to the brigade, including Inspector Clarke, as intelligence officer, Sub-Inspector Abraham, who acted as A. B.C., and Sergeant Newson, who was senior non-commissioned officer of signallers. The object was to sweep the eastern Transvaal from the Delagoa Bay line to the Zululand border; and a column started from Springs on the 28th January with a convoy of 450 vehicles.

Heavy rains fell on some days, and supplies failed altogether for awhile owing to wagons that were expected from Utrecht being hung up in Elandsberg, the men being dependent entirely on food they could capture from the burghers. No commissariat supplies reached the column either, from the 19th January until the 15th March, and during the greater portion of that time the horses were almost without rations. General Dartnell crossed the Intombi River and reached Vryheid, after which he marched to Louwsberg, to make a sweeping movement towards Zululand. The column travelled to Utrecht, Newcastle, and Charles-town, where General Dartnell handed over the command to Colonel Bullock.

CHAPTER 14

The Defence of Mahlabatini

One of the most serious conflicts in which the Natal Police have taken part was the defence, during this war, of the magistracy at Mahlabatini, on the 28th April 1901.

About a score of the police under Sergeant Locke had been brigaded with the Natal Volunteers for some months at Dundee, when they received orders to entrain for Zululand. From the Tugela they rode up to Melmoth, where a standing camp was pitched for some weeks until orders were received for them to leave their kits and go on a four days' patrol to Mahlabatini, to which place they rode, establishing a camp outside the court-house. Every morning before dawn a patrol of four men was sent along the road towards Emtonjeneni, and this patrol went out as usual on the day the attack was made. As the men were riding past a *mealie* patch, about two miles from the camp, a shot was fired, and one of the patrol galloped back to camp reporting the incident.

The whole force was quickly saddled up, and rode out under Sergeant Locke, with Mr. Wheelwright, the magistrate, and Colonel Bottomley, who happened to be there. They rode quickly down the road, and made a thorough search of the *mealie* patch, but discovered nobody, so they went along the *veldt* towards the Emtonjeneni store, about three miles away, until they came to a place where the road divides, the main track passing to the left, and a path going straight on through some *wattle* trees. The magistrate, with four men, went along the road to the left, galloping to the top of a ridge, where they came under a hail of bullets. The sun was just rising, showing the troopers up very clearly on the skyline, and providing an excellent target for the Boers, who were concealed in the trees.

On hearing shots, the advance party of the men who had gone

along the path got into skirmishing order, and entered the trees, where they were ambushed. They were shot down to a man, every one of them receiving two or more wounds.

The remainder of the troop hastily opened out, and arrived on the scene at a gallop, just as a Boer named Van Neikerk, more courageous than the others, came out of the trees to demand the surrender of the whole troop. This was refused, so he instantly fired, hitting one of the horses; but he in return received a bullet fired by Trooper J. Smith.

The police dismounted and took cover, spreading well out. They fired whenever they saw the slightest movement in the direction of the enemy, and after the fighting had lasted some hours the Boers were driven off.

The dead and wounded troopers were placed in a police wagon. Sergeant Locke had been very badly injured within an hour of the opening of hostilities. He was found lying on the ground with his head on his saddle, Van Neikerk, also badly wounded, being near him. Most of the men had gone back to camp, and there were few left to attend to those who had fallen. Sergeant Locke was with difficulty lifted on to the wagon, which went slowly towards the camp, but as the jolting was so bad a stretcher was improvised. No natives had been seen about all day, but fortunately at this moment a party of thirty of them in full war paint appeared.

They were told to carry the stretcher in which Sergeant Locke was lying, but they were in a violent frame of mind.

"We cannot do it: we want to fight," they replied emphatically. It was only when the muzzle of a revolver was held close to the Induna's head that he ordered eight of his men to act as bearers, and this they did with reluctance.

The list of casualties was:

Killed:—Sergeant Collett (who in one leg alone received seven wounds), Trooper D. Cameron, Trooper Salmond, and Trooper Nelson.

Mortally wounded:—Sergeant Locke and Trooper Aldwinkle.

Wounded:—Trooper Smith.

Sergeant Locke died the same evening, and Trooper Aldwinkle expired about a month afterwards. Trooper Smith recovered, and is now a warder at the central gaol at Pietermaritzburg.

On the morning following the attack the survivors dug graves for their dead comrades, this being a difficult task, as the ground all round consisted of shale. As nothing better could be found to mark the spot where the bodies lay, rough crosses made from biscuit boxes were erected over the graves .

The defence had been maintained by 3 non-commissioned officers and 19 troopers of the Natal Police; it was afterwards discovered that the enemy had numbered about 150, and the little British force killed 11 of them. The rest went back, and, thinking they had been opposed by a regiment, shot their native spies, who had told them that there were only a few men of the police there. When they discovered how many troopers there really were at Mahlabatini they sent along a disconcerting message to the effect that they would pay a visit to the camp on the first moonlight night and wipe out every man there.

Two distinguished conduct medals were won by members of the Natal Police during this skirmish. One was awarded to Sergeant Smith, who was promoted to be a first-class sergeant, and the other went to Sergeant Evans, who was promoted to sub-inspector.

The following telegram was sent by Lord Kitchener on the day following the fight:—

Please express to the chief magistrate and Civil Commissioner, Zululand, and to Natal Police, my appreciation of the gallant defence of the Mahlabatini magistracy, by the magistrate and staff and field force of the Natal Police. I greatly regret their heavy loss, but in such a brilliant action losses are inevitable. Please send names of any men who have distinguished themselves.

The following official message was sent by the Prime Minister:—

The Government has learnt with deep regret of the loss of so many brave lives in the attack on the Mahlabatini magistracy yesterday morning. It desires, however, to express its admiration of the brilliant manner in which the Natal Police field force acquitted itself on that occasion, when attacked with overwhelming strength, with the result that the attack was repulsed and the enemy were defeated. I beg of you to be good enough to convey this expression of appreciation to the remaining members of the field force who took part in this engagement.

Chapter 15

Hunting the Enemy

On the day following the attack on the Mahlabatini magistracy, General Dartnell's column, which had been taken over by Colonel Bullock, moved to the neighbourhood of Blauw Kop on the Vaal River, round which it wandered for some weeks, making unsuccessful efforts to capture small bodies of Boers who moved about very rapidly, and continually sent very sarcastic heliograph messages.

A small number of the enemy were taken near Amersfort, and others were captured while sleeping on the banks of the Vaal. Several men were shot by the enemy during the first ten days, and on two occasions the troops were shelled. A combined movement was made under General Sir Bindon Blood, and for some time both the police and their horses, besides the rest of the force, were on half rations. About sixty oxen were lost within twenty-four hours through poverty and exhaustion, the animals being kept eight or nine hours in the yoke during each trek.

A grass fire swept through the camp at Ermelo, and left many of the men in a disastrous plight. There were several nights of intense frost, and heavy rains towards the end of May caused such heavy losses amongst the transport animals that the rate of progress was reduced to one mile a day. The horses and oxen were given five days' rest at Standerton, after which the men went south to Rolfontein, and then on to Wakkerstroom to pick up more supplies, returning again to Standerton, where the command was taken over by Brigadier-General Spens.

General Dartnell had been offered another command, and the police went down to Pietermaritzburg to join him, but there it was found that the Government desired him to remain in the colony during the visit of the Duke and Duchess of York (the present King and

Queen).

Elaborate arrangements were made to ensure the safety of the Royal party, 400 of the police being amongst those who guarded the railway from Durban to Pietermaritzburg. Every culvert bridge, cutting, station, and road-crossing was kept under observation, and in spite of this the train ran over a horse near the Umsindusi Station. After the pilot train had passed the animal broke loose from a platelayer's cottage in the darkness and got on to the track just as the Royal train approached.

Before leaving, the Duke asked a number of questions concerning the Natal Police, in which he evinced great interest. He remarked that they were the best dressed body of khaki-clad men that he had ever seen.

On the 27th August General Dartnell took command of the Imperial Light Horse Brigade, to which were attached a body of the Natal Police. The brigade marched up to Harrismith near the border of the Free State, and from there took a large convoy of provisions for Bethlehem. All the natives having been evicted from their *kraals* on the route, no information was available concerning the movements of the enemy; but while the transport was crossing the Eland's River, about 400 Boers charged down upon the advance guard, retiring when the Imperial Light Horse dashed up. Slight opposition was offered on one or two of the following days, and the column marched into Bethlehem on the 8th September. From there a combined movement was made in the Brandwater Basin, the enemy again coming in contact with the column on the 18th September.

As it was reported that the Boers intended making a raid into Natal from the north, the column marched back to Harrismith, being in touch with the enemy almost the whole way. At Harrismith it was learnt that 1500 Boers were moving down into Natal by way of the Nkandhla district in Zululand. General Dartnell was ordered to take the 2nd Imperial Light Horse to the Zululand border, which he did, going by train from Harrismith to Pietermaritzburg. Just after he had started, the Boers attacked the Mounted Infantry of the Dublin Fusiliers at Itala Mountain, near Nkandhla. The British force lost 80 men, but were unmolested by the enemy on the following morning while retiring to Nkandhla. Not far away, at Fort Prospect, a strong body of Boers attacked the British garrison. The Zululand native police assisted in the defence, which was successful.

On the 29th September Sub-Inspector Mansel was ordered to take

MEMORIAL AT PIETERMARITZBURG TO POLICE AND NATAL
TROOPS WHO FELL IN THE BOER WAR OF 1899-1902.

a convoy of 36 wagons from Melmoth to Fort Prospect, with an escort of 20 members of the Zululand native police. The convoy started shortly after midnight, the road being reported clear, but before long they were attacked by the Boers. Resistance was impossible with such a small escort, and all the wagons were lost. Sub-Inspector Mansel was taken prisoner, but the native police managed to escape. The following day, on their own initiative, they attempted to recover the convoy, but the task was too much for them. Five of the Zululand Police were killed in the first attack, and two fell when they attempted to retake the wagons. Later in the day the sub-inspector was released, and he got back to Melmoth on foot.

At this time another detachment of Natal Police was constantly patrolling and searching the farms in the Babanango district and a portion of the Vryheid district, sometimes by themselves and sometimes with the 5th Mounted Infantry, there being several small skirmishes. A post was established at Emtonjaneni, and there a considerable number of police remained for over a year until peace was declared.

At the close of September 1901, General Dartnell, with his staff and a number of police, left Pietermaritzburg for Eshowe, and overtook the column which had been ordered for Melmoth; but as the invasion of the colony by the Boers had been defeated, the troops returned to Harrismith, over a week's march by road.

In the middle of December the Imperial Light Horse Brigade, under General Dartnell, arrived at Eland's River, where it was stated that General De Wet was at Kafir Kop with 400 men, other commandoes near bringing the strength of the enemy up to 1200. The men under General Dartnell were ordered to Wit Klip, sixty miles away, each man carrying four days' rations. When they got there it was reported by natives that De Wet had left the *Kop* the previous evening, with the intention of attacking a convoy at Eland's River. General Dartnell decided to follow them, and the next day a surrendered burgher informed him that the Boers were going to attack his troops at the Langberg with seven commandoes.

As they approached Tiger Kloof the advance-guard, which consisted of Imperial Light Horse, was heavily fired upon, and a field gun also opened fire on the brigade, but the shells failed to explode, and did no damage. The column closed up and was threatened on the left by a party of Boers, upon whom a *pom-pom* was directed. The firing lasted for about an hour, and then most of the enemy drew off in the direction of the Langberg, and worked round to the rear, where they attacked Colonel Briggs' regiment of the Imperial Light Horse, which lost four officers and had seven or eight men wounded. In the middle of the afternoon the Boers retired and the brigade bivouacked near Tiger Kloof.

Few records are left of the doings of other branches of the force during the war. Some officers were detailed for service with the Utrecht-Vryheid Mounted Police, which did duty in those districts until peace was declared. Non-commissioned officers and troopers were attached to various columns, where their services as guides were exceedingly useful. In the few maps that were available, little was shown besides the main roads, the paths not being indicated at all; and as it was necessary on many occasions to avoid the main roads, the police had to lead the troops along *kafir* tracks. They also acted as interpreters and signallers.

A good deal of disappointment was created amongst the police on account of the fact that though many of them were in the field until the close of the war, only one or two, attached to General Dartnell's Staff, received the King's Medal. The conditions laid down for this decoration were that men must have completed eighteen months' service in the field, some portion of which must have been outside the colony in the year 1902, and that they must have been under the command of a General Officer.

The medal was given to the Cape Police and the Cape Volunteers; and the volunteer staff in Natal also received it, although they did not complete eighteen months' service, and saw no service after September 1901. The detachment under Sub-Inspector Hamilton at Emtonjaneni were actually encamped within the Transvaal border, but the General Officer Commanding in Pretoria contended that these men were not under a General Officer. A great deal of correspondence passed on the subject of the medals, but without avail.

CHAPTER 16

A Visit to England

The conclusion of the Boer War brought little rest to the members of the Natal Police. The reserve force consisted of 200 men of these troopers, and they were attached to the Border Police force.

The men under Sub-Inspector Hamilton moved down from Emtonjaneni to Dundee, where they joined in the march, with the Natal Border Police, to Vryheid, remaining there until the following October. The reserve then left for Pietermaritzburg, and after refitting, went out on a long patrol, through the Umkomaas Valley to High Flats, afterwards going to Ixopo, Mabedhlana, Indawane, Bushman's Nek, Underberg, and Bulwer—a round the force had made many times before.

Ten members of the corps were selected to represent the Natal Police at the coronation of King Edward VII. These men were Sergeant Ingle (who was drowned eight years later in Lake Sibayi, Zululand) and Troopers Black, Bradshaw, H. S. N. Brown (subsequently killed at Impanza during the last Zulu rebellion), H. Campbell, Edwards, Harrison (also killed at Impanza), Morgan, and F. W. Stephens. This body, under Inspector Mardall, was attached to the Natal contingent under the command of Lieutenant-Colonel Greene, of the Natal Carbineers, and on arrival in England was encamped with other contingents at Alexandra Park.

In the early part of 1903 there was trouble with the natives down in the neighbourhood of Umzinto, near the Umpambinyoni River. Faction fights assumed serious proportions, and as it was feared that the inter-tribal combats might get beyond control, the police were hastily sent down from Pietermaritzburg .

A force of about 30 men, under Sub-Inspector Dimmick, made a quick trek in pouring rain to the scene of the fighting, where a number of the natives had been killed. Very soon afterwards the field force, under Sub-Inspector Hamilton, also arrived from Ixopo; and the operations were directed for about a couple of months by Colonel Mansel.

Strong patrols moved through the troubled area to quiet the natives, who were in a very quarrelsome mood for a long time. The troopers endured considerable hardships, food not always being obtainable, and heavy rains during the first few weeks did not add to their happiness.

At Indudutu there was great excitement amongst the natives, who had assembled in considerable numbers and were prepared for battle. On the 27th January 1903, a large party of Saoti's warriors crossed the Umpambinyoni, intent on slaying Ntembi's faction, but the latter fled, whereupon the invaders burnt their *kraals*. The natives scattered over a wide area of exceedingly rough country, and the task of the troopers was a difficult one.

About eight huts were burnt before the natives calmed down somewhat, the arrest of a number of the assailants having this effect. The headquarters' detachment was sent back on the 12th February, but Sub-Inspector Hamilton's men were not able to leave the district for months, and afterwards they were engaged far away in the northern districts, the natives there being in a very unsettled state. The detachment got back to Pietermaritzburg for Christmas, the field force having been out for four years and four months without a break.

In the April of 1903 the reserve force and all available men in the districts were engaged for some time in the difficult task of taking a census, after which the reserves were sent to Durban to meet the first batch of Chinese labourers that had been taken over to work in the Transvaal mines. The Chinese were guarded night and day by the Natal Police.

The corps lost its oldest and best friend in the early part of 1903, when Major-General Sir J. G. Dartnell retired on pension. He returned to England, and though he is thousands of miles away from the force which he commanded for nearly thirty years, his interest in it is as keen now as it ever was.

The men who served under General Dartnell revere his memory. He had the courage of a lion and the heart of a woman. He engaged the confidence of his men and made their troubles his. His condemnation and commendation were just, and made those who received them better men than they had ever thought to become. He was as faithful to those under him as they were to him, and they loved him as he loved them. General Dartnell erred only in his charity and mercy. Today the old troopers speak of him as a man and a man they would follow into Hades because of the faith they had in "Hell-fire Jack" to get them out again.

As regimental as a button-stick, General Dartnell was terribly severe when the occasion warranted severity. Once a couple of troopers named Cantley and Johnson had been out fishing, and their boat's moorings came adrift. There were some almost water-logged skiffs near, and the men jumped into one of these, one rowing after the vanishing boat and the other bailing out for dear life. But, bail as he would, the old craft sank within a few yards of shore. Johnson would have been drowned had not his colleague helped him, and they scrambled up the shore.

Bedraggled and cheerless, they were walking along, when to their horror they met the General. For a moment he eyed the pair severely.

"Have you two fallen into the water?" The question was rasped out in a tone of severe disapproval. When angry he had a curious habit of holding the fingers of one hand in the air, and this was known by everyone to be a sure sign of coming punishment. His fingers were held well aloft on this occasion.

"No, sir," said Cantley, wondering what was coming.

"Has this man upset you in a boat?" he asked, addressing Johnson. The fingers were waving furiously.

"We went out in a boat that sank," said Johnson, "and he pulled me out, sir."

"Go to my room," replied the General, in his severest tones. "I am living in a hut up there on the right. You will find a bottle containing whisky. Drink half of it—and see that Cantley has the other half."

And the general walked off without waving his fingers again.

General Dartnell was succeeded as Chief Commissioner by Colonel Mansel, C.M.G., who had been one of the earliest members of the force, having joined in 1874 as sub-inspector. He retired in 1882 in order to take charge of a force of native police in Zululand—later known as the Zululand Police. When Zululand was absorbed in 1897 the European officers who had had control of these natives became members of the Natal Police, with seniority according to the date of appointment. This made Colonel Mansel second-in-command, until Major Dartnell retired.

These changes were quickly followed by the appointment of a

Parliamentary Commission to inquire into the working of the force and to suggest any necessary alterations. The Commission travelled all over the colony, and took evidence from civilians, Government officials, and members of the Natal Police. Many of the Commission's recommendations were adopted by the Government, the corps benefiting considerably in consequence. One suggestion was that a certain proportion of first-class sergeants should be allowed to marry, and many non-commissioned officers have since taken advantage of this opportunity.

CHAPTER 17

The Rebellion of 1906

There is little doubt that trouble had been brewing amongst the natives for a long time before they openly rebelled in 1906. The *kafir*, always suspicious when something he does not understand is taking place, was puzzled in 1904 when a census of the colony was ordered. It was explained to the various chiefs, in front of gatherings of Zulus, that the Great White King desired to count his people, and that they need not fear that taxation would follow. The census was taken, but on its heels came the poll-tax under which each adult Zulu had to pay £1 a year for the privilege of being allowed to live—a very unfair tax which was withdrawn in 1910. It is one of the most striking characteristics of the Zulu that he deeply resents being misled by Briton or Boer, and the imposition of the tax, following on an official assurance that none was to be imposed, stirred still more deeply the existing unrest.

For a considerable period the Ethiopian preachers had been dinning into the heads of the natives their gospel of Africa for the blacks, who were convinced the day was not far distant when the white man would be swept off the land, leaving all his goods and the fruit of his work for his coloured brother.

Dinuzulu professed to remain loyal to the colony, but strange messengers were noticed passing between him and the chiefs in Natal; and the disaffection gradually increased, the natives actually killing white chickens and white goats in anticipation of the general clearance of the whites. They expected support from Zululand, and were told of "a great flame" which was coming from there to exterminate the white man. They left their work in the towns and returned to their *kraals* in large numbers. The police stationed in Zululand reported that Dinuzulu was receiving messengers, but for their pains they were laughed at in some quarters, the authorities lulling themselves into a sense of security and peace until it was too late.

When certain well-known natives were reported to have visited the Usutu *kraal* a prominent official expressed the opinion publicly that if the police could not send correct reports they would be better out of the country. Those reports, which still exist at the police headquarters, form interesting reading in view of after events. A detachment of the corps under Sub-Inspector Ottley spent the greater portion of 1905 and 1906 on the Umsinga mountain, where the Ethiopian preachers were hard at work, and the reports they then sent in were subsequently verified in every particular.

The poll-tax fell due on the 1st January 1906, and the first sign of open rebellion followed almost immediately. In some districts the money was paid; in others the natives refused point blank to submit to this taxation. The latter attitude was adopted at Mapumulo and Umtwalumi; and at Henley about thirty natives, armed with assegais and spears, threatened to kill the magistrate of the Umgeni division, Mr. T. R, Bennett, who was collecting the money from the people of Chief Mveli. The chief's brothers identified the recalcitrant natives, and warrants were at once issued for their arrest.

On the morning of the 8th February a small party of police, consisting of thirteen Europeans and four native constables, with Sub-Inspector Hunt at their head, hastened by train from Pietermaritzburg to the scene of the disturbance. They made their way to Hosking's farm in the Byrne district, near Richmond, a trooper and a native constable being left there in charge of the pack horse. A steady rain was falling and a dense mist covered the hills as the main body of men pushed their way on to Majongo's *kraal*. This was hastily surrounded and three Zulus were arrested, but one of the troopers noticed that on a ridge above a mass of armed natives were watching the proceedings. Hesitating to cause unnecessary bloodshed, Sub-Inspector Hunt clearly instructed his men that they were to regard their duty as police duty, and not to use firearms excepting to protect their own lives.

Two troopers were left to guard the prisoners at sundown, and the sub-inspector led the rest of his little band straight up the hill towards the *assegais*. When they were within hearing a halt was called. Indistinctly the natives were seen in a very defiant attitude, and they were advised both by the sub-inspector and Miswakene, the native sergeant, to lay down their arms. This they showed not the slightest inclination to do, and as the darkness was rapidly making the position more difficult, Hunt ordered his men to return to the *kraal* and await daylight.

Their old fighting spirit roused and long suppressed, the natives took this withdrawal of the police as a signal to vent their fury, and in a few moments the actual fighting in the long rebellion had begun. The Zulus shouted, "If you take the prisoners there will be bloodshed," and suddenly charged.

In the darkness none could discern clearly what was happening, but a shot was fired, presumably by Hunt. The Zulus made a savage attack, and *assegais* shot through the air. Hunt's voice could not be heard, and Sergeant Stephens rallied all the men round him at a wire fence. They were Troopers Van Aard (the interpreter), Arnold, Hardgreave, M'Clean, Olive, Wood, Clarke, and Norval. The natives soon vanished, and then it was discovered that Sub-Inspector Hunt and Trooper Armstrong had been killed, while Sergeant Stephens had been severely wounded with an *assegai*. The bodies were recovered early next morning by a party of police under Inspector Lyttle.

This first little tragedy of the rebellion was afterwards reported upon by a board of inquiry as follows:

> We regret to say that too much leniency was shown by Sub-Inspector Hunt to the natives after they had threatened his party with their weapons, and this leniency was caused by the fact that the police are in the habit of going amongst large bodies of armed natives and dispersing them, the natives never previously having seriously resisted the European police on such occasions.

On the day following this brief skirmish, martial law was proclaimed by the Governor, Sir Henry M'Callum, and a number of the colony's forces were ordered to mobilize for active service, the troops being augmented by the Natal Police and twenty native constables under Colonel Mansel. These concentrated at Thornville Junction. A patrol had in the meantime been sent in pursuit of the rest of the natives who had taken part in the fight, but nothing was seen of them for a couple of weeks, although the search was kept up continuously.

A combined movement of all the troops mobilized was made, and the rebels' crops and *kraals* were destroyed. The rebels even eluded an *impi* got together by the loyal chief, Mveli, but one of the men, one Bunjwana, was caught on the 25th February while the cliffs near the Umlaas River were being searched. The police moved in skirmishing order along the hill until they discovered the remains of food,

TROOPER POLICE CROSSING THE TUGELA DURING
THE REBELLION OF 1906.

TRANSPORT CROSSING THE TUGELA (1906 REBELLION).

showing that the rebels had recently been there. Bunjwana, securely handcuffed, was taken to a very steep precipice where he said five of the rebels were hiding. Sergeant Wilkinson, with five of his men, descended a steep slope and gained a narrow ridge along which they crawled for fifty yards. They just had room to pass along, there being a sheer descent of about two hundred feet from the ridge.

Bunjwana, still handcuffed, was forced to take the lead, Wilkinson prodding him now and then with the business end of a revolver to remind him that it was an affair to be taken very seriously. Every man on the ledge knew that the natives who were in hiding could shoot them as they crawled. At last they came to a position from which they could see the crevices into which the fugitives had crept.

"Tell them to come to us," said Wilkinson to the prisoner, "and if there is any treachery your brains will be the first I shall blow out."

Bunjwana shouted to his friends that the game was up, but the rebels would not leave their shelter at first, fearing they would be fired on. The sergeant told them they would not be hurt if they threw down their weapons and walked with their hands up. After a while they did this, and so bitter was the feeling against them, that it was with the utmost difficulty that Sergeant Wilkinson prevented his troopers from killing them then and there. The men were secured and conveyed to the top of the precipice, where they were handed over to Sergeant Court. They had had in their possession a Natal Police revolver and a quantity of ammunition—taken from the body of Hunt.

Another of the men involved, named Uvela, was caught the same day at Mr. Smith's farm, Fox Hill. For their valuable assistance in helping to trace these men, three farmers, named Howard, Dobson, and Boyd, were thanked by the Government.

A search of the Enon bush had been made by Mveli's *impi*, who came upon some of the rebels, killing three and capturing a number of others; and twelve men in all were charged at Richmond on the 19th March with murdering Hunt and Armstrong. They were also charged with public violence, having taken up arms against the Government. The trial lasted a week, and all the prisoners were sentenced to be shot, representatives of the surrounding tribes being warned to be present, but a cable was received suspending the execution for the further consideration of the Home Government.

The colonial Ministry promptly tendered their resignation, as they felt that the authority of the Government must be upheld at that critical juncture. The interference of the Home Government was deeply resented, and wildly excited meetings were held in the region of Richmond. A proposal to lynch the natives was freely discussed, but ultimately, after several cables had been exchanged, the Home Government recognised that the decision of this grave matter rested in the hands of the Natal Ministers and the Governor. The order suspending the sentences was rescinded, and the Ministry resumed office.

As the murdered men were members of the Natal Police force, it was decided that the police should provide the firing party. At ten o'clock on the morning of the 2nd April the prisoners were marched down to a secluded valley near the village for execution, the ceremony being attended by a number of headmen, European residents, and schoolboys who played truant in order to see the grim performance. The natives accepted their fate with that calm indifference which characterizes them.

"Do we sit or stand for it?" some of them asked casually while black bandages were being tied over their eyes a few seconds before their bodies were riddled with bullets.

There was a man named Bambata—a chief, who ended his days in a particularly unpleasant fashion—living in the land of thorns in Umvoti County near the Tugela and ruling over a tribe known as the Amazondi, which is the Zulu equivalent of "The Haters." He was an ill-tempered brute with an extraordinary love for *kafir* beer, and vague ideas on the subject of other people's property, cattle-stealing being amongst his amusements. On account of his peculiarities he was deposed, his younger brother, Funizwe, being placed at the head of the tribe, a trustworthy Induna named Magwababa being appointed Regent. Bambata went to Zululand—a trip which he did not undertake for any good purpose—and then, recrossing the Tugela, began to prowl about the country in the vicinity of Keate's Drift. While he was skulking there with his men he received instructions by messengers from the Government to appear in Greytown. An impertinent reply was his only answer, and as there were strong reasons for suspecting that he was urging the natives to rebellion, it was decided to arrest him.

Much trouble and the loss of several lives would probably have been avoided had the action of the police not been hampered in the first instance when the warrant was issued. Colonel Clarke had been ordered to leave headquarters with sixty-five of his men for Greytown, to execute the warrant. They were joined by forty men of the Umvoti Mounted Rifles under Lieut. Nuss, and Colonel Clarke decided to surround the *kraal* where Bambata was known to be at night. The men were encamped a few miles out of Greytown at a point overlooking the thorn country, and the two officers rode out together, so that they might lay their plans with every chance of success. They made a long detour in order to get near the *kraal* unobserved, and soon found that Bambata was sleeping with one eye open. He had no intention of being surprised if he could help it. Silent Zulu sentinels were posted on the high peaks overlooking the road ready to signal the alarm.

The two officers returned with their plan of attack completely mapped out. Bambata was in the trap and they were ready to capture him. To their disgust they found on their return to the camp that an urgent message awaited them from the authorities, stating that the expedition was to return to headquarters, as it was too dangerous!

A week later, the authorities again changed their minds, and sent Colonel Clarke out with a detachment of seventy-one police to endeavour to fetch Bambata in. On the 8th March a force of 130 police and 40 Umvoti Mounted Rifles entered the thorn district at daybreak, intent on capturing the ex-chief dead or alive. He had now left the *kraal* where he had been nearly trapped, and was skulking about in the Impanza Valley, an extensive dip between towering hills, covered with impenetrable bushes of thorns, cactus, and prickly aloes. A road from Greytown runs through the valley to Keate's Drift, and in the centre of this wild and lonely district there was a hotel kept by Mrs. Marshall. The occupants of this hostelry were in a state of alarm, the windows of the establishment having been broken by large stones in the night, and the people there declared emphatically that they feared they would all be murdered unless Bambata were captured.

The force .marched up the right bank of the Impanza Valley over mountainous country. They could only move in single file until they reached the foot of a high, steep precipice at the head of the valley. This had to be negotiated, and the men clambered up as well as they could, finally reaching the *kraal* of Umfihlo, only to learn that the fugitive had slept there the previous night and had since left. He had evidently bolted in a desperate hurry just before the arrival of the troops, for there was meat still cooking in pots, and clothing was scattered about.

The troops went towards Van Rooyan's farm, and on the way saw three mounted natives dashing across the country in the distance. They took a gap in a stone wall at a flying leap and vanished—and a few moments later the police learnt to their chagrin that one of the trio

NATAL POLICE AT BREAKFAST AT MIDDLE DRIFT, WHILE IN PURSUIT
OF BAMBATA (1906 REBELLION).

TRANSPORT CROSSING THE TUGELA (1906 REBELLION).

MAN-HANDLING WAGONS UP MACALA HILL,
DURING THE REBELLION OF 1906.

was Bambata, and that he had declared his intention of going straight on to Zululand.

As nothing could be gained by staying there, the force returned to Pietermaritzburg, instructions being telegraphed to the authorities in Zululand to arrest the fugitive there, but the elusive ex-chief could not be traced.

His next move was a bold one, for he descended on Magwababa, the Amazondi Regent, and carried him off from his Natal home. He was followed by the Greytown magistrate, Mr. Cross, together with a number of police, who were fired on at the Impanza Hotel. Taking advantage of the presence of the police, the occupants of the building left it and hurried on to Keate's Drift, being disinclined to face the danger attending the journey on the road to Greytown.

Again the main body of the police were ordered from Pietermaritzburg to the thorn valley, where a force of 180 men arrived, and moved out in the direction of Botha's farm overlooking the Impanza road leading to the hotel. The rebels had cut the telegraph wires from Grey town to Keate's Drift, but a message sent *via* Umsinga and Pietermaritzburg from Keate's Drift was received by the police appealing for help for some women and a child who were unable to get away owing to a crowd of hostile natives blocking the road.

Colonel Mansel, who was in charge of the police, decided to go to their assistance at once. Ten men were left to look after the tents and wagons, and the rest moved down the steep hill into the valley at a brisk trot. They went cheerfully, in spite of the fact that they were already dog-tired, having been travelling all night and moving continuously; but for four of them it was the valley of death.

As they approached the Impanza Hotel they surprised two natives on horseback, who abandoned their animals hurriedly and bolted into the dense thorns, the horses being secured by the police. At the hotel there was an amazing scene of wreckage. It had been left unguarded since the occupants made their hasty flight to Keate's Drift, and the natives, discovering it was at their mercy, had broken into the place. How many of them entered it cannot be guessed, but when they left it everything breakable was broken. They discovered the liquor, and one may form an idea of the wildness of the scene when it is stated that they drank whisky and other intoxicants to the value of nearly a hundred pounds.

There was an ostrich farm adjoining the hotel, and the natives had ruthlessly stripped the tails of as many birds as they could catch, feathers being left strewn on the ground. An ox had been slaughtered—the Zulu develops a craving for meat when under the influence of alcohol—and its remains were scattered about.

Armed natives were seen on the ridges in the distance, and it was clear that the police would have been attacked on the road had their manoeuvre not been sudden and unexpected. Before nightfall they pushed on to Keate's Drift, where it was found that Sub-Inspector Ottley and his detachment had made a very rapid march from Umsinga and barricaded the hotel. There were three ladies there, Mrs. Marshall, Mrs. Hunter, and Mrs Borham, together with a European child. Colonel Mansel desired to convey them back to the camp at the other side of the Impanza Valley, and for a while there was difficulty in persuading them to leave shelter, but at last a carriage was procured and they got into it.

Darkness was now falling, and the return journey had to be made through the snake-infested valley along the tortuous track overhung on one side by mountainous slopes covered with boulders, and sloping away on the other side into the lower part of the valley. Before they started on their ride they knew there was a horde of natives hanging about, many of them under the influence of liquor, and all of them only waiting a suitable opportunity to plunge their *assegais* into the body of a white man. An ancient native not in sympathy with Bambata's doings, warned the police that they would be attacked in the Impanza Valley, and that as the track was narrow and the men would not be able to turn easily, the rebels would rush at the rear-guard.

Every possible precaution was taken against a surprise, but the nature of the country prevented flankers from being thrown out. Dense bushes of prickly thorn skirted the track in places, and orders were given that whenever these thick clumps were approached the men were to dismount and fix bayonets.

A more trying situation for the nerves of the men would be difficult to imagine. The first part of the ride, as far as the dismantled hotel, was accomplished in safety, and there Mrs. Marshall desired to search for a number of her wedding presents, including some which she treasured highly. As the place had been turned upside down by the Zulus this occupied about half an hour. Just prior to the halt one or two natives had been seen hurrying along in the half light shed by the moon.

A few of the wedding presents having been recovered, the force left the hotel and mounted the hill leading to the camp. There were four men ahead acting as scouts. Fifty yards behind them came the advance guard under the command of Inspector Dimmick, and another 150 or 200 yards in the rear was the main body with Colonel Mansel in charge, the carriage containing the ladies and child being in their midst. The little procession had gone a few hundred yards and arrived at a bend in the road with a towering hill at one side, when suddenly a dense mass of *kafirs* rushed out of the thorns at the foot of the hill.

The natives, who had been lying in wait, went straight for the rear of the advance guard and at a close range fired a volley. Nearly every one of them seemed to be armed, and a hail of badly aimed bullets whizzed past. Several horses crumpled up in a few seconds, and one man was hit. The police, being mounted, with their reins in one hand and a rifle in the other, were at a disadvantage.

The first volley was followed by a wild dash on the part of the natives, who got to close quarters with their *assegais*. Half maddened with drink looted at the hotel, and wholly savage, they stabbed and threw their weapons with considerable effect.

It must be recorded to the credit of the white men that though the attack came with dramatic suddenness after a long ride, during which they were held in constant suspense, they acted as calmly as though they had been on the parade ground. Riderless and wounded horses began to plunge about in the dark, but there was not the least suggestion of confusion amongst the men.

The advance guard turned immediately the attack was made, and as the Zulus rushed in they clubbed them with the butt-end of their rifles. Steadily they fought their way back towards the main body, which had quickly dismounted and begun to shoot at the black, moving mass. The *kafirs*, between two fires, were checked to some extent, and the advance guard pushed their way through them, and then in a temporary lull of hostilities formed up awaiting orders.

Some of the men who had been dismounted were picked up, and Trumpeter Milton, who had been badly stabbed in the back, was placed on a horse. Their rifles were hastily slung alongside the saddles, and drawing their revolvers, they made a quick rush to the main body.

After their first check the natives worked round the bush and attacked both flanks, sometimes getting within a few yards of the column, but the thorns were so thick at that point that they could rarely be seen.

It was a very hot corner for some time, and to this day nobody knows how long the skirmish lasted. There was neither time nor opportunity to look at watches, but apparently the firing lasted about half an hour. The Zulus had chosen an excellent position for their attack, the bush and darkness giving them such an advantage that they might have been able to wipe out the whole column had their heads been cooler and their aim more accurate. Gradually they retired farther into the thorns, where it was practically impossible to follow them. The troopers took the attack so lightly that an attempt was made to induce the natives to charge again, but without avail. The Zulu war-cry was heard at first, and later deep voices were heard shouting *Ngene* (which meant "Come along into the bush"), but they did not venture into the roadway again.

After a considerable pause, it being still uncertain what the natives' next move would be, the officers discussed the situation, and the sad task of picking up the dead and wounded was performed. Each of the dead men had between twenty and thirty *assegai* wounds, the natives having stood over their bodies as soon as they fell and stabbed them time after time. It was found that the casualties were:

Killed.—Lance-Sergeant Harrison and Troopers Ashton and Greenwood.
Wounded.—Major Dimmick, Troopers Dove, Braull, and Emanuel, and Trumpeter Milton.
Missing.—Sergeant Brown.

Eventually the advance was resumed, although, had the ladies not been present, the force would undoubtedly have remained there until daylight and raided Bambata's location. The ladies had displayed remarkable coolness during the attack, and when the march was resumed they got out of their carriage, which was utilized for conveying the dead and wounded. For some distance the natives followed, dodging from bush to bush, firing occasionally, though without effect, and hurling abuse; but after a while they disappeared altogether. The ladies covered the rest of the journey—about eight miles—out of the Impanza Valley on horseback, and camp was reached at 2 a.m., the troopers being thoroughly exhausted.

In his official report to the Minister of Defence after the skirmish Colonel Mansel wrote:

"I would bring to your favourable notice the excellent behaviour of the men, who were cool and quiet, and obeyed every order with the greatest alacrity; and also the behaviour of the advance guard in fighting their way back to help the main body. In the doing of this most of the casualties occurred. I would also bring to your notice the gallantry of Major Dimmick and Trooper Folker and others who brought in Trumpeter Milton who was severely wounded, Folker carrying him in front of his saddle. The gallantry of Major Dimmick and Trooper Folker in bringing this man in under most desperate circumstances is deserving of the V.C."

One of the bravest actions performed that night stands to the credit of Trooper Guest. The moment the first attack was made some of the horses in the advance guard bolted straight ahead in the direction of Greytown. Amongst these was a terrible brute ridden by Guest, who could not pull up for a considerable distance. When he stopped he could distinctly hear the noise of the fighting, so he wheeled round and galloped back in the darkness.

Trooper Emanuel's horse had been stabbed, and collapsed. Emanuel fell, and received the blow of a heavy *knobkerry* in the centre of his forehead, which almost crashed his skull in. He had just fallen and would soon have been finished off, as he was quite alone, when Guest galloped up, making his way through the blacks to the advance guard. His unruly horse was terribly excited, but when he saw Emanuel he pulled up, and got the fallen trooper on to the back of his animal, carrying the wounded man through to his comrades. This was done by Guest at the risk of his own life, and he was awarded the Distinguished Conduct Medal, the same honour being bestowed on Trooper Folker for carrying Trumpeter Milton.

The night's troubles were not over even on arrival at the camp. The voices of the natives were heard nearby, and another attack was feared. Although this was their second night without sleep, the men were called out again for picket duty. They stood to arms until dawn, hearing mysterious calls and the barking of dogs in the distance, but nothing exciting occurred.

Sergeant Brown's body had not been discovered in the darkness, and it was not known for certain until the roll-call in the morning that he had not returned with the little force. Two days later his mutilated remains were found in the bush alongside the path where the fighting had taken place. He had been one of the most popular members of the force, and as his body was badly hacked with *assegais* it was with a feeling of relief that his comrades realized that his end had been sudden. He had been dragged into the thorns and quickly killed.

Today there stands a lonely grave at the head of the Impanza Valley, opposite the place where the main camp had been pitched. It is within a few yards of the roadway, miles from any habitation other than widely scattered native *kraals*. At its head stands a monument erected by the comrades of the four men who died righting bravely in one of those little British fights that never come before the British public.

Chapter 18

After Bambata

Soon after the Impanza fight, reinforcements in the shape of the Umvoti Mounted Rifles, four guns of Natal Field Artillery, and four companies of the Durban Light Infantry went up to join in the hunt for Bambata. The police moved off at dawn, skirting the hills in the direction of Keate's Drift, overlooking the Impanza Valley, but found no trace of the rebels, and returned to camp at dusk. It was during this expedition that the mutilated remains of Sergeant Brown were discovered.

On the 8th April the police were under orders to join Colonel Leuchars' force, but as it was persistently stated that the rebels had gone over the border into Zululand, permission was obtained to join in the chase after him there. Great difficulty was experienced in getting across the Tugela, at Middle Drift. The water was low, but the bed of the river consisted of huge boulders, round which the wagons had to be drawn, the whole of the track being covered either with stones or soft sand. There were two wagons, each drawn by ten mules, and one drawn by sixteen oxen. So laborious was the task of crossing this place that the men were hauling, pushing, and moving stones the whole day before the three vehicles were got to the other side, and the party bivouacked on the bank of the river.

There news was received from a storekeeper that the rebels had passed, going into Zululand the previous day; and the police also met a party of civilians who had been after the rebels and missed them. The most enthusiastic of this crowd was a one-legged man whose misfortune in no way deterred him in the chase. He rode with the point of his wooden leg stuck in a jam tin instead of a stirrup iron.

The next day Fanefili's store, south of the main road between Eshowe and Nkandhla, was reached, and there the detachment were met by Troopers Smyley and Cartwright, who had ridden from Nkandhla through the forest to deliver a message from the district officer to the effect that the forest road was unsafe, as many natives had been seen in the district. Having delivered their message, and stayed the night there, Smyley and Cartwright went back to their station by the road concerning which they had given the warning.

Colonel Mansel decided to take another route—Galloway's road—to Nkandhla, sending the wagons round by Eshowe and Melmoth. The march was a long and tiring one, over mountainous country, the police being accompanied by nearly a hundred of the Zululand Police on foot. The colonel was informed that Sikananda's tribe, which was in a state of rebellion, might attack the party at any moment, but the troopers pushed on as rapidly as possible, and it was dark when they reached the Nkandhla gaol, both men and beasts being exhausted. There had been great uneasiness amongst the garrison there, and the advent of the police was greeted with cheers from the Zululand Mounted Rifles, who were stationed there to the number of about a hundred. With the total force now in the gaol yard the *laager* was safe even if every *impi* in Zululand had hurled itself against the solid walls; but the natives were not so foolish as to try the experiment.

The horses were picketed in the yard, and the cells were occupied by thirty women and children. Incidentally, a son was born to Mrs. Charles M'Kenzie in the gaol. It was a boy, and was promptly known as "Bambata M'Kenzie."

Pickets outside the *laager* had an exciting time, for rumours of coming attacks were constant. So difficult was it to follow the movements of the enemy that practically every day even the friendly chiefs brought in news that an *impi* not far away was going to make an attack at dawn. Naturally such warnings could not be disregarded, and many a sleepy trooper cursed the friendly natives when he had to roll out at some unearthly hour only to find that nothing had happened.

There was a barbed wire entanglement round the gaol, and the troopers slept by the side of the trenches just within the wire, the orders being that as soon as an alarm was given the men were to enter the trenches. One night when it was raining hard, a shot was heard, waking everybody up. The outlying pickets were at once called in—some of them did not need any calling—and everybody stood to arms for hours. Nothing happened, however, and later it leaked out that the shot had been accidentally fired by one of the native police. Scares of this kind were continually occurring.

In the middle of April a number of civilians working on gold mines in the district, wishing to join in the excitement of warfare, asked permission to picket Signal Hill. This was granted, and the change enabled stronger patrols of police to go out. They nearly always found natives on the edge of the Nkandhla forest, evidently placed there to watch the movements of the force encamped in the gaol.

Bambata was reported on the 23rd April to be in the vicinity of Qudeni Hill, so Colonel Mansel set out with every available man at ten o'clock at night. No rations were carried, as it was not expected the men would be away very long, but the march was kept up inter-mittently all that night. The force, having failed to round up the rebels, returned to the *laager* at six p.m., having been out for twenty hours. Some of the horses were knocked up, and the troopers, who had had nothing to eat since they went out, were ravenous.

The following day orders came for the police to move to Fort Yol-land, together with the Zululand Police. The transport again made the tour *via* Melmoth and Eshowe. A quantity of rifles and some ammuni-tion were taken to Melmoth, where about 160 people were huddled together in the greatest discomfort, and constantly alarmed by native scares. The transport outspanned a few miles beyond Eshowe, and at dusk Sergeant Neville was sent out to them from Eshowe to state that two miles away a chief was arming and would attack the transport at night. As there were only five men, one of whom was unarmed, escorting the wagons, a fight would have been more exciting than successful, but reinforcements, consisting of a hundred mounted men and infantry, were sent out at midnight.

No attack was made, and it was discovered later that there had been an assembly of natives. These had gathered together to attend a wedding. They passed near the transport the next day, peacefully enough, but the police had been kept on the *qui vive* all night.

The main body of the police, which went to Fort Yolland by the Galloway road, had an equally exciting trip. Passing along the edge of the bush, they encamped on the top of a very high hill; and at dusk the forms of many Zulus were seen watching in the distance. There was no water either for the men or horses that night, and both were parched after the long and tiring march. The animals were ringed together, and as there seemed every prospect of an attack at any moment, sleep was out of the question. Every trooper spent the night, wide awake, sitting back on his saddle which was lying on the ground, wondering from which direction the rush would come and when he would next

A WELCOME DRINK AT A DRIFT ON THE TUGELA (1906 REBELLION).

A TRANSPORT WAGON OVERTURNED ON BAD ROADS
DURING THE REBELLION OF 1906.

see water. The only thing they had had to eat was bully beef. They munched it in melancholy silence on the top of the hill, and this salt-saturated substance, when eaten alone, produces an amazing thirst. The rumour was spread in the night that there was a stream a quarter of a mile away, and a few of the men, entirely disregarding the danger of being *assegaied*, or the penalties incurred by leaving the camp, crept away. Though they did not admit having gone to the stream, there is no doubt whatever that they did, in spite of the risk of death.

It was later shown that a large *impi* was going to make an attack, and heavy loss of life was averted by Colonel Mansel's decision to make a quick dash towards Fort Yolland when the first streaks of dawn appeared. With all speed the horses were saddled and hastened down the hill, at the bottom of which there was a *spruit*. Both the troopers and their animals were longing for water, but strict orders were given that no stop was to be made for a drink as the *spruit* was forded. With the stream running up to their knees the horses struggled to get their heads down to it, but had to be urged straight through to the other bank.

The trek to Fort Yolland was accomplished so quickly that the natives lost sight of the detachment, who reached their destination without being fired on. The discomforts there, however, were considerable. All the men were put on half rations, and they had to sleep in tiers on a steep hill. It was almost impossible for a man not to press on the trooper sleeping just beneath him, and occasionally a weary individual, losing his balance, began to roll down over his comrades. A few acid comments would be made at such moments, for the men were not in too good a temper, and gradually they would fall off to sleep—until a similar incident occurred again.

The chief Mfungela remained loyal, and he arranged to signal by means of a fire when he expected to be attacked. On the night of the 2nd May the signal was made, and the police hurried out to his *kraal*, only to find that the alarm was groundless. They returned to camp just as the Zululand Police arrived from Eshowe.

At three o'clock on the morning of the 5th May a strong force, consisting of 175 Natal Police, 100 Zululand native police, 90 Naval Corps, 30 Natal Mounted Rifles, and 50 dismounted men of the Durban Light Infantry, moved off in the direction of the Nkandhla forest. Behind them marched 600 loyal natives, chiefly men of Mfungela's tribe. At the top of the Komo Hill the mounted troops off-saddled for about an hour and a half, and then the march was continued along the road past Domville's store, which had been looted, until they came to a path leading to Cetewayo's grave.

A few hundred yards from the track there was a Government forester's hut, and this was filled with rebels, who waited until the Zululand Police, under Inspector Fairlie, were well within range, and then opened fire on them. The shooting only lasted a minute or so, the rebels leaving their shelter and bolting into the forest. One man of the native police only was wounded.

The force soon reached open country again, and descended the Bobe Ridge, leading down to the Insuzi River. The slope was very steep in places, and while the Natal Police were dismounted and leading their horses in single file, a body of several hundred natives, who had been lying in wait with Bambata behind a small eminence, charged down on the advance guard of the Natal Mounted Rifles and the native police. The Rifles—there were only about half a dozen of them—there came back at a gallop, with the enemy almost on top of them. The moment the mounted men cleared the front the enemy rushed straight at the native police, who stood their ground magnificently, and in a few seconds had the foe in check. The Natal Police hurried up, and for a little while there was a sharp exchange of shots. Lead fell like hail in the ranks of the enemy, until they broke and, leaving a hundred dead on the ground, fled down the ridges on either side.

This was the only time during the rebellion that the police were present when the Zulus charged in open country in the daylight, nor did they make more than one or two charges in the daylight all through the war. Their confidence on this occasion was due to a statement made by their witchdoctor, when he went through the ceremony of preparing them for battle, to the effect that his "medicine" would turn all the white men's bullets into water the moment they left the muzzle of the rifle. They were extremely valiant until they discovered that the bullets that were flying amongst them were very real; and then their courage oozed and they fled, Bambata with them. He was seen flying over the top of a hill on a white horse.

A large number of Zulus were on the surrounding heights watching the skirmish, and judging by the manner in which they were seen moving through the forest, they had not anticipated the force going down the Bobe Ridge, but had thought they would keep on the main road to Nkandhla, where an attack had been contemplated. It was quite clear that the troops were surrounded, because there was a good deal of sniping from every direction, particularly at the rear, where the Durban Light Infantry were firing for some time.

The enemy were not pursued, and, having cleared their front, the men turned towards Fort Yolland. They crossed a stream which flows into the Insuzi, and after many of them had had a refreshing draught a number of dead Zulus were discovered in the water. These were evidently men who, having been wounded, had crawled away to die.

While everybody was crowded into the stream it was noticed that the natives were coming down the hills. They advanced in twos and threes until they got within range, and then started sniping. The rearguard, which was now composed of Natal Police, fired back, and the Zulus disappeared for a time. It had been decided to bivouac for the night, but the position was so unsafe that, though everybody was thoroughly exhausted, and night had come on, the order was given to march back to Fort Yolland—a dozen miles away. The infantrymen were almost in a state of collapse after the day's hard work, and most of the mounted men gave up their horses to those who had none.

While one *spruit* was being crossed two troopers, who were the last men in the rear-guard, had an experience which was somewhat unnerving. The path down to the stream was narrow, the men being hemmed in by bush until they could only go two abreast. The long procession took a tremendous time to get over the *spruit*, and while the men were crossing the two troopers had the unenviable task of standing alone at the top of the path leading down to the drift, with bayonets fixed. There was no room for anyone else, so the rest of the rear-guard went on and were a score yards away awaiting their turn to get over the *spruit*.

Meanwhile the Zulus crept up unseen and unheard, until the two men heard the peculiar guttural war-cry quite close to them in the trees, and a shot was fired. Fortunately it missed. All the time they remained at their post the two men knew that the natives might get through the bush on to the path leading to the *spruit*, and cut them off hopelessly. The sniping was kept up with painful regularity. One Zulu appeared to have a .303 rifle. They could hear him moving about in the bush, and distinguished the crack of his weapon from that of the other old elephant guns and muzzle-loaders when he fired. The two troopers were particularly pleased when the moment came for them to hurry on after the rest of the rear-guard.

At a *donga* a little farther on the dozen Natal Police, who still constituted the rear-guard, came upon a Maxim pack-horse, with two or three men trying to readjust its burden. The little body of police helped them, all the time dropping farther and farther behind the procession. The delay lasted ten minutes or a quarter of an hour, and they had no idea how far off the main body were, for there was dead silence, save for the crackling of a *kraal* which had been set on fire. As the flames shot up the party in the donga found themselves in a brilliant glare, giving the snipers an excellent opportunity to practise shooting.

One or two of the police were sitting on a rock, and a rustling was noticed in the bush. It was the native with the .303 rifle, and for a few tense moments he could be heard making his way nearer and nearer. At last a crack rang out, and a bullet struck a rock within a foot of the place where Trooper Scott was sitting. His companions remember fragments of his hasty remarks to this day.

When the Maxim was readjusted they hurried up the hill on the other side of the *donga*, and endeavoured to get in touch with the column. The pack-horse, however, was exhausted, and two or three of the police had to push it up the steep slope, although they were thoroughly tired themselves. This further reduced the strength of the rear-guard, which struggled on till the foot of a large hill leading to Fanefili's store was reached, and here the straggling end of the main body was overtaken. That last wearisome climb seemed unending, and had an *impi* rushed down, nothing could have saved the men, for they were beaten. There were still four miles to tramp to Fort Yolland from the store, and nobody needed rocking to sleep when they got back to camp.

CHAPTER 19

Mome Gorge

The back of the rebellion was broken by the massacre—it was not a battle—in the Mome Gorge, on the 10th June. The police, to the number of about a hundred, under Sub-Inspector Esmonde White, were attached to Colonel Barker's column in the vicinity of Cetewayo's grave, when three men rode through the bush to deliver a dispatch from Colonel M' Kenzie to Colonel Barker, giving him orders to waylay an *impi*. Colonel M' Kenzie was encamped on the top of the heights, and as the dispatch had to be carried a distance of about fourteen miles through the enemy's country, and through the Nkandhla forest, in the dead of night, he called for volunteers from amongst the ranks of the Zululand Mounted Rifles. Troopers Johnson, Deeley, and Oliver were chosen for the dangerous but important duty. Had they failed it is possible that very few of the enemy would have been killed in the Mome Gorge. They succeeded in reaching Colonel Barker at 1.15 a.m., and the dispatch they carried ran:

> You will please move at once with all available men (leaving sufficient for the defence of your camp) to the mouth of the Mome Gorge. I have information that an *impi* is coming from Qudeni to enter the Mome Valley between now and dawn. Try to waylay it. . . . You must take your Maxims, in case you meet the *impi*, which is reported to be of considerable strength.

It was pitch dark when the police were ordered to saddle up. Colonel Barker's column consisted of three squadrons of the Transvaal Mounted Rifles, a section of the Natal Field Artillery, a Maxim and one Colt gun of the Transvaal Rifles, and 100 Zululand native police, besides the Natal Police. This force was moved along the valley of the Insuzi, strict orders having been given that the march was to be performed as quietly as possible because it was not certain where the enemy were.

About 50 of the Natal Police were told off to escort the gun of the Transvaal Rifles, and this, as it was hauled over the stones up the hills, made a row that could easily have been heard a couple of miles away, in spite of all the men's efforts to make as little noise as possible. On the force rounding the shoulder of a hill near the gorge they could see fires dotted about in the valley, which is shaped in the form of a horse-shoe. There were fully three-score different fires counted, the Zulus evidently having a rest after their long march. Either their sentries had not heard, or had ignored the rattle of the guns over the boulders, for no sign of alarm was observed, though nothing could be seen except the distant points of light. Hundreds of men lay sleeping in the depression, utterly unconscious of the presence of the British force, which gradually and silently spread over the hill-tops until the natives were surrounded, trapped, and doomed.

Strict orders were again sent round that the utmost care was to be observed in avoiding making noise, and Colonel Barker planted his men quickly and stealthily.

Inspector Fairlie, with the native police, and Lieutenant Betting-ton, with the native levies, were sent out to occupy a position over the gorge, with the object of blocking the entrance and preventing the Zulus from reaching the thick bush, at the edge of which they were sleeping. They lost their lives through superstition, for had they gone a little farther and slept in amongst the trees they would have been safe; but no native would dare to enter the Nkandhla forest—the place where Cetewayo's remains lie—after nightfall.

Two squadrons of the Transvaal Rifles, with a Maxim, were placed on the ridge at the east of the horse-shoe, and another squadron, with the 50 Natal Police and big gun, took up their position on the western ridge. Other guns, with an escort of Natal Police, were placed on a kopje to the south, to cut off the enemy's retreat in the direction of the Insuzi.

All this time, apparently, the *impi* slept peacefully. Besides the darkness, there was a slight mist, and though not the form of a single Zulu could be distinguished, someone, through impatience or nervousness, fired a shot. A moment or two later pandemonium reigned.

No fighting force ever organized could have made much of a stand against such an appalling stream of lead as that which poured down on to the sleeping natives. At comparatively close range shrapnel was hurled into their midst, and from everywhere round them big guns, Maxims, *pom-poms*, and rifles were belching forth shot as fast as the men could work. Aiming was done by guess-work in the direction of the fires, but it was remarkably successful, for rows and rows of Zulus were afterwards discovered dead in their blankets. They had been riddled as they slept.

Startled from sleep, many of the natives grasped their weapons hastily and tried to form up into a body, but the odds against them were so overwhelming that they could do nothing, and the slaughter was complete when the first streaks of dawn stole across the sky. A few Zulus crept away and escaped, but the valley was lined with hundreds of torn bodies, and the sight when day broke was one which brought a touch of nausea to nearly every white man who had taken part in the shooting.

Bambata and Mehlokazulu, and other leaders, were amongst those who got out of the valley. They, with the remnants of the *impi*, passed along the bed of the stream, but only fell into the hands of the column under Colonel M'Kenzie. Bambata was killed while endeavouring to escape into the main bush. For purposes of identification, his head was cut off. Mehlokazulu, who also fell, had been one of Cetewayo's fighting generals, and is said to have been in command of the force which crossed the border into Natal prior to the Zulu War of 1879, and, having secured two coloured women, refused to give them up. This incident to some extent helped to cause that war.

There was a small bush at one side of the gorge, and when it was light enough to see properly, the police were sent to clear it. A good many Zulus were turned out, and were shot as they ran, but Sub-Inspector White's men had some narrow escapes owing to a number of the natives "playing 'possum." Pretending to be dead, they lay still, and then got up suddenly to stab the nearest white man. Several of the Zulus who had attempted this trick were shot just as they were going to use their *assegai*. One of the enemy was lying apparently dead across a path, and Sub-Inspector White and several others stepped over his body. A trooper, more inquisitive than the others, looked closely at him.

"This cove is alive. I swear I saw him wink," he called out, and fired point blank at the Zulu with his revolver.

The shot missed, and the "dead" man promptly scrambled to his feet, starting to bolt down a side path. He would not have got far, for several revolvers were levelled at him, but Mr. White told his men not to fire. The trooper who shot at the native on the ground had had his opportunity; now the Zulu was given a chance, and he disappeared, possibly escaping altogether.

Later in the day the troopers and Zululand native police joined Colonel M'Kenzie's column and drove the bush, many more rebels being killed, several of them being shot in the trees up which they had climbed. Only about twenty of the Natal Police were able to take part in this last drive, most of them being tired out. They had had sixteen hours' work, and the marches had been over the roughest possible ground. They had carried some rations, but were hungry, thirsty, and exhausted when, long after sundown, they arrived back at Colonel Barker's camp.

It was estimated that over five hundred Zulus were killed during the day, and only one of the British force met his death. This was Captain Macfarlane, D.S.O., of the Transvaal Mounted Rifles. Only eleven of the attacking force were wounded, one of these being Trooper F. Fergusen, of the Natal Police, who was stabbed in the groin with an *assegai*.

CHAPTER 20

Exciting Night in the Bush

A day or two after the Mome fight a signal came by heliograph, with the last rays of the sun, ordering the police, under the command of Sub-Inspector White, to join Colonel M'Kenzie's force—about ten miles away—at once. From the neighbourhood of Cetewayo's grave they were to march through the bush that night, leaving their wagons behind. Afterwards Sub-Inspector White admitted that that march was as trying as any he ever undertook.

The sun had set long before they started, and there was only the faintest light. With the officer in charge, at the head of the party, there were "Tricky" Johnson, Oliver, and Deeley (the Zulu Mounted Rifles men who took the dispatch to Colonel Barker which led to the Mome fight), Sergeant-Major Ingle, and Ndhlovu, a native sergeant who has seen warfare under many conditions, and whose assistance has at times been most useful. Sub-Inspector White knew the path over which his men had to travel, having been over it before, and what he knew of it was not reassuring, especially as they dared not show a light, for it was not known where the enemy might be lurking in wait for them.

There was danger of a sudden attack every yard, for the bush was supposed to be infested with rebels, and the path was so narrow that it would only admit of one horse being led at a time.

When they got into the bush they encountered inky darkness, and the men—there were well over a hundred of them—had to keep hold of the tail of the horse in front of them as they crept through the gloomy place, hemmed in with thick trees, each of which might have concealed natives. They had gone about half-way along this track, and the men were beginning to congratulate themselves on the fact that they would soon reach the main road—a wider track closely hedged

187

in with bush, where they would at least have been able to make some sort of resistance—when those in front pulled up sharply. Ndhlovu, feeling his way along the path, at the head of the procession, with Mr. White at his heels, found the way was blocked.

A number of large trees had been felled by the Zulus and lay right on the track. The detachment had walked straight into a deadly trap and were so closely wedged in that had the natives been in the bush on either side the troopers would have been massacred in a few moments. It was too dark to see anything at all, and the track was so narrow that it was utterly impossible for the horses to turn. There seemed to be no prospect of going either forward or backward.

Ndhlovu, baffled for a few moments, began to feel his way through the felled trees. They had been placed lengthways on the path, with their tops facing the troopers—a hopeless barrier in the circumstances. At last he came back to Mr. White and reported that he had found a possible passage through. With almost uncanny skill in the darkness he led the way over fallen trunks, round bushes and between trees, until at last they came to the track once more, and the whole detachment, hanging close on to one another, followed, nobody daring to strike a light lest he should be instantly pierced with a Zulu's *assegai* or hit on the head by his nearest comrade as punishment for his folly. They had come out on the "main road" to the top of the bush where there was a little more room; and owing to the nature of the cover on either hand the men marched on foot in sections of fours, leading their horses with one hand and holding their revolvers with the other, the rifles being slung on the saddles.

The party owed their lives to the fact that the Zulus never dreamed that a force would go through the bush at night. They had laid their clever trap to operate in the daylight, and had actually been on the spot up to a little while before the troopers arrived, this being shown by fires which were still smouldering in the bush when the police came upon them.

Once they reached the open country they soon got to the place where Colonel M'Kenzie had pitched his camp—only to find that he had moved. Weary and hungry, they hunted about, and it was midnight before they found the column. There must have been a curious feeling of security in the camp, for the sentry had to be awakened at the headquarters' lines before the arrival of the police could be reported. It was impossible to procure fodder for the horses, which had to be ringed for the night as they were. The men were without food, and

NDHLOVU, A TYPICAL SERGEANT
OF THE NATIVE POLICE

CAKIJANI, THE REBEL

only had a blanket each as extra covering. For many days they suffered bitterly in consequence, getting their meals anyhow and lying awake half the night shivering with cold. Some of them even dug holes in the ground in order to get a little shelter, and it was weeks before they recovered their wagons with such comforts as they contained.

During the operations round Cetewayo's grave, Sub-Inspector White on one occasion had charge of the transport, some of the wagons belonging to the Durban Light Infantry. As the roads were bad and it was necessary to move quickly, Mr. White had given strict instructions that nobody was to ride on the wagons. He was astonished, a little later, to notice a figure huddled up on the top of one of the vehicles, and, riding over quickly, told the man somewhat curtly to get down.

"Don't speak to him like that, sir, please," said someone attached to the infantry; and the huddled-up figure remained motionless.

"What do you mean?" replied Mr. White. "I gave orders that nobody was to ride."

"But he always rides, sir. Please leave him there."

Somewhat puzzled, the sub-inspector looked more closely at the figure and found it was that of a very old, grey-bearded, wrinkled man who could not have walked the distance to save his life.

"And pray how long has he ridden?" asked the sub-inspector.

"Oh, for many years, sir. We take him about with us everywhere. He's our mascot!"

And Methuselah was left undisturbed on the wagon.

One of the most remarkable figures in the rebellion was one Cakijana. There is no doubt that but for him the trouble would never have reached the proportions it did.

Coming of lowly stock—he had four brothers pulling *rickshas* in Pietermaritzburg—Cakijana had a wonderful brain, and remarkable power over his fellow-Zulus. In the early stages of the rebellion he reported to various chiefs that he had come from the Usutu *kraal*. Dinuzulu subsequently denied that Cakijana was his emissary, but many of the natives believed it; and in this way Cakijana first obtained his influence.

He became a veritable fire-brand, travelling rapidly about northern Natal and Zululand, stirring up strife wherever he went. Before this he had been imprisoned for theft; but he was no ordinary thief. By the sheer power of his own personality he became one of the great Zulu generals. He took part in the attack in the Impanza Valley, and murdered four natives during 1906 because their views did not agree with his plans.

After the storm and stress of the rebellion, Cakijana, with Mayatana, Rolela, Tobela, and several others, wandered about Zululand, armed. Cakijana always stated that he was the agent of Dinuzulu, and created much unrest. Finally he gave himself up in Pietermaritzburg, but was only sentenced to seven years' imprisonment, turning King's evidence against Dinuzulu, who was charged at Grey town with having caused the rebellion. After a lengthy trial Dinuzulu was acquitted on all counts excepting that of harbouring rebels, and was deported to the Transvaal, where he still remains.

Since the rebellion ended, the Natal Police have had a comparatively quiet time. One portion of the field force was sent to bury the bodies of those who had fallen at Insuzi, where the Transvaal Mounted Rifles had beaten the rebels; a strong detachment was sent to patrol the district of Nongoma, under Assistant-Commissioner Clarke; and Inspector Dimmick took a body of men through the native locations in Zululand, the object of this being to impress the Zulus and show that the white men still had a good fighting force at their disposal. There were about 130 men under Inspector Dimmick. A patrol covering many hundreds of miles was started from Nongoma, the force going up into Zululand in September 1907, and passing through the districts of Nkandhla, Mahlabatini, Ceza Bush, and the Usutu country to Nongoma, where they were kept on patrol until the arrest of Dinuzulu in December.

There was a large display of British activity at the time, besides the police there being over a thousand militia near when Dinuzulu surrendered to the authorities at Nongoma.

The troopers, under Inspector Dimmick, resumed their forced marches after that, many natives in various districts being compelled to surrender their arms. The orders were to "keep on the move." Both men and horses were severely tried by the continuous marching, which lasted practically without a break until the end of the year.

Another wave of economy swept over the colony shortly afterwards, and the Government reduced the strength of the Natal Police by 226 men, this practically abolishing the field force. Since then there have been one or two small disturbances, such as faction fights, both in Natal and Zululand, but these were quickly suppressed; and the natives today are more tractable and peacefully inclined than they have ever been.

The present Chief Commissioner of Police, Colonel W. J. Clarke, was appointed to that office in November 1906. He has a longer record of service with the police than any other man in the corps today, and he has done that which no other man in the force has ever succeeded in doing—he joined as a trooper and, working his way up gradually from the ranks, became Chief Commissioner. Colonel Clarke was a recruit in April 1878, and took an active part in the early troubles. He was with Lord Chelmsford's column when it arrived at Isandhlwana on the night of the disaster there, and has acted as dispatch rider on several occasions.

Mr. Clarke was promoted to be lance-corporal in 1880, and corporal a few months afterwards, becoming sergeant in 1882, sub-inspector in 1889, and inspector shortly afterwards. He became Assistant Commissioner of Police in 1904, and was acting Chief Commissioner during the greater part of 1905.

Colonel Clarke was practically the first officer commanding the field force in 1896-97, under General Dartnell. The statement will probably not be disputed that he is the cleverest police officer in Africa. He has a genius for organization, and it is largely due to this that the Natal Police, with their fine fighting record, are the only body of men in Africa who are at the same time highly efficient policemen and good soldiers.

COLONEL CLARKE,
CHIEF COMMISSIONER OF NATAL POLICE.

CHAPTER 21

Headquarters

Owing to the difficulty of getting suitable recruits, the Natal Police are at present quite a hundred and twenty men under strength, and there are fewer troopers at the barracks at Pietermaritzburg than there have been for a long time. The handsome building is on the top of a hill overlooking "Sleepy Hollow," as the town is sometimes called, and catches any breeze there may be on the hot summer days near Christmas. Here, for many years, the recruits have been enrolled and put through their early drills. No very hard-and-fast rules are laid down concerning recruits. They must be single men over 5 ft. 7 in. in height, and physically fit, because those who enter the corps must look forward not merely to the romance of being mounted soldier-policemen amongst the Zulus, but also to enduring hardships, and enduring them cheerfully.

The recruit only remains at headquarters a few months as a rule before being drafted to an out-station. There, in times of peace, he has a life which a hard-working man in England would regard as a perpetual holiday on horseback. In times of war and rebellion, all the manliness that is in him is brought out; he treks and rides and climbs until his powers of endurance are taxed to the limit. The corps can make no use of weaklings or shirkers, and it has been the making of hundreds of men who would in all probability have drifted through life aimlessly, without a suitable opportunity to develop the best part of their characters. There was a striking instance of this in a roving character who went out from England many years ago to join the Natal Police. He had been rather wild as a youth, but the idea of joining the force appealed to him, so he walked straight to headquarters on arriving at Pietermaritzburg and enlisted.

He had taken out with him a letter of introduction from his people to a Natal farmer who had lived near his home, but did not get an opportunity to pay the call. Years afterwards, when turning over his kit, he came upon the note, and, wondering what it was, read it. The letter was in the following terms:—

This is to introduce a young fellow who has never done any good for himself, and we are sending him out to join the Natal Police. If you think it advisable, you might like to see him. From what we know you had better not.

The point of the story is that the young wanderer afterwards became—and still is—one of the best and most highly respected Inspectors the corps has ever had.

There have been men in the corps from Oxford and Cambridge, and every public school of importance in England. For some reason Cheltenham boys have been particularly prominent in the police. Since the Union of South Africa was effected the recruits have consisted chiefly of young Dutchmen, and as trade has improved a number of well-educated men have left the corps to take up very good posts, for which their training has particularly fitted them.

The recruit is first taken on as a probationer for a month, and, unless he develops undesirable habits, is enlisted as a second-class trooper, drawing pay at the rate of 7s. a day. He signs on for three years' service, being promoted to first-class trooper at the end of a year, his pay being raised to 8s. a day. If re-engaged after three years' service he draws 9s. a day, and after six years he is paid 9s. 6d. a day, in addition to any extra pay he may have qualified for.

Some alterations will be made under the new regime, but in the past the troopers bought their own horses and kit, the payment being spread over the first three years of their work, and when they left the money they had paid for their horse was refunded, their kit also being put up for auction. At headquarters, messing and forage costs the trooper about 3s. a day, but his expenses are considerably reduced when he gets to an out-station, where fishing-rod and gun generally provide welcome additions to the menu.

During the first few months the trooper goes through mounted and foot drill, and as he has lectures on law and other subjects to attend besides "stables" and other duties, his time is fairly well occupied. Life begins to grow sweet for him when he becomes a non-commissioned officer, though promotion has not been very rapid in recent years owing to the fact that the men who have held the good positions remained where they were in the hope of living to draw a pension. Lance-sergeants (there are no corporals) receive the same pay as a first-class trooper; a man's salary is increased by a shilling a day when he becomes a second-class sergeant, and another shilling a day when he becomes a first-class sergeant. A sub-inspector receives £300 a year, this rising to £400. An inspector first receives £450, which rises to £550 a year.

The present strength, including all ranks, of white men is 680, the authorized strength being 800. There are also 1106 natives in the corps and 105 Indians.

The headquarters barracks will accommodate 200 men and the same number of horses, though there are rarely so many at Pietermaritzburg owing to the demands of the out-stations.

Nearly every trooper who has left England to join the corps cherishes the ambition to visit his own country, so he often saves both leave and pay for the first few years until he is entitled to a holiday consisting of three months on pay and then a month or two without pay.

Here is an incident in the life of a gentleman trooper. An elder son, who chafed under the conventionalities of life at home, went to South Africa and joined the corps in its early days. Amongst his family acquaintances were the Governor of Natal and his wife. A day or two after the trooper had joined, a lady friend handed him a small parcel and asked him to give it to the Governor's wife. The trooper sent a note up to Government House, asking what he should do with the parcel, whereupon His Excellency wrote inviting him to luncheon. Having finished "stables" and his other morning duties, the trooper put on his best Bond Street clothes and, looking very spruce, started out. "Puffy" Stean, who was very regimental, and would like to have seen his men always in uniform, saw him leaving the barracks.

"Here, young Johnnie, where are you off to?" he asked.

"I have obtained leave, sir. I'm going to Government House," replied the trooper.

"Ho! Indeed! And what might you be going to do there?" inquired the sergeant-major, bristling.

"I'm going to lunch with the Governor, sir."

"So!" said "Puffy" quietly. "There's a drain here that needs cleaning out."

Knowing that it would be folly to kick against the pricks, the trooper put on overalls and, rolling up his immaculate linen, obeyed

SQUAD OF RECRUITS AT DRILL.

RECRUITS AT DRILL

orders. "Puffy" had chosen the task well, for the only possible way of cleaning the mud away from this particular drain was to scoop it out with one's hands. "Puffy" watched him scornfully for a few moments and then walked away.

Having completed his task, the trooper took off his overalls, and, with the aid of sundry toilet requisites, removed all traces of his labour. Shortly afterwards the hand that had been dutifully scooping mud from the drain was shaking that of his Excellency the Governor and that of the Governor's wife. "Puffy" loved to see obedience, and the new trooper earned his everlasting respect that day under trying circumstances.

"Once upon a time "there was an officer in charge at headquarters who dearly loved a fight. It was not seemly that one in his position should take part in a game of fisticuffs, but he yearned to do the next best thing—to be a spectator. The second-in-command knew of this, and, as he was equally interested, he privately arranged with the troopers that when there was to be a fight between two men they were to settle their dispute at a certain place where he could see all that happened without being seen himself. Many a fierce combat was waged at this place before the eyes of the officer in charge and his second-in-command, but one day a struggle was interrupted by a sergeant, who put the opponents under arrest, and next morning they were brought before the officer in charge, accused of fighting.

The contest had been a particularly interesting and exciting one, and the sergeant proceeded to relate, entirely incorrectly, how one man had struck the other. Impatiently the officer in charge listened for a while—until he was unable to stand it any longer.

"It's an infernal lie, sir," he said angrily.

And then, realizing that he knew too much about the affair, he had to dismiss the combatants hastily before he got deeper into the mire.

"Puffy" Stean was a keen enthusiast, and the interests of his corps were next to his heart. This led to his being placed in an awkward position at headquarters on one occasion. An influential young farmer, who owned a large estate, vast herds of cattle, and a useful banking balance, called at the barracks. "Puffy," mistaking him for a prospective recruit, rushed at him, told him he would be perfectly satisfactory, ordered him to draw his preliminary kit—consisting of a couple of blankets, a mess tin, and a combination knife, fork, and spoon—and told him to visit the tailor to be measured.

Having a sense of humour, the farmer obeyed, and "Puffy" congratulated himself on having added a smart man to the ranks. After drawing his kit the farmer returned to "Puffy" and asked to see the commandant.

"What the deuce do you want with him?" asked "Puffy." "He's too busy this morning to be bothered with recruits."

"But I'm not a recruit," replied the farmer, "and Colonel Dartnell is a personal friend of mine whom I have called to see."

"Puffy" nearly exploded with wrath, and to make matters worse had to apologise profusely before he could get back his blankets.

There have been some changes in the personnel of the force during the last year or two, but as a corps the men are a splendid, abstemious body and a good fighting force, with intimate knowledge of a wild and mountainous country. They take a keen interest in their work, and with constant exercise under the most healthy circumstances possible, are as hard as any similar body of men in the world. The majority of them are magnificent horsemen, who in the course of a day's patrol cover country which stout-hearted hunting men in England would dread to travel over even in the heat of the chase. These patrols are made over *kafir* paths which lead over *kopjes* covered with crags smashed by lightning and intersected by dangerous *dongas*—deep gullies quickly washed out by violent storms.

The members of the force are especially good at rifle shooting, and have won a great number of trophies. The one thing insisted on by the Chief Commissioner is that every man should be a good shot, not only at targets, but at field firing and unknown distances. The Government of Natal has always been liberal in the supply of ammunition, and there are no districts in which the men do not get practice, at least once a month.

Recruits are not now enlisted in England, (at time of first publication), but young men who are prepared to pay their passage out would be accepted, provided they could pass the medical examination

CHAPTER 22

At the Back of Beyond

A lonelier life than that led by a member of the Natal Police away on some out-station in the far north of Zululand, perhaps a couple of hundred miles off the nearest railway, it would be difficult to imagine; and yet it has some indefinable attraction for the men. Just as the call of the East gnaws eternally at the soul of a wanderer who, having once passed into the magic at the other side of the Suez Canal, has returned to hum-drum old England, so the lonely life in Zululand grips those who have once grown accustomed to its peculiar charm. A man may be stationed for eight or ten years at a place like Ubombo, which is 150 miles from the railway, or Ingwavuma, which is even more remote, with only a few *kafir kraals* in the district, and still be contented, although his only white neighbours consist of a magistrate and a store-keeper.

At such places there is usually a sergeant in charge of the station, and he may have one, or possibly three European policemen to associate with. Speak to him of the Strand and Regent Street and a curious look comes into his eyes. He is living his life in the wilds, with little else than Zulus and snakes for companions, and is missing, year after year, all the good things that wonderful London has in its store-cupboard. He is human, and when you remind him of these things he will tell you with a touch of *pathos*, which he would not like you to see, that he really would like to go home again for a while, "because things do get a bit slow sometimes here, don't you know."

And yet he could no more live in London for the rest of his days than he could fly. A murderous Zulu rushing at him with an *assegai* he would tackle without turning a hair, but a motor 'bus coming round a corner suddenly in Regent Street would startle him so much that he would develop a craving to be back in the wilds amongst the snakes

POLICE CAMP AT GLEN ROSA, ALEXANDRA COUNTY.

POLICE CAMP AT GWALIWENI, ON THE BORDER OF SWAZILAND.
ONLY ONE WHITE FAMILY LIVES WITHIN 30 MILES OF THE PLACE,
WHICH IS SIX DAYS' RIDE FROM THE RAILWAY.

and *kraals.*

The men at headquarters at Pietermaritzburg have dozens of companions to associate with, both in barracks and in the town, and yet the majority of them prefer to be on an out-station. On the occasion of the coronation of King Edward VII. a number of men were called in from the back blocks, some of them having been there for years. They went to London and thoroughly enjoyed themselves, but when they got back to Natal they asked to be sent back to their solitary posts.

A man who has grown to love life on an out-station cannot readily tell why he loves it, though he will say vaguely that it is "fine." He has plenty of hard work, but he has also plenty of clean, healthy pleasure. His expenditure is nothing *per annum* beyond the necessaries of life. He has his own horse, and opportunities to go out with his gun after game both small and big.

This strange fascination of the out-stations even holds good at such fever-stricken places as Maputa and Enselini, in the low-lying districts of Zululand, where malaria is very prevalent in the summer, and the men's diet consists solely of tinned meat and crushed *mealies*, supplemented by such things as the troopers can shoot.

There is nothing quite like the room in which a member of the Natal Police lives when he is in the wilds. Someone has drawn a very accurate picture of it:—

A small wooden sofa without any head,
By day made a couch, by night made a bed;
A chair with three legs, propped up with a stick,
An allowance of candle, all tallow, no wick;
A pen-and-ink sketch of some pretty face,
A short double-barrel, half stuck in its case;
A carpet that doesn't half cover the floor,
A target chalked out on the back of the door;
An old Reitbuck skin, by way of a rug,
Whereon sits a terrier, pointer, or pug;
Apparatus for washing, a foot tub, a pan,
Extract of Orders, and half of a fan;
A fawn-coloured glove, a lock of dark hair,
Both highly prized, from some lady fair;
A couple of razors, an old ostrich plume,
A fishing rod, shot belt, a rifle, a broom;
A tumbledown candlestick smelling of brass,

The "N.P." drill-book and a cracked looking-glass;
A mould to load cartridges, a piccolo, flute,
The bowl of a calabash, and half of a boot;
A loaded revolver, kept at half cock,
A gun-case, a cash-box, lacking a lock;
A treatise on "Zulu," a bottle of port,
A shield from Impanza, an unfinished report;
Two assegais, a knobkerry, and a half-smoked cigar,
Some Boer tobacco in an old broken jar;
A letter from home and the orderly book,
A hat, and a powder-flask hung on a hook;
Some pairs of old boots, a part of a novel,
One-half of the tongs and a bit of the shovel;
A large book of photos, a Zulu costume,
And towels and slippers all over the room;
An easy armchair, only lacking its back,
A sketch in burnt cork of some wonderful hack;
A pair of cord pants with a whip in the pocket,
A tea-caddy open, containing a locket.
In the midst of this chaos, as gay as you please,
On a rickety chair, perched quite at his ease,
A pipe in his mouth, his feet in the grate,
Sits the overworked trooper a-cursing his fate.

Next to the magistrate, the sergeant is the most important person within many miles. On him devolves the whole responsibility of the station; and though life may be grey and uneventful for very many months at a stretch, he must be prepared to act, and to act quickly, when the occasion arises. Unrest amongst the natives occurs periodically, and though only whisperings of it may have reached the ears of the white men, an open rebellion might break out at any time. At such moments the Natal Police have proved their merit, quelling the disturbance either with tact or a sudden display of authority.

The work of the men on out-stations consists chiefly of going on patrol and dealing with such things as faction fights and cattle-stealing. The Zulu dearly loves a fight, and if he gets the opportunity of attacking an enemy with a couple of sticks, the pair of them will keep at it, hammer and tongs, until one or the other falls with a dent in his skull. On these occasions their uncles and cousins have a habit of joining in, until the affair becomes serious and someone stands a good chance of being killed.

ZULUS PAYING DOG TAX TO A TROOPER ON PATROL NEAR
INGWAVUMA, ZULULAND.

NATIVE CARRIERS BEARING KIT USED ON CENSUS DUTY.
THE MAN CARRYING SEVEN CHAIRS TOOK THEM 20 MILES A
DAY ON HIS HEAD.

As a general rule the fiercest of faction fights end abruptly when the police arrive, for the native greatly respects the force, although he does not particularly mind going to prison, especially for fighting, which to his mind is far from being a reprehensible pastime. Natives have been known to save up their money in order to have a good fight and then pay the inevitable fine. In cases where nobody has been killed, and only sticks have been used, the penalty is usually about £5 to £10 for the ringleaders, and 30s. to £3 for those who only joined in for the fun of the thing. A Zulu gets miserable if he cannot have a fight now and again, so he has many excuses for a fray, though it generally concerns the lady of his dreams.

There were 166 Zulu prisoners arrested at Mapumulo towards the end of 1912 for taking part in a faction fight, in which one man was killed and forty injured. It was the most serious affair of the kind that had taken place for many years in the district. The Mapumulo court-house was not nearly large enough to hold the delinquents, so they were arranged in rows outside. The jailer filled the prison "to the brim," and was unable to take them all in, so fifty of the natives were allowed to go, their chiefs being made responsible for them.

The hardest work on an out-station is the annual inspection of the hut and dog taxes. Every *kraal* in the district has to be visited, however remotely it may be situated, and this often occupies four months.

The difficulties of this tedious inspection are manifold. It is strictly contrary to regulations to warn the natives to meet at different places so that they can show their hut tax receipts and dog licences to the police, but this arrangement is unavoidable at times. Like his more enlightened brethren, the Zulu goes out paying calls sometimes, and on these occasions he consumes a goodly quantity of native beer. Often the police climb over rough country and call at *kraal* after *kraal*, only to find that the men are away at a beer-drink. The children and dogs fly into the bush as soon as a patrol appears on the scene, and the receipts cannot be found. Sometimes the head of the *kraal* will remain away day after day, going to different beer-drinks, and as it would be a physical impossibility for the patrols to call every day until he happened to be in, his dogs are counted and a message is sent telling him to produce his tickets at the police camp.

The troopers occasionally go on a patrol extending over 80 or 100 miles, and this is a considerable undertaking when, owing to the danger of horse-sickness, they have to go on foot. This malady, caused by a mosquito bite, ends in the animal choking suddenly before its owner

166 PRISONERS ON TRIAL FOR TAKING PART IN A FACTION FIGHT

is aware that it is ill. So prevalent is this trouble at certain seasons of the year that even at headquarters fires have to be lighted in the stables at night to smoke the mosquitoes out. Another disease that has to be carefully guarded against is *nagana*—a slow but almost certain cause of death to the horse. It is caused by the bite of the tsetse fly. It would be crass folly to tether a horse out all night in Zululand in the hot weather, and so the trooper sometimes has to walk.

Almost the only thing to think about on an out-station is police work, and consequently the men get keenly enthusiastic about their duties. After a raw recruit has spent six months drilling and studying routine at headquarters, he is usually drafted off to some more or less lonely post, and the effect of this on him is curiously noticeable. A youth who showed little or no aptitude for the work while in the hands of the drill instructor, suddenly develops a sense of responsibility when he finds himself tackling his duties.

However remote the station may be, discipline is invariably maintained just as strictly as it is at headquarters. A sergeant and a trooper may be together in some lonely place for years, each dependent almost entirely on the society of the other all that time, but discipline is never relaxed, even though the two men may be good friends or have grown to hate the sight of one another. It is a severe test of good-fellowship to be thrown into the company of one man year after year at a benighted corner of the earth where nothing ever happens; but ill-feeling hardly ever crops up, perhaps because the men realize that they have to put up with each other.

Some of them grow strangely quiet and subdued after spending a long time in the back blocks, and for a little while after their return to headquarters there is something aloof about their demeanour. This has given rise to the jest that all men who live on an out-station in Zululand for a long time go mad, or, as they put it, suffer from "Zululand tap"—though nobody seriously believes it.

The deadly monotony sometimes tells on them a little. Three men were sitting round a camp fire not long ago far from the madd'ing crowd at the headquarters canteen. The trio had been talked out for months, and there was no earthly prospect of seeing a stranger for a long time. An air of depression hung over them as they sat silently pulling at their pipes.

"Good Lord," said one wearily, "nothing interesting ever happens in this rotten hole. You always know what's coming months in advance."

"You don't know what's going to happen now," said another, as he reached out for a case of cartridges and threw them into the fire.

Half the chimney was blown out, but nobody was hurt. Something had happened—and all three felt much happier for days afterwards.

Fortunately, extraordinary things do happen on back-stations now and again to relieve the monotony. One of the most remarkable official reports ever made came from Vant's Drift, on the Buffalo River, in the autumn of 1905.

While on patrol, a trooper called on a Dutch farmer, who for over twenty years had been sorely puzzled by oft-repeated statements that weird, inexplicable noises were heard on a part of his estate. The farmer, who still lives at Vant's Drift, was much afraid of being laughed at, and the trooper, growing interested, could only extract the Dutchman's story from him bit by bit.

Before the last Boer war he had been in the habit of sending sheep down to the part of his estate where these mysterious noises were heard, every lambing season. It was quite four miles from his house, in a valley through which a stream runs. A white man was always sent to take charge of the animals, and he had to camp out.

Sane, sober white men, on several of these occasions, returned complaining vaguely of the loneliness of the place, and saying they would not remain there as they were disturbed in the night by curious noises which they were unable to trace. The farmer invariably had the greatest difficulty in persuading his men to stop in the valley any length of time. He might have imagined they were joking but for the fact that they grew quite insolent if he persisted in asking them to go back to the sheep. New men invariably returned to the farm after spending two or three nights near the stream. So persistent did the complaints become that the farmer determined to go to the place himself and find out whether there was any foundation for the rumours; but the war broke out, and it was not until 1905 that he got a forcible reminder of the affair.

A few weeks prior to his telling the trooper of his troubles he had sent a man down to the old place to look after some sheep, but the man returned in a hurry and said he dared not stay there another day alone. He begged that someone should be sent to keep him company, or that he could, for preference, be relieved of the duty altogether.

The Dutchman, now keenly interested, questioned the man closely and got from him an account of what had frightened him. He said that every night he had been disturbed by hearing the sound of a woman wailing loudly, and the crying of a child. At first he took no notice of it, but the noises continued for such a long time, and seemed so near, that he went out of his hut to discover what was wrong. He could see nobody, however, although he could still hear the wailing, which appeared to come from farther and farther away, until at last it died away in the distance.

Wondering what was the matter, the man called up his native boys. Their reply rather amused him. They said they, too, had heard the noise of crying, but there was no woman anywhere near, nor a child. They declared the place was evil and bewitched. There was no *kraal* within a couple of miles, and no native dared to pass the place at night.

Laughing, he returned to his hut, but he felt somewhat creepy the following night when the same thing happened. It began to get on his nerves when he heard it night after night, and on some occasions, he declared, he saw a dark, indistinct shape which was surrounded by "a faint wavering light which came and disappeared with the wailing."

The natives also told him they saw the object, and at last, thinking that some practical joke was being played upon him, he lay in wait with a very tangible shot gun. It was a dark night, and he waited patiently for the spook for some hours. At last it appeared, wavering and howling as usual. Taking careful aim when it was within range, he emptied both barrels at it, expecting to see the object collapse. But to his horror nothing of the sort happened. The figure went on making a dismal row as before, and after floating about for a while vanished in the distance.

This was too much for him, and he went straight to the farmer early the following morning. When he left the place his native boys left also, refusing to remain without the protection of the white man.

The farmer promptly sent for two or three of his neighbours, all matter-of-fact men, and they decided to camp out at the place "for the fun of the thing." It was an eerie expedition, but they took it more or less as a joke, and pitched a square tent under an overhanging rock, on a slight rise overlooking the stream. After their evening meal they turned the lights out, lit their pipes, and waited to see what would happen. Soon they were startled to hear the wailing of a woman. The sound was clear and distinct, and seemed to come from immediately behind the tent. It was an uncanny experience, and they listened breathlessly until they also heard the crying of a child.

There was very little breeze, and as the sound died away the tent collapsed; one man received a blow which dislocated some of his teeth, and another had his arm broken. They all made a dash to the tent flap, just as the tent was pitched on to a small *plateau* overlooking the stream.

There was a shadowy form near, with a light floating over it, gradually gliding away in the direction of the water; and the hills echoed with the piercing shrieks of a woman in dire distress. The party of investigators had seen all they desired to see, and without waiting another moment, cleared off, nor did they stop until they reached the farmer's house.

The trooper, as much interested as the Dutchman's neighbours had been, suggested making an expedition to the place, and the farmer agreed to show him where these events had occurred. They started straight away, a native carrying a spade and pick, as it was suggested that the victim of some tragedy might have been buried by the side of the stream. They followed a track across an undulating plain, and climbed a steep rise where they found themselves looking into a deep, secluded valley, along which the stream flowed. They had to climb down a sharp descent, until they came to a large semi-circular cave which receded into the hill to a distance of about ten yards, a ledge of rock forming a natural roof about twelve feet above their heads. It was altogether a wild, isolated place to which only an occasional sheep was likely to penetrate—but this was the spot on which the tent had been pitched on the eventful night when two men were hurt.

The wailing had arisen immediately behind the tent, so the trooper started digging there enthusiastically.

He was prepared to dig up the whole surface of the cave if necessary, but he had not been delving very long before he came upon the complete skeletons of a woman and a child.

The bones lay about three feet below the surface, and had obviously been there a long time. The district surgeon, who was called, said he fancied the large skeleton was that of a European woman. The police were never able to solve the mystery as to how it got there. At the request of the farmer the skeletons were given a more suitable resting-place, and the farmer never had occasion to complain about ghosts again.

The trooper who investigated the matter, and dug up the skeletons, is now on the headquarters staff—where he keeps two curious ashtrays, each consisting of half of the woman's skull.

Ghost tales abound at all the police camps in Natal and Zululand, probably because there is hardly an old station at which a trooper

Police camp at Loteni, near Basutoland border.

Police camp at Nqutu, Zululand.

has not committed suicide at one time or another. Estcourt Fort has a very-well-known spook. Years ago a member of the corps walked up the stairs with jingling spurs, carrying saddlery, and a few minutes later he put a bullet through his brain. Now and again very serious-minded troopers open the door when they hear the clanking of a man mounting the stairs, and, on seeing nobody there, remark, "Oh, it's only the ghost."

The laying of a ghost at Mid-Illovo in 1903 caused a good deal of excitement. It had been common knowledge for years that the police camp was haunted. Various people swore they had seen the spook on several occasions, and it began to take an active part in the life of the troopers, for every morning jugs, dishes, joints of meat, and other things disappeared, and were afterwards found in various parts of the grounds.

Matters became so serious that the men kept their revolvers ready loaded, and one night they were awakened by the crash of breaking crockery, and the wildly excited yell of "I've got him," uttered by Trooper Smith.

The other three members of the corps snatched up their weapons and dashed up to the entrance of the mess-room, where they found Smith declaring he had seen the milk-jug dancing about by itself. This sounded so idiotic that his comrades thought he had been dreaming, but at that instant there was another crash, accompanied by moaning.

Smith and one of his colleagues dashed round to the back, and mounted a wooden partition over-looking the mess-room. From this position they enjoyed the creepy sensation of observing the milk-jug floating about in nothingness. They fired simultaneously. The jug dropped, and something could be heard rushing about in the darkness.

At this thrilling moment Trooper Woolley arrived with a light, and then it was seen that the disturbance had been caused by a *kafir* dog. It had evidently been in the habit of helping itself in the camp at night-time, and on this occasion had got into trouble by wedging its head in the milk-jug. As the light approached, the dog tried to get out of the window, but two more shots rang out, and then a fierce fusillade started. Bullets were sent flying in all directions, but the mongrel jumped through a broken window-pane and was not seen until the following day, when a herd-boy reported that he had found its body half a mile away. It had been hit in seven places, the lower jaw being completely blown off.

Life is not altogether without its humours on the out-stations. Some time ago a circular was issued to the police urging each man to carry permanganate of potash, which, if applied quickly to a snake-bite, is often effective. An Indian messenger rushed up to the home of a police officer near Pietermaritzburg and begged for a man to be sent down to a house near, where a snake had bitten someone . Hastily snatching up some permanganate of potash and a lancet, the only man available ran to the patient, meanwhile telling the messenger to go to the police station with all speed and send a doctor along. The messenger had just carried out these instructions and left the police station, when an Indian woman, sobbing hysterically, limped in and exhibited a wound in her leg. She was in a state of wild excitement, but could not speak a word of English.

Taking in the situation at a glance, and knowing that snake-bites need very prompt attention, the men on duty made her sit down, and with a lancet cut the place at which she pointed, afterwards rubbing in permanganate of potash thoroughly.

They were engaged on this operation when the district officer happened to walk in.

"What have you got here?" he asked.

"Snake-bite, sir," said a trooper, as he rubbed in the drug.

"Why, you haven't cut the wound nearly enough," replied the district officer. "I'll have a go at it."

He applied the lancet afresh, and rubbed in the drug liberally, the woman bearing the pain stoically.

"There!" said the district officer at last. "She ought to be all right now. You should do a job like this thoroughly."

An Indian constable came in.

"Here," said the district officer. "Ask this woman what sort of a snake it was that bit her."

The man obeyed.

"She says she knows nothing about a snake, sir, but came to show you where her husband had been hitting her," explained the Indian constable.

The subject of the treatment of snake-bites was a delicate one to broach to that district officer for months afterwards.

At Greytown, in 1905, when the field force was stationed there, about forty horses belonging to the troopers broke loose and stampeded wildly at five o'clock in the morning. One or two men who attempted to stop them were powerless, and the animals disappeared in

213

A TYPICAL OUT-STATION GROUP, AT MAHLABATINI, WITH THE NATIVE POLICE AND SPORTING DOGS

a body in a few minutes at full gallop. Search parties were sent out, but the animals had covered too great a distance to be recaptured easily. To the astonishment of the orderly sergeant at the Pietermaritzburg headquarters, nearly fifty miles away, a dozen of the horses galloped into barracks at 4.30 the following morning. Amongst them was one animal which had been going dead lame for days. It was afterwards found that they had not travelled on the main road, but had made a detour *via* York.

A comical story is told of a field force returning to headquarters from northern Zululand. The horses were being entrained under the supervision of a sergeant who had an exalted view of his own ability. In the dull glare of many lanterns, the scared animals were being driven into a row of cattle-trucks that lined one of the platforms.

"How many beasts are you getting into those boxes?" demanded the sergeant.

"Ten, sir," replied the orderly.

"Ten! why, man alive, you'll have to squeeze at least fifteen in," replied the non-commissioned officer, heatedly.

"It can't be done, sir. They're already over-crowded," replied the orderly.

"I'll show you how to put horses in," said the sergeant; and he started to drive the animals into a box with care.

"That makes fifteen," he said at last, with great satisfaction. "I told you it could be done. Is there room for any more?"

"Room for three more, sir," a recruit replied, casting his lantern round.

"That makes eighteen!" observed the sergeant; and three more horses were entrained.

"Full up?" inquired the sergeant.

"Room for three more, sir," said the recruit imperturbably.

Somewhat surprised, but hiding the fact, the sergeant ordered the requisite number to be driven in.

"Still room for three more, sir," cried the recruit.

By the time forty-five horses had been entrained in the box, even the sergeant began to show signs of amazement.

"What on earth do you mean, idiot?" he shouted, as the recruit droned out the same remark which by now was becoming monotonous. "Room for three more, do you say?"

"Yes, sir. There's room for one—two—three—FOUR—more!" counted the recruit deliberately.

Natal Police taking their midday meal at Ndumu, Northern Zululand, while on census duty.

At that moment a night-clerk dashed up breathlessly.

"The stationmaster wants to know what on earth you are doing," he panted.

"Tell him," replied the sergeant, with a satisfied smile, "that I have just succeeded in entraining forty-five horses in one cattle-box—and there is still room for four more, so we shan't want the other boxes."

"Heavens, man!" replied the night-clerk," there are nearly fifty horses tearing up and down the line, and everything's going to the dogs."

"There's room for heaps more, sir," broke in the recruit. "There isn't a blooming horse in that box."

Then the mystery was explained. The door at the opposite side of the cattle-box had been left open, and almost as fast as the horses had been entrained they had escaped at the other side.

Practical jokes sometimes relieve the monotony at out-stations, with rather alarming effect on occasions. There was a violent-tempered trooper who had a perfect horror of cats, and when things grew dull one night another trooper tied a cat to a tree near the ill-tempered individual's room. He also balanced a bucket of water over the man's door and attached a string to the cat's tail. When the irritable trooper had settled down to read, his colleague gently pulled the string on the cat's tail. A mournful wail went up again and again, whereupon the easily angered trooper snatched up his gun with the intention of shooting the animal. As he dashed out of the door the practical joker at just the correct moment pulled another string which he had fastened to the bucket of water.

More furious than ever, the trooper with the gun turned his attention to his tormentor, and there was a keenly exciting chase until the culprit dashed into his room and locked the door behind him.

The cat-hater was in such a violent temper that the proceedings did not seem at all likely to end there, so the fugitive hastily piled boxes against the door—through which a shot came just as the fugitive was climbing out of the window at the back. It hit the bed instead of the trooper, who rushed round to the front, jumped on to his adversary's back and took his weapon away before any further damage was done. It was quite a quarter of an hour, however, before the angered man could be persuaded to enter the other trooper's room. Then they both laughed, inspected the dent made by the bullet on the bed, and divided all that was left in a decanter between two glasses.

The man who pulled the cat's tail was Trooper Fairlie—now an inspector in the force.

An exciting incident was related to the writer by an inspector of the Natal Police.

"I was a trooper on an out-station," he said, "where two Irishmen had a bitter quarrel, and late one night the ill-feeling grew to such a degree that it was decided to fight a duel. Things had been deplorably slow for months, so we were all delighted at the prospect of a little pleasant diversion. Two of us were appointed seconds. It was agreed that one principal should go out with his second and hide, and the other was to follow a few minutes afterwards. They both had carbines, and the man who saw his opponent first was to fire.

"They tossed to see which should go out first, and my man lost. It was pitch dark when we followed a little while afterwards, and very warily we peered about for some time, but nothing happened. In a fit of absent-mindedness I struck a match to light my pipe, and our opponent, who happened to be quite close, blazed away with his carbine. This so startled me that I hit my principal in the middle of the back with a *knobkerry* which I had taken out with me.

"'I'm killed,' he groaned, sinking to the ground.

"The other principal ran up and stooped over his enemy's prostrate form.

"'Good Heavens, Larry,' he cried bitterly, 'I've shot yez! Now it's meself I'll shoot.'

"So overcome was he with grief that he probably would have done so had he not—only with the utmost difficulty—been persuaded to believe the fact that the bullets had been extracted from the cartridges before they were placed in the carbines.

"The incident brightened us all up for days. The duellists were the best of friends ever afterwards, and nobody was a penny the worse excepting my un-fortunate principal, who complained of a pain in his back for some time."

It is during times of rebellion that the isolated troopers are most liable to an attack of "nerves." Physically, they are as fit as men can be, but a subtle feeling of uneasiness creeps over them when the natives are in the mood for a rising. Nothing definite is stated to the white men, who never know exactly when to expect an outbreak, or in what form it will come; but after living amongst the Zulus for a lengthy period they learn to detect signs of unrest which foreshadow the coming of the storm. Generally there is a telephone at the magistracy, though this cannot be relied on in case of fighting, because the natives have discovered the advantage they gain by cutting the wires. Cunning, and yet bland, the Zulus have to be watched closely when there is unrest amongst them, and the troopers get into the habit of "sleeping with one eye open" until the danger subsides. Before actually making an attack the Zulus drive their cattle away, and store their grain in pits, consequently these moves are watched for very anxiously.

A man literally carries his life in his hands in the back-blocks sometimes when he has been inquiring into a murder, especially if the murder has been a political one; and it is more by good fortune than skill or wits that he learns of his danger. Sergeant F. L. Wilkinson had a particularly trying time in this way at Nkandhla, just after the Zulu rebellion of 1906. He had gone over to Mahlabatini in connection with the murder of Mr. Stainbank, the magistrate, and a native made an important statement to him, but subsequently said he would not repeat it in court. Soon after another Zulu observed to the sergeant, in front of a magistrate—

"If the white man who has been sent here to work up this case implicates our chief he will be removed." This was a polite but firm intimation that Wilkinson would be killed if he interfered.

That was the first warning he received. For more than six months afterwards he was constantly dogged, and narrowly escaped death on several occasions. Time after time he was warned by friendly natives to be on his guard, not to use the same paths more frequently than he could help, and not to stay at the office late at night, as there were certain Zulus who were bent on assassinating him sooner or later.

On one occasion one of Sergeant Wilkinson's colleagues was nearly killed in error. Two armed natives leaped out of some bushes as a trooper passed, but fortunately discovered their mistake in time and ran away.

On another occasion the sergeant had gone thirty miles from Nkandhla to arrest a rebel. He discovered that the native's father had died, and the native was going to a *krantz* to perform some medicine rites at night. Wilkinson decided to go to the *krantz*—a lonely enough place for any heathen rites—and trap him there. While he was dogging the movements of the rebel, he, in turn, was being followed by two men who were awaiting a favourable opportunity to shoot him. When Wilkinson was far away this came to the ears of the Nkandhla magistrate, Mr. B. Colenbrander, who sent a mounted messenger warning the sergeant and recalling him. He was told he would be courting certain death if he remained out, so he returned.

The perpetual knowledge that one is being followed by murderers in Zululand is enough to try the stoutest heart, but Sergeant Wilkinson continued to investigate a number of political murder cases which needed very delicate handling. Friendly natives at Nkandhla constantly repeated warnings to him, and nearly every night during the six months he slept in a different room or changed the position of his bed, expecting any moment to hear bullets crash through the window.

On the 8th September 1907 he returned to Nkandhla, after following a man who was suspected of having murdered the chief Tshishili, and was told that he would be killed that night unless he were careful. At midnight he had a cup of coffee with the magistrate— his political enemies afterwards suggested that it was not coffee—and left with Detective Rathbone for the police station. Rathbone, when leaving him, on the way, pressed him to take a lantern, but the sergeant preferred to go without one. His life was again saved, a few moments later, by an odd impulse which led him to turn off the main road, and make a detour of fifty yards. He had gone home hundreds of times by that road, but never before had he made the same detour: the next morning it was proved that two men with firearms had been lying in wait for him behind a hedge in the part of the road he avoided. Had he not gone round he would have been shot in the back.

On arriving at the police station he went straight to his bedroom, pulled down the blind, which left a two-inch gap at the bottom, got into bed, read for a few minutes, and then turned out the lamp. The moment he did so a shot was fired through the window, which was about a yard from his head. A revolver bullet passed within an inch of his face, and his cheek and nose were cut by splinters of falling glass. In almost every case of murder in the district for some time previously two shots had been fired. Realizing this in a flash, the sergeant instantly squeezed himself between the bed and the wall, waiting for a few torturing seconds for the second bullet. It came—and would have killed him had he leaped up after the first shot. It buried itself in the floor close to him. A moment later he had reached his revolver, and, shouting to awake his colleagues in another room, ran outside. A figure was disappearing in a gap in an adjoining plantation, and Wilkinson fired but missed. As he did so Trooper de Ros hurried out, also armed, and together they searched the neighbourhood for quite an hour, but without success.

There is every reason to suppose that the man who fired at Wilkinson was subsequently shot by the Natal Police at Mbekamuzi.

POLICE CAMP AT KNOXWOOD.

THE OLD POLICE CAMP AT NDUMU.

When a member of the police has to make a long journey in remote districts, far from the railway, he treks from one police camp to another, and need hardly ever sleep in the open on such a trip, the camps having been distributed practically all over Natal and Zululand.

Built by the men themselves in Northern Zululand. It is nearly a week's journey from a railway station.

The comfort of being able to put up at one of the camps every night does not, however, fall to the lot of the police when they are moving about at full speed during war times. Some trooper who had tasted the full joys of trekking has placed his impressions on record in the *Nongqai*, [1] the quarterly magazine of the police. His views are shared very generally by those who have been through it. Here they are:

Ride in the rain, ride in the sun
(They both beat down like hell),
From this camp to some other one,
And you've got to hurry as well.

Camp in the wet, camp in the dry,
On the hill, the valley, or plain;
You hope to God you may not die
Before you see home again.

Fall in for guard, fall in for drill,
It's all in the long day's work;
You get no rest unless you're ill,
Or are one of the rotters that shirk.

Fight like the devil, fight, seeing red,
With never a thought of retreat,
Remembering that you're a long time dead,
And a deuced hard lot to beat.

Drink what you can—anything wet,
And pray for the wine that is red;
But when it's the grape juice don't forget
To drink for your pals who're dead.

The principal duties which the members of the force have to perform in the out-stations are:

Frequent and vigilant patrolling.

---

1. Meaning those who wander—the Zulus' name for the Natal Police.

The suppression of tumults, riots, or breaches of the peace.

The detection of crime and the arrest of offenders.

The execution of criminal warrants and summonses.

The prevention of cattle being driven about the country without passes, and the prevention and the detection of the stock thefts.

The prevention of natives travelling about the country with firearms or *assegais* (without the written permission of a magistrate), and the seizure of all such weapons.

The inspection of licences in the various districts.

The collection of statistics for the annual blue book.

The issue of passes to natives.

The discovery of stolen property.

Escort of treasure and prisoners.

Acting as messengers of magistrates' courts.

Attending stock sales and inspecting slaughter-houses, with a view to tracing lost or stolen stock.

Inspecting hut and dog tax licences.

Acting as Customs and Excise officers.

Acting as postmasters.

CHAPTER 23

The C.I.D.

In a dingy little office in Pietermaritzburg there is one of the most remarkable Criminal Investigation Departments in the world, and it has handled some of the grimmest tragedies and most extraordinary crimes that ever taxed the ingenuity of a police officer. The C.I.D. owes its existence to Colonel Clarke, who fathered it and practically built it up with his own hands.

In 1893 the officers of police were invited by the authorities to submit schemes for the re-organization of the various police forces in the colony. Mr. Clarke submitted one, and inserted in it a C.I.D. Subsequently, when a number of changes were being made, he was entrusted by the Attorney-General with the task of putting the department on a working basis. That official stated in Parliament that he did not think they had any one who was capable of taking charge of the department properly, and Mr. Clarke was only given a year's trial at first. How well he acquitted himself may be judged by the fact that he remained in authority there for nearly eleven years, though he was away for considerable periods with the fighting forces during that time.

The work of a C.I.D. consists of taking over cases from the various stations that cannot easily be dealt with by the police there. Mr. Clarke had been promised a free hand and every assistance: when he came to start he found "every assistance" consisted of the use of the services of one native constable, and the only C.I.D. work that individual was capable of performing was sweeping the floor and running messages— slowly. A furnished office was provided: the furniture consisted of one barrack-room table and one form. The first task that faced the department was to impress upon the police all over the colony the very fact that there was such a department at work. A great many circulars had to be issued to the different stations, and the authorities refused to grant Mr. Clarke the simple apparatus necessary for duplicating letters. The C.I.D. chief had seen the working of the C.I.D. at Scotland Yard, and therefore was able to model his department on the lines of those employed in London; but with such an inadequate staff it was extremely difficult to work any system.

Very slow progress was the natural result of finding almost overwhelming odds against the work, but gradually one man after another was added to the staff, including both Europeans and natives. The Europeans chosen had to be detectives capable of doing very delicate work.

It soon became apparent that a staff of trained, intelligent natives would be of very great service to the department, for the Zulu detectives could go amongst their chattering brethren and get to the root of a mystery, in some cases, long before any European would succeed. In theory this sounded excellent: in practice the absolute childishness of the average Zulu (in some matters) was a serious obstacle. Some hundreds of natives had to be tried before a candidate of any promise whatever could be found, and even then they were no good until they had had a great deal of training.

Not ten really good native detectives were chosen out of quite a thousand men who were tried.

One of the greatest problems was, and still is, to get a native detective who could be depended upon to conceal his identity. The Zulu dearly loves to show his authority, and boys were constantly taken off cases because they had disclosed their business. On one occasion a native detective, sent out to make inquiries in the wilds, was provided with an old and ragged suit for the purpose. He turned up at the place, and worked on the case for a couple of days, and then blossomed out in all the glory of police breeches and gaiters.

Another boy spoilt his case through an affair of the heart. He did excellent work until one of the maidens in the district took his fancy. The police were at a critical stage of their investigations, when the girl told the native detective, who had purposely been clothed in rags, that she could not have anything to do with him because he was not in a position to keep her properly.

"That is all right," he said. "Not a word! I am working for the Government."

The girl promptly told everybody that he was not what he appeared to be, and the police had to leave the case.

Two men were chosen to go out on a sheep-stealing case. For over an hour they were coached carefully, and warned to use the utmost discretion. They were dispatched in the role of wild-cat-skin sellers, and suitable stock-in-trade was bought for them. Looking very wise, the pair of them went out, but apparently they put their heads together for a couple of hours to solve a knotty problem as soon as they had the opportunity. Then they returned to the C.I.D. and explained that they could not very well go as they were because they had no arm badges on to show that they were members of the police force!

On another occasion Mr. Clarke sent two native detectives to Woodside to make inquiries into a case of theft, and when he followed them the inhabitants of each *kraal* that he passed on the road told him that his detectives were at a certain farm. The Zulu officers on their way to this farm had visited each *kraal* and told the natives that as they were detectives there must be no sheep-stealing while they were in the district.

There is one great difficulty which the native detective has to contend with. When a Zulu is seen wandering about the country every black who meets him asks what his business is, where he has come from, and where he is going to. The arrival of a strange native is always reported to the local chief, and the whole tribe grow very suspicious of him until they know everything about him.

It is a hopeless task to send a native to make inquiries amongst his own tribe, for he will rarely give them away. Knowing enough to hang a man, he will often return to the C.I.D. and say he cannot find anything out at all.

Very rarely can a native detective be discovered who works as well when alone as he does with a European member of the force. They will obey orders and ferret out things quite well while with a white man, but when by themselves they have no initiative, and lose interest.

Once a native is "wanted," the police in the neighbourhood of his *kraal* are informed of the fact. A book is specially set apart for notices of this kind, and the native constables are periodically informed whom to inquire for. In their travels amongst the *kraals* they frequently find that some of a "wanted" man's own people, or even his neighbours, know exactly where he is; for though he may not have returned to the district, he has a habit of sending messages. His utter inability to keep a still tongue is as frequently the cause of his own undoing as it is that of his friends.

The C.I.D. in certain work rely very much on native constables, who in this way have special facilities for obtaining valuable information, but in intricate cases they can rarely be depended upon, for they are much too inclined to jump to a hasty conclusion from which they cannot be turned.

Naturally only native detectives who have a perfectly clean record can be taken on, and prior to the introduction of the finger-print system it was by no means an easy thing to make certain that some demure, smiling, black candidate had not just finished several years' imprisonment under another name, for horse-stealing. The proportion of Zulus who have never been in prison is not nearly as large as it might be, for, with their queer outlook on life, they do not regard a term of imprisonment as anything to be ashamed of, but merely as an inconvenience. Nor does the prisoner's own family think any the worse of him for having been very justly sentenced; he is welcomed back to his *kraal* by his parents as though he had only been away for a holiday.

Mr. Clarke worked single-handed up to the end of 1894, and gradually the C.I.D. became a power in the colony. It was then dawning on the police that such a department had come into being. The request was made to the Chief Commissioner that the C.I.D. should be responsible for all returns of crime, and the reports were accordingly sent to the department, which in that way got into closer touch with the police.

In 1895 the chief of the C.I.D. managed to get a clerk to assist him in the work, which was rapidly growing, and from that time onwards the department became more and more useful. The task of identifying criminals who had been convicted before was often a problem, and Mr. Clarke began to take a keen interest in the finger-print system. At that time it was little understood or appreciated, but the chief saw it had immense possibilities in the colony. Having made a thorough study of the method employed at Scotland Yard, he attempted in 1898 to induce the Natal authorities to adopt the system, but was told that there were not sufficient criminals in the colony to justify it, and that the colony was not advanced enough. Determined to show that it was not only useful but highly necessary, he introduced the system at his own expense. Nearly everyone was opposed to the idea, and the chief had all his work cut out to convince the sceptics before the scheme was at length officially approved.

It was a long time before the various magistrates began to show confidence in the finger-print system, but its accuracy having now been established it is relied on very considerably.

Some years after it was adopted Mr. W. H. Wilkes, one of Pietermaritzburg's leading solicitors, was a pronounced sceptic, so the C.I.D. authorities told him he could leave his finger-prints at the office and make a test, by getting the officer in charge at some back-station to send another set of his prints up to headquarters, and seeing how quickly they traced the first impressions.

The prints filed are classified under three headings, *viz*. European, Asiatic, and native, and the solicitor was told he could enter his prints under any heading he chose without their being informed on the point. He accordingly had his finger-prints taken, and these were filed away in the Indian section. Mr. Wilkes laughed, and to make certain of baffling the C.I.D. he said nothing about the matter for well over a year.

Then he went into the police station at Eshowe and had prints sent from there to headquarters. They were sent in as those of an Indian, the only stipulation that had been made being that he should stick to the same nationality. Without hesitation, the officer at work picked out the original impressions, and the lawyer became a convert.

In innumerable instances prisoners have disputed their previous convictions. Where the case was an important one this has necessitated warders from far distant prisons being called at much expense; but not in one single instance has the system been at fault in the colony, nor do those who have studied it properly believe that a mistake can be made providing the prints are clear.

In two prints bearing a general resemblance, it is improbable that they will have some mark or characteristic in common. But if it be admitted that there is one chance in four of such a thing, there is only one chance in sixteen of their having two similar characteristics. This system of multiplication can be carried on, in order to show the reliability of finger-prints, until one finds that the chances against two people having thirty-two similar characteristics are countless millions to one against.

To be certain that no error can occur, it is the custom of the C.I.D. never to take a finger-print from glass into court unless there are nine different points of similarity. The records show that in about forty cases since 1903 convictions have been secured as a result of prints being found on glass. Failure to show previous convictions may be caused by bad prints, which in some cases cannot be classified. In many cases convictions have been obtained on finger-print evidence alone, and in others native housebreakers have been traced and imprisoned through leaving the prints of their fingers behind.

A case of considerable interest occurred in Durban recently. A house was broken into and £30 in gold was taken. Someone had broken the fanlight and climbed in that way. It was suspected that a native servant knew something about it, but on being questioned he denied all knowledge of the theft, and the police were left without any clue whatever excepting toe-impressions on some of the broken glass. The somewhat puzzled native allowed the police to take the impression of his toes, and this, together with the carefully preserved glass, was sent to the C.I.D., which reported promptly that the marks on the paper and glass had been made by the same toes.

The native's possessions had been searched without any money being found. His brother was away at his *kraal*, and a detective took the opportunity of searching his box in the presence of the suspect. When £19 in cash was found there the native regretfully admitted his indiscretion, adding that this was part of the money he had stolen. He was awarded ten strokes and a month's hard labour. Had it not been for the toe-prints a conviction would never have been obtained, for there was no other direct evidence. No other case of using prints made in this way with the foot has ever been known in Natal. The marks were very clear, even though the native had always walked about in bare feet. It is not likely that Scotland Yard has traced a man by toe-prints, because the bare-footed burglar is a rare exception in England.

Long after the C.I.D. had become an indispensable factor in police administration, the official delay in providing necessary equipment was almost humorous—except in the eyes of the C.I.D. staff. After the finger-print system was adopted a request was made for some sort of a washstand, which was very necessary, as the officers were constantly getting their hands ink-stained while taking prints. The request was refused, but as experience showed that several requests had to be made before anything was forthcoming, Mr. Clarke perseveringly went on asking for his washstand for nine years, and at last in sheer desperation sent out for one without obtaining permission and put it down on his accounts.

He was surcharged for the amount on the ground that he had done this thing without authority, so he had to pay for it himself. When, however, the Police Commission of 1903 was sitting, the important matter of the washstand was gravely put before that body, and the money was refunded to the chief.

For over eighteen years a requisition has been sent in annually from the C.I.D. for some sort of matting to cover the wooden floors, which resound with heavy steps when people are walking about there. Each year the Public Works Department has sent a man down specially to measure the rooms and passages, and on being told that he has taken the measurements before, he has said, "Oh, but this is another requisition."

The C.I.D. is still waiting for its bits of matting.

There was a painful shortage of chairs, and visitors had to stand when they called at the department. For quite six years a requisition was sent in annually for a further supply of chairs, but the authorities were obdurate.

At last Sub-Inspector Hunt—who was murdered in the first tussle of the 1906 Zulu rebellion—put in a pathetic request that half a dozen packing-cases might be sent down to the C.I.D., so that the visitors could be invited to sit down occasionally. Apparently the humour of the suggestion appealed to those in authority, for six chairs were promptly supplied.

Today, (at time of first publication), there are more sets of fingerprints at the C.I.D. in Pietermaritzburg than there are at any other similar office in the British Empire, including even Scotland Yard. The colony has only 1,100,000 inhabitants, and of these 214,734 different people had left their impressions up to the time the last returns were made. There are the criminal records of 146,875 people in the pigeon-holes awaiting reference when the men go through the hands of the police again, and the finger-print system has proved the previous convictions of 131,315 culprits.

Of all the impressions taken 12,800 are those of Europeans, 118,000 Asiatics, and 215,040 natives; these figures including the duplicates which are made when a man is convicted a second time or on subsequent occasions.

No native constable is enrolled now until his finger-prints have been taken and his record searched. Sometimes this search reveals astonishing results, men who have spent several terms of imprisonment calmly offering their services to the police. But for the finger-prints there would have been 730 criminals, who otherwise seemed perfectly satisfactory, in the force.

One striking instance occurred some time ago. An Indian wished to be enrolled in the police, but Inspector Meiners was informed by the C.I.D. that the man had been convicted in 1903. This the coolie denied indignantly. He said he had never been in prison in his life, and he was willing to go through any test to prove the fact; and as the man was so emphatic the inspector returned the papers to the C.I.D., asking whether a mistake had not been made. The finger-prints were again checked, and Mr. Meiners was informed that the impressions were certainly identical. The suggestion was also added that the prosecutor in the case should be traced and questioned on the subject.

Before this man could be found the coolie was given full particulars of the conviction referred to in the records of the C.I.D., and was told the name of the man who prosecuted; but he remained unshaken. Not wishing to do him an injustice, Mr. Meiners had the prosecutor traced, and it was not until the two men were brought face to face that the coolie gave way and admitted having been sentenced.

In returning the papers, Inspector Meiners wrote: "The value of the finger-print system has been proved once more."

Every indentured Indian landing in the colony has had his finger-prints taken since early in 1903. Prior to that, in the majority of cases, coolies who absconded had to be sent to the Protector of Indian Immigrants at Durban for identification, but in hundreds of cases he was unable to say where they were indentured. Under the new system the absconding Indian's finger-prints are sent to the C.I.D. by post. In five minutes the point is settled and the man returns to work. During the last nine years the C.I.D. has dealt with 6437 men in this way. This is of great assistance to the employer of labour, for in the old days he had to pay the railway fares of the coolie and his escort, often over a considerable distance. It also saves the employers thousands of pounds, because whether an Indian absconds or not the employer has to pay the Government £5 a year during the period of indenture, to cover the *coolie's* fare from India and back.

The system also prevents the Government from losing a good deal of money. If an Indian desires to remain in the country after his indenture has expired he must pay an annual tax of 3, and he is prevented from avoiding this by means of the finger-print system.

Dead bodies are frequently found on the *veldt*, and taken from rivers, and the greatest difficulty is experienced sometimes in identifying them. In forty-eight cases the C.I.D. have been able to find out who the man or woman was by means of finger-prints after all other means had failed.

When a warrant is out for a man on some serious charge, and the police are unable to find him, the matter is greatly simplified if he has been imprisoned before. The fact that he is "wanted" is added to his record at the C.I.D., and when he is handled by the police next time on some other charge the old warrant is dealt with. So far the department has received information of the failure to execute 561 warrants, and the system has led to 259 of these being executed subsequently.

Of those people who have escaped from prison since 1902, 75 have been returned to the cells by the use of finger-prints.

A man is classed as an habitual criminal when he has committed three or more serious crimes. The list shows so far that these consist of 166 Asiatics and 1062 natives. The number of European habitual criminals is exceedingly small in proportion.

During the last nineteen years 2318 different cattle thieves have been convicted, some of these having ten or a dozen different thefts entered against their name.

It frequently occurs that finger-prints result in suspected people being proved innocent. There was an instance of this when a European named Maurice Edmonds disappeared under mysterious circumstances, and was subsequently found drowned. Foul play was suspected, and there seemed every reason to suppose that the man had been murdered by two Zulu women.

Their finger-prints were taken, and in a few moments their records were turned up, showing they could not possibly have had anything to do with the affair as they were both in prison at the time.

In all cases where a native gives a receipt on Government business, this, besides being witnessed by two Europeans, bears the stamp of his thumb, so that he cannot dispute the payment afterwards.

An additional check on old "lags" was provided when a photographer was added to the staff. Each prisoner undergoing sentence in the Central Courts at Pietermaritzburg is photographed, the prints being placed amongst a wonderful collection of pictures. The photographer is an expert in making enlarged photographs of finger-impressions on glass, and in several instances his work in this direction has led to criminals being convicted.

There are filed the photographs of 12,714 individuals, 1646 of these being Europeans, 1923 Asiatics, and 9145 natives.

One reason why the C.I.D. is particularly useful is because the Europeans who are sent out to different districts on a case are not known locally. They go long distances, and often spend many months away unravelling a mystery. Their task is utterly unlike that of the

English police detective, for their work is largely in connection with half-civilized blacks, many of whom do not speak a word of any language other than their own. In cases of murder—nine out of every ten of which are committed by natives for the purpose of obtaining their unholy "medicine"—and plundering, the detectives often have to spend a long time trekking from place to place on the *veldt*, stay out all night keeping watch on a suspected *kraal*, and ferret out a criminal who is as subtle as any ever dealt with by a Scotland Yard officer. The detective is constantly in danger, for when the Zulu turns into a ruffian he is a particularly rough specimen to handle, and has no fear whatever of the consequences of any desperate action he may take.

To extract information from a native is generally a task requiring infinite patience. A C.I.D. man may have to talk to a Zulu for hours on every subject under the sun before he can touch on the matter with which he is concerned. He may be certain that the native can tell him what he wants to know, and the native may know what he is after, but if it were discussed early in the conversation the Zulu would profess entire ignorance, or even get up and walk away. Sometimes it is necessary for a detective to talk in this way all day before he dare mention the affair he has on hand.

The men who "get on" in the Natal C.I.D. are those who are strictly sober, good linguists, and have an almost superhuman trick of keeping on a man's trail when all hope seems to have gone.

Some of the older hands in the C.I.D. speak the Zulu language almost like a native, and, after having spent a lifetime studying the subject, understand the complex nature of the native as well as they understand each other. They also speak Dutch, Hindustani, Tamil, and Urdu, and bits of other tongues used by the thousands of Indian *coolies* in the colony. There are also many excellent linguists in the force who are not on the C.I.D. staff. The men get extra pay as soon as they can make themselves understood in any of the more useful languages, a third-class linguist drawing is. a day extra; second class, 1s. 6d. a day; and first class, 2s.

No case of murder is ever dropped in any circumstances, it being followed up sometimes for years, as happened in the case of a girl murdered at Estcourt. The murderer disappeared, but he was found a dozen years afterwards, tried, found guilty, and hanged.

There was a mystery near Dundee early in 1911 which it seemed absolutely impossible to solve at first. A European, named Lazarus, who was driving to the St. George's Colliery, was found shot dead, sitting in his trap, and a purse that contained £3 had been taken from his pocket. There was no clue whatever, and Detective Grant, who was sent to investigate the affair, was baffled for some time.

A native in the district, named Francis Ngcobo, had been convicted two years previously for pointing a revolver at a girl, but the revolver had never been found. Grant, in chatting discreetly with the natives, found that Francis still carried a revolver. It was a small one, and the Zulus said that the bullet taken from the dead man's body was the same size as those fired by Francis. The man was arrested on suspicion, and the detective found that several natives had seen him sitting on a stone near the scene of the crime just prior to the murder. Bit by bit the chain of evidence was pieced together, Grant discovering that though the prisoner had been trying to borrow money—and failing—before the murder was committed, he was not short of cash afterwards.

Finally Francis was committed for trial, tried before a jury, and convicted. He admitted his guilt before the execution took place.

Five years ago there was an alarming epidemic of burglaries in Pietermaritzburg, and though several good detectives were set to work they could find out nothing for some time. At last impressions were discovered on a window that had been entered. These were photographically enlarged, and all possible classification combinations were worked out. Owing to the fact that the impressions were incomplete, the search lasted two and a half days and 1142 files were examined. Then the prints were found to agree with those of an old criminal. Nobody knew where he happened to be at the time, so his photograph was circulated, together with a full description of him.

Two men went up to the Togt Office (where natives have to report what work they are doing) a few days afterwards, when an officer recognized the "wanted" man by his photograph. He was promptly put in prison, and his companion, on being searched, was found to have stolen property in his pockets. The detectives got to work amongst the associates of the prisoners, and in a little while they had under lock and key the whole gang, who had been concerned in more than a score of cases of house-breaking and theft within a short time. Two of the men were even brought back from Ladysmith.

Just a year afterwards the housebreaking started again in the same city, and a burglar left in one house two table-knives which he had stolen from another place. He also left traces in the form of fingerprints on a fruit jar in one house and on a bottle in the second place.

These showed that the burglar was Moses Kanyile, an habitual criminal who had just been released after serving a term of imprisonment. Within a few hours, as Moses was leaving the town, he was stopped. He was unable to explain away a loaded revolver, a coat and waistcoat, and a silver pencil case which were part of the property missing from the two houses, and he was removed from further temptation for a period of five years.

The late Chief Justice of Natal, Sir Henry Bale, remarked when summing up in the case that finger-print evidence had been of the utmost value.

The Zulu criminal is as wily in his way as his white brother who operates in Brixton, only he travels about a great deal more. He has a wonderful assortment of *aliases*, and without the finger-print system would be such a difficult creature to deal with that one wonders how the police managed to do their work effectively before it was introduced in Natal. A thief had escaped from prison in Cape Town, and the authorities there notified the C.I.D. at Pietermaritzburg of the fact, enclosing copies of his finger-prints. There was nothing filed concerning him, but some months afterwards a man was arrested in Durban for house-breaking. When his finger-prints were examined it was found that he was the man who had escaped in Cape Town, though he, of course, did not give the same name. In countless instances *kafirs* would be able to avoid imprisonment by merely changing their names if it were not for the finger-prints.

Far more prisoners escape from gaol in Natal than in England, not because the prisons are insecure, but because the native guards cannot always be trusted. When a member of their own tribe is in custody they are not at all unlikely actually to help him to get away. Another reason for the numerous escapes is that the Zulu criminal is very daring, and if he thinks there is the faintest hope of getting away he will make a desperate attempt.

There is only one case on record, however, of a man condemned to death escaping. A loyal native, named Deyikana, was spying in the rebels' location at Umsinga in 1906, when he met half a dozen natives who recognized him. He started to run, but they struck him down and beat him. One of his assailants, Mucuwendoda Ntombela, then gave him a fatal blow. The murderer was subsequently tried and sentenced to death.

On a Tuesday morning—he had just been told that his sentence had been confirmed and that he was to be hanged at Ladysmith the following Friday—a native guard helped him to get away from the condemned cell at Dundee. He pushed the murderer up on to the ledge of a window, and Mucuwendoda scrambled to the roof, from which he dropped over the wall. This was done at 8 a.m., while the white gaoler was at breakfast, and nobody saw the prisoner go, because this part of the building was not visible from the yard. Thus, within three days, less an hour, of the time at which he was to be executed, the *kafir* got away.

Condemned men are allowed certain privileges, amongst them being the use of snuff. Mucuwendoda was missed as soon as an official went along to give him his day's allowance of snuff. In three minutes every police officer in the place had been called, and a hue and cry began. They first got on to the man's track by finding footprints on a flower-bed where he had climbed over the wall, and on being questioned the overseer of a road-repairing party said he had seen a native running in the direction of Mpati Mountain, which is about three miles from Dundee, and on which there are a number of coal mines.

Every available man, including native constables, took up the chase, and the fugitive was seen in the distance running at full speed. He had vanished by the time his pursuers reached the mountain, which formed an ideal place for hiding, being covered with great valleys, huge rocks and trees. Throughout that day the place was thoroughly searched. The local chiefs were called upon to send their tribes out to assist the police, but though every part of the mountain was explored, and the mines were visited, they could not find the man who was nearly due to be hanged. The district officer, and indeed all the prison staff, were in a state of great alarm, and some acid messages passed along the telegraph wires that day.

To make matters worse, a terrible storm came on that night, and the mountain was enveloped in a dense mist until 10 a. m. the following morning. Under these conditions the search, though pretty hopeless, was kept up in vain.

Parched and hungry, the murderer crept from his hiding-place late on Wednesday night, having turned his clothes inside out to hide the fact that he was in prison garb. Unperceived, he made his way down the mountain slopes to the flats behind Talana Mountain, towards the Buffalo River. It was midnight when he reached Mr. Gregory's farm. Knocking at the entrance of a native *kraal* he asked for food. It is not usual for a native to make such a request at that hour of the night, and as the head of the *kraal* had heard of the prisoner's escape he invited him in, telling his two sons to fetch food for the stranger. He also added quietly that they were to bring back some stout *reims* (ropes made from cow-hide), and when they had done so Mucuwendoda was overpowered and tied up.

To the unbounded delight of every one at the prison, the natives arrived there with the missing man soon after three o'clock on Thursday morning. The district officer was informed by telephone of what had occurred. Half afraid that the good news could not really be true, he dressed hurriedly and drove to the prison to look at the captive. He saw the man trussed up in irons, and then heaved a sigh of thankfulness, for though nobody could in reality have been blamed for the escape, excepting the guard who helped Mucuwendoda out, it had been a pretty anxious time.

The murderer, after his adventures and disappointment, was utterly unmoved, and spoke of his doings with as much indifference as though he had no personal interest in the affair. He explained to the district officer that he had been hiding in an ant-bear hole, over the entrance of which he had drawn a stone. From there he had watched the searchers during the daylight, and at one time, he said, he could easily have put his hand on the boots of Trooper Baker.

That morning the district officer, glad to see the back of such a slippery scoundrel, sent him down to Ladysmith by the 7.5 a.m. train, and the man was well and duly hanged at the appointed hour on the Friday.

His fellow-tribesman who had assisted him to escape had meanwhile been sentenced to six months' hard labour.

The prince of Zulu gaol-breakers is Mfanyana *alias* Nkane. The latter name, which he probably bestowed upon himself, signifies impudence and pertinacity.

Nobody knows what his early criminal record is, because that dates back to the time before finger-prints were taken; but, on being discharged from prison in Johannesburg many years ago, he made his way along the railway line to Natal, breaking into nearly every railway station on the route. As he approached Charlestown, which is on the border of the Transvaal, the Natal Police were looking out for him. At the various railway stations he had gone into the office and rifled the safe, generally carrying it out bodily. He had three assistants who followed him about, but he never used more than one of them at a time when engaged on a thieving expedition.

He celebrated his arrival at Charlestown by entering the office of the resident Justice of the Peace. There he stole the safe, carrying it off on a trolley which he annexed from a neighbouring Arab store. He made a quick trek from there to Newcastle, and broke into the offices of a lawyer and several other people, smashing the safes and extricating their contents.

A member of the Natal Police, while on patrol about two miles from Charlestown, came across the Charlestown safe on the *veldt*. He went straight back to camp to report the matter, and when he returned with assistance half an hour afterwards Mfanyana had just left the place, taking the trolley with him.

One of the police was informed that a tall native had been seen pushing a trolley towards Volksrust, and as there was reason to suspect that this was Mfanyana, the Transvaal police were warned to put a special guard on at the court and at the pass office in Volksrust. Soon afterwards the native entered the court, but could not obtain anything of value there, so during the night he went to the pass office, where several of the Transvaal police were sleeping. Opening the window cautiously, he entered the room, and without making sufficient noise to awake the men, he picked up a very heavy safe—one which no ordinary white man could lift, and carried it out, stepping over a native constable who was asleep in the doorway.

From here Mfanyana went to Wakkerstroom about twenty miles away, where he broke into the magistrate's office and took away various articles. He returned quickly into Natal, and stole the safe from the office at Mount Prospect railway station. He carried it some distance on a trolley, and tried to force it open with a pick, but failed; so he moved on to Chariest own, and entered the house of Mr. Gardiner with a duplicate key.

Unluckily for him, on the night Mfanyana broke into the Mount Prospect station, Sergeant Ker, of the C.I.D., happened to be there on another case with two of his native detectives, and learning that a tall native had taken a ticket to travel on the down *kafir* mail, he went to the station with Mr. Gardiner's native servant, having meanwhile planted his own native detectives at the exits. Mfanyana was there on the platform, and as soon as he saw the detective with the native servant he tried to bolt, but was secured. In his hat were three gold watches and two or three bunches of safe keys, the proceeds of twenty-three burglaries.

The police had found that while he was in Charlestown he had constantly been with a native named "Charlie." This man was promptly put under lock and key also, and in his bundle was found a good deal of stolen property. While he was being searched, another native came along and asked for "Charlie." On the principle that one may judge a man by the companions he keeps, this individual was also taken in charge, and at his house more stolen property was discovered. A hat and a pair of boots found on the trolley near Mount Prospect station were proved to be his.

The following morning one of the native detectives was searching the hut of "Charlie" when a fourth member of the gang came along.

"I hear the white detectives have got 'Charlie,'" he said. "Are you working for these Europeans?"

The detective admitted that he was.

"Oh," said the fourth culprit, "they have not got us all. I have a lot of the keys at my place."

The native detective smiled blandly, invited the man in, and shut the door until assistance arrived. In this way the whole gang fell into the net.

All four were committed for trial, and while imprisoned at Newcastle, awaiting that unpleasant ordeal, they amused themselves by holding the head of an Indian under water in a bath while they took £4 out of his pocket. For this incidental affair they were each awarded six months' imprisonment and twenty lashes.

When they stood in the dock charged with having stolen various safes, the evidence showed that it took six Europeans to carry one of the safes, and both the Judge and jury expressed doubt as to whether Mfanyana, even aided by one of his assistants, could have lifted it. The safe was taken into the court by a dozen native constables, whereupon Mfanyana, who had heard and understood what had been said, stepped on one side quickly and lifted the safe and the table on which it stood, unaided.

He was sentenced to four years' imprisonment with fifteen lashes, and then he declared that he would never have been captured had it not been for the death in the Pretoria gaol of Umgulugulu, "the king of native thieves." This unfortunate event, said the safe-thief, had broken the spell which he had against arrest by the detectives.

The governor of the gaol at Pietermaritzburg afterwards expressed the opinion that Mfanyana was the most unruly convict, either black or white, that he had ever had to deal with. He committed many offences while serving this sentence, and on two occasions was given twenty-five lashes.

It was not very long after Mfanyana had been sentenced that he escaped—in the January of 1908—and made his way back to Newcastle. There he broke into a railway refreshment-room and a house. He stole some liquor, and was recaptured while lying in a drunken sleep on the outskirts of the town. Ten years were added on to his term of imprisonment on account of this escapade.

There was some trouble owing to the man being in leg-irons while he walked through the street to the court, but it was explained by those who had to handle him that he was such a dangerous character that they dared not march him along like an ordinary prisoner. That their fears were somewhat justified is shown by the fact that Mfanyana attempted to escape six months later (for which he received ten lashes), and a little while afterwards in some mysterious way got out of his cell at the Pietermaritzburg gaol, climbed over a wall, and got away at 5 a.m. He was not lucky on this occasion, for he was seen hiding in a bush on the outskirts of Pietermaritzburg, and once more was placed behind the prison bars, before midnight. For this he received a further sentence.

Mfanyana was now getting desperate. His one craving in life was to regain his freedom. He openly stated that if he could not get away he hoped they would hang him. One day he got into the room where the warders keep their arms, and, securing a revolver, made his way out into the yard. He shot at the first man he saw, and after firing several times, pulled the trigger while the muzzle of the weapon was within a foot of one of the warders, who to this day thanks his lucky stars that for some reason the cartridge missed fire.

The culprit was secured and taken back to his cell, and, when tried for attempted murder, was sentenced to six years' additional imprisonment, but he escaped not long afterwards, and on being recaptured was given fifteen more lashes.

Mfanyana was, naturally, a constant source of anxiety to the authorities at Pietermaritzburg gaol, and as it was not considered that he was safe there, he was removed to Pretoria, where he was made so secure that there is little doubt but that he will spend the rest of his days in prison.

The sentences against this prison-breaker are known to amount to twenty-one years, without such terms that he may have served prior to the introduction of the finger-print system. It is also recorded that he has had a total of one hundred and ten lashes for his sins.

In Pietermaritzburg and Durban there are municipal police forces which are not under the control of the Natal Police. All criminal work there is handed over to the C.I.D., there being a branch of the department in Durban.

Lawless characters who are known to the police have a somewhat restless time. The C.I.D. is in constant touch with that haunt of villainy, Johannesburg. As soon as a criminal settles down there a little of the secret machinery of the police force is set to work, and the undesirable being is warned that he had better move on as he is being closely watched. Generally speaking, every criminal of any importance gets to Johannesburg eventually, and works his own particular game until things get too hot for him. Every winter there are thousands of people from up-country in Durban, including a tolerable sprinkling of criminals, and yet there is very little crime there, comparatively, because the men are aware that the eyes of the C.I.D. are on them. The incoming boats at Durban are also closely watched.

The C.I.D. is now, (at time of first publication), under the control of Inspector Earle, who was one of the first men called in to assist Mr. Clarke in the early days. Mr. Earle has held his present position for seven years.

CHAPTER 24

Witchcraft

In the gloomy interior of a grass hut there is a shrivelled figure bending over a pot, the contents of which the shrivelled figure stirs slowly as they boil on the fire of wood. The hut reeks with smoke, there being no ventilation save the occasional puffs of wind which come through the little entrance not three feet high. The whites of the eyes of the. stooping man roll as though he were in pain, while he mutters some weird incantation. He has done this thousands of times, for perhaps he is a hundred years old, and did the same thing for the never-to-be-forgotten Chaka. He squats on his haunches and peers into the pot from time to time, as though cooking *mealies* and watching their progress.

But the pot contains the melted fat of a human being who has been specially murdered for the purpose. This is one of the *abatakati*—one of the witchdoctors preparing *muti*.

He sincerely believes that with the aid of this liquid neatly bottled and corked he holds the power of life and death over the friends and enemies of his clients. Those who consult him, too, have implicit faith in his power. *Muti*, or medicine, is a generic term embracing not merely medicine to be taken internally and externally, but charms of all sorts, which are firmly held to have supernatural power.

There are over a thousand native doctors, or herbalists, licensed to carry on their trade in Natal and Zululand, these men curing various ills by means of simple treatment; but witchcraft is a criminal offence, and the *abatakati* work their spells furtively. Their unholy practices date back farther than any white man can trace, and even when the *kafir* was living in his natural wild state they were an offence against the tribal laws. In the districts where the Zulu is becoming more civilized, witchcraft is not so extensively believed in, but even today, (at time of first publication), there are many districts in which a native, if his crops were bad, would murder someone and take certain parts of his body so that *muti* could be made of it. This is dried and burnt, the smoke being allowed to blow across the crops to improve them; if it does not, the *muti* clearly has been made improperly. The substance from which *muti* is made, and the manner of its application, depend entirely on the mood of the witchdoctor. So childishly convinced are the natives of its efficacy that they will readily run the risk of imprisonment, or even death, in order to get it.

One of the commonest requests put before the *abatakati* is for a love charm. A Zulu youth, enamoured of some dusky maid, pays a live goat, or perhaps a beast, to have a spell cast over her. The youth may be given a twig or a root, with instructions to put it near the place where she will come to draw water at dawn. Sometimes she learns what is taking place, and, if she be susceptible, her heart goes out to her lover. That has been good *muti*. Should she spurn him, the *muti* has either been poor, or she has defied its influence. Generally she does not, or cannot, show defiance. When the girl knows that her lover has applied the medicine spell to her, the idea that it will cause her to give way, whether she cares to or not, grows so powerful, and works on her nerves to such an extent, that in a fit of something akin to hysteria she eventually does become one of his promised brides.

Gentle though the Zulu is, or appears to be in many of his ways, he has crude ideas on the subject of killing people, and it is by no means an uncommon thing for the girl who scorns her lover's *muti* to be murdered by him.

Away down in the Umzimkulwana Valley, in a desolate and forbidding region near Hell's Gates, there dwelt an uncanny-looking little Zulu named Mtanti, who had achieved much renown as a witchdoctor. It was known throughout Alfred County that his spells were the finest procurable and worked wonderfully. On this account he was looked upon with awe and the deepest reverence. In October 1898, two lovelorn natives named Gomfe and Mbowa approached him deferentially and begged that he would give them *muti* that would cause the maidens they adored to reciprocate their devotion. Mtanti considered the difficult point gravely, and then promised that their wish should be gratified so long as they paid his fee, though he also stipulated that they must assist him in the matter.

On the edge of the native location a man named Kay had a lonely farm, and his solitary house-servant was a ten-year-old boy, Gijimani, the son of the witchdoctor. Kay, though of a retiring disposition and inclined to live the life of a recluse, was universally liked by his scattered neighbours, both black and white. Apparently he had not an enemy in the world. Mtanti paid a visit to his son, spending the night in the boy's *kraal*, but when all was quiet he got up, called his assistant, a native named Sibalweni, and joined the two lovers who were waiting near. The four men entered Kay's house and deliberately killed him with *assegais*, the witchdoctor afterwards cutting away a portion of the dead man's windpipe.

In this ghoulish fashion he was to obtain *muti* which was to work a love-spell. When the farmer's body was discovered the police found that their most valuable witness was the boy Gijimani. With that surprising frankness which characterizes the Zulu in his natural and "uncivilized state," he told how his father had come to the farm and gone out during the night. It was clear that robbery was not the motive, for nothing of value in the house had been touched. As soon as the hue and cry started all the four men implicated disappeared, and the police began a search which lasted for months, the case creating a great deal of excitement, because at that time the murder of a white man by a native was an extremely rare event.

The murderers were at last captured, Mtanti and his assistant being run to earth in Pondoland, about forty miles from the scene. While the search was in progress the boy was carefully guarded, there being every reason to suppose that his father, if he got the opportunity, would kill him.

One of the striking features of the trial was the unhesitating and straightforward manner in which the child gave evidence against his father, exhibiting no more compunction in telling all he knew than he might have shown if the man had been an utter stranger.

The two lovers were sentenced to penal servitude, while Mtanti and Sibalweni were hanged in Harding gaol in the presence of native chiefs and headmen of the division. After the execution many natives were called in to see the bodies still swaying at the end of the ropes; for the impression was very prevalent amongst them that the occult power of Mtanti was so great that he could defy the white man and even return to life if they killed him.

Although witchcraft was always an offence, the belief in it was so great that many of the chiefs employed the *abatakati*. It is related of Chaka that at one time he had too many witchdoctors in his retinue. He had methods peculiar to himself of thinning out the ranks of undesirables. One day the blood of a goat was sprinkled near the entrance to his *kraal*. This might have been the work of an enemy trying to cast a spell over the great chief, or it might have been various other mysterious things. Chaka assembled his mystics and ordered them, one after another, to "smell out" the person who had done it.

Their task was singularly difficult, as Chaka had done it himself, and each witchdoctor who named the wrong person was dispatched to his forefathers without ceremony. Only one wise old man, who possibly had his suspicions, said vaguely, "Zulu," [1] indicating that the great chief had done it, and he was rewarded with the privilege of living.

The ordinary Zulu, however, does not admit the possibility of the witchdoctor making a mistake, and this is proved by his belief in the ceremony of obtaining information from a witch.

When he goes to consult the mystic the latter sapiently remarks, "You have trouble."

"*Yizwa*" [2] replies the troubled one emphatically, violently clapping his hands. The witch then knows he is on the right track and proceeds accordingly to guess the wants of his client, whose only reply is "*Yizwa*" and clapping. The client has a very fair idea of the identity of the person who has done him an injury, or thinks he has, and he says "*Yizwa*" less enthusiastically when the mystic is questioning in the wrong direction. So the game goes on, very much like that of "hot and cold" played by thousands of children in England, and there is only one vital difference.

The client firmly believes the witch is discovering his enemy for him, and the game played in this way may eventually lead to the death of some perfectly innocent person. The mystic, by a process of elimination, having narrowed down the field of inquiry to one person, declares that individual to be guilty, and the client ends up by getting *muti* to put a spell on him, or to kill him, according to fancy.

Murders committed by means of witchdoctors' medicine often present the greatest difficulty to the police. Some poisonous concoction placed in food or drink has the desired effect, and it is invariably only because of the Zulu's utter inability to keep his own counsel that the truth leaks out and the culprit is hanged. Often the police are perfectly aware of the facts but still cannot get a conviction, proof being the stumbling-block. Owing to this habit of putting medicine

---

1. This, of course, was Chaka's "surname."
2 "Hear thou!"

into food and drink it is the custom at a native beer feast for the host to take the first sip. This is an indication that there is no ill-feeling. It only shows that *muti* was put in afterwards if one of the guests dies next day.

Up to a few years ago murders of this kind were much less frequently detected, because an analytical examination of the stomach was not insisted upon. In cases where poisoning was suspected the onus of proof rested with the Attorney-General, in the absence of any one capable of making a scientific examination. The "cat trick" was usually resorted to. If a cat died after being fed on the suspected parts it was assumed that the dead man had been poisoned.

According to the Zulus, no man ever dies a natural death: life is always ended by the use of witchcraft. When a man expires his friends call in a witchdoctor to "smell out" the person who placed on him the fatal spell. Generally the witchdoctor puts the blame on the richest native in the district. In Pondoland in particular not long ago no native dared to accumulate comparative wealth, for the moment he displayed any sign of opulence a witchdoctor would declare he had worked a fatal spell, and the man was hounded down, his cattle being ruthlessly taken from him.

The *abatakati* send out horrid messengers to the people. When a hyena's strident cry is heard, the natives know it has come from a witchdoctor, and is screaming, "I've got you. I'll have you." This ill omen is certain to be followed by some unspeakable calamity. The doctor rides abroad on a wolf, baboon; or a goat, and it is astonishing how many natives have seen the *abatakati* prowling about in the moonlight on such unserviceable steeds. Nothing would shake their conviction that they really had seen such an apparition.

There is one form of killing one's neighbour in Zululand which the natives declare to be very effective. The ceremony is known as *pehla*, and is only performed in very secluded places, because nobody besides the *amadhlozi* (the spirits) must know what is going on. There is one other good reason why prying eyes must not observe the rite: many Zulus have been killed by order of the chiefs for practising *pehla*. There are certain herbs and leaves which have to be placed in a *calabash* and stewed and stirred. After a while there rises a froth, and at the psychological moment the Zulu softly calls out the name of his enemy. This, if done properly, is certain death to the victim; if he should not die, that is the result of the herbs not having been correctly mixed. Great care has to be exercised in seeing that the right ingredients are used, for some herbs produce an infallible love-charm, and an error might cause awkward complications.

Another way of murdering an enemy without subsequent trouble is to place a certain herb in one's mouth and puff one's breath into the victim's nostrils. The Zulu places great faith in this method, though there is no danger of the murderer being poisoned in the operation

Many of the witchdoctors in remote places are undoubtedly wonderful toxicologists. They know the medicinal value of every herb and root that grows in their country, and are able to compound subtle poisons which would baffle a Harley Street specialist. It is a recognized fact amongst the Natal Police that many a man whose death has eventually to be attributed to natural, or unknown, causes has been sent to his grave by means of poison. Some of these poisons leave little or no trace of their presence, and where the death takes place a full day's journey from the district surgeon's station, it is a couple of days before he sees the body. In an extremely hot climate the task of proving murder is impossible in such circumstances.

As a result of his extensive knowledge of herbs, the witchdoctor performs wonderful cures sometimes, and this doubtless accounts in a large degree for the native's faith in him. The patient, however, has to take his chances as to whether he gets natural or supernatural *muti*.

The natives' faith in these doctors has led to some of the oldest white colonists also believing in them, for they will call in the Zulus to "smell out" stolen cattle or other property, and even to "doctor" their families.

A somewhat interesting experiment was made a few years ago by two medical men who decided to leave London, settle right away from civilization in Natal, and combat the Zulus' blind faith in native witchdoctors, using the most approved modern scientific methods. They ran up tin and iron shanties, and it was possible for the blacks to be treated in the wilds with all the medical skill that could be obtained in the best of hospitals. The experiment was an utter failure. In six months the two doctors had to abandon their rural shanties and admit that they had been beaten by native superstition.

Even near the larger towns of Natal today, (at time of first publication), there lurks the fear of the *abatakati* (which means literally, "Those who only lack fur all over their bodies to make them animals"), for the human heart makes very good *muti*. Workers going home in the evening between the vast wattle plantations peer uneasily into the dark depths of the trees, constantly dreading the descent of a *knobkerry* on their pates, after which they would be cut up and parts of them boiled down into efficacious jelly.

Children and young girls not infrequently disappear, and though the police cannot always be certain of the fate which has overtaken them, it is often safe to assume that the little ones have fallen victims to these ghastly rites. Occasionally the mutilated remains of an infant found in an ant-hole tell their own grim story.

When a young chief arrives at the age of puberty he is doctored for the benefit of his tribe in general, and himself in particular. If the witchdoctor should require some portion of a human being for the *muti* he may send a native to obtain it. The instructions are given in the quaint Zulu idiom. The doctor would never dream of saying, "Go, get me the ear of a white man." If he wanted such a thing he would put it thus: "A loathsome creature that enters its *kraal* on two legs stands in my way. I desire its ear." A white man does not have to go on all fours to get into his house, but a *kafir* does to get into his hut.

A witchdoctor of Pondoland had to give *muti* to a chief, and he deputed a native to get certain portions of a child's body. A half-caste living in the district, named Jerome Oakes, had a little daughter who was just beginning to toddle. In searching for good *muti* a Zulu puts all scruples on one side. In this case the native had actually been brought up with the baby's mother, having been her father's servant for more than twenty years. One morning the child wandered away from the house, up a water *sluit*, and circumstantial evidence showed that the native murdered her there. The police had practically no evidence to work upon excepting marks of blood on a stone in the *sluit*, and their task proved a long and baffling one.

The half-caste, distracted through the loss of his daughter, hampered rather than helped the police, and, such is the faith in witchdoctors and their kind, he begged and prayed Sergeant Esmonde White to let him go to one of these creatures and consult him. He declared that the police did not understand such matters and begged for money to pay the necessary fee. Oakes became such a positive nuisance that the sergeant gave him a coin in order to get rid of him, and the half-caste went straight to a blind old hag who lived miles away.

He returned and told a peculiar story which there was every reason to believe was true. He said that the sightless witch was squatting at the entrance to her *kraal* by herself as he rode up, and when he approached she addressed him by name and told him he had come to look for his child. Somewhat surprised, he dismounted, handed the coin to her, and prepared to start the *ukubula*. [3] On receiving the money she started off rapidly, saying the child was dead, but they were looking in the wrong direction (which happened to be true). Then she stopped suddenly, with an angry snarl, and threw the money back at the half-caste.

"The white police have given you this," she said savagely. "I know nothing about the child. Go!" Nor could the sorrowing father persuade the witch, in whom he had the profoundest faith, to say another word; so he returned and handed the coin back to the sergeant.

After a protracted search the police discovered the child's clothing in the native's *muti* bag, and sufficient evidence having been obtained, he was tried, found guilty, and hanged.

If a chief thinks he is losing his power he calls his witchdoctors together for advice; and on occasions they decide to *ukumisa*, or strengthen him. This is a very solemn process, and involves the death of some man in the tribe who has left another tribe to join them. The *abatakati* have the victim murdered, and certain parts of his flesh, mixed with herbs and roots, are made into *muti* powder.

Surrounded by his tribe, the chief takes a dose of this concoction. He squats in front of it and dips first one hand and then the other into it, swallowing the stuff in quick gulps. Meanwhile, other *muti* having been made out of powdered orchids and other things mixed with water, every man present is sprinkled with it, after which the natives go away from the scene, being very careful not to look back, which blunder would undo all the good.

A case of this kind occurred quite recently within sixty miles of Pietermaritzburg.

On occasions the neighbours of an *umtakati* take very extreme measures when they deal with him.

Near to the Manyuseni Hill, in the Mpofane Location, about thirty miles from Greytown, people were dying rather rapidly early in 1910, and all the natives believed that they were being killed by Mbemu, who was known to be able to put death-spells on those whom he did not like.

One night the hut in which he lived alone was seen to be in flames, and the next morning he was found close to the ashes of his home, dead and covered with burnt grass. He was literally wounded from head to foot with *assegais*, and a number of *assegai* heads had been left in his body.

---

3. Ceremony of getting information.

Every Zulu in the district, however carefully questioned, displayed utter ignorance of the affair, and after a few days the police were compelled to stop inquiries. Long afterwards they discovered that nearly every native had known all about it, but would not give a hint to the police because they considered it a proper course to have taken in killing Mbemu, in view of his having put death-spells on so many other people. In spite of the work put in by Detective R. E. Stevens, it is probable that the truth never would have come out but for the idle chatter of two women. Quite six months after the murder took place the news reached the police that a native and two women had actually seen the crime committed. One of the women told a friend "in confidence," and the friend repeated the news, as it was the choicest bit of scandal she had ever heard.

A few days later four men named Nongqai, Mashayinkomo, Latsheni, and Mbotshwa were arrested. At the time of the murder Nongqai's mother had just died, and his father was dying. Convinced that this was the work of Mbemu, Nongqai took the other three men with him late at night and set fire to the thatch of their victim's hut. The four stood by the small door, *assegais* in hand, and when Mbemu rushed out, aroused by the fire, they plunged their weapons into his heart. Terribly wounded, he staggered a few yards, and then fell, whereupon the murderers stood over him and stabbed him time after time. They covered him with dry grass and set fire to it. A pair of Nongqai's trousers, covered with blood, and cut into pieces, were found a few hundred yards from the burnt hut.

The next morning Nongqai and Mashayinkomo were dancing jubilantly at a *kraal* a mile away, and singing their own praises, a number of natives standing round. The police arrived there by chance an hour or two afterwards, but nothing was said of the triumphal dance.

At the conclusion of the preliminary trial Nongqai admitted his guilt, and that of Mashayinkomo and Latsheni, but said that Mbotshwa was not with them. This was probably due to a curious form of revenge. When they saw the evidence was getting too strong for them Mashayinkomo and Latsheni declared that Nongqai killed the man single-handed, and Mbotshwa preserved silence on the point. This silence saved his life, for though they were all sentenced to be hanged the sentence on Mbotshwa was afterwards reduced to penal servitude for life.

There was a peculiarly drastic method of dealing with witchdoctors, particularly those guilty of body-snatching, up to twenty or thirty years ago. It may prevail today, (at time of first publication), but the natives are so closely watched by the police that they have little opportunity of murdering a witchdoctor without being found out. Certainly they would do it if they thought they would go undetected.

The *umtakati* was seized, and a number of short sticks were thrust into his body. Each stick had two prongs, the object of these being to create additional pain when the twig was twisted. This was continued until the witchdoctor became unconscious, whereupon the sharpened end of a *knobkerry* was stuck into his frame.

This ceremony was carried out with due solemnity, after which the dying witchdoctor was conveyed to his *kraal* and deposited with his wives, the single word "receive" being uttered by the men. The mention of that word was quite sufficient to indicate the fate that had overtaken the victim. A screen was put round him and he was left there until he died. It was a severe lesson to other witchdoctors in the district for a little while, but others would begin to practise the unholy rites very soon afterwards.

Even after a Zulu is dead he has not finished with the dread power of the *abatakati*, for his friends and relations watch over the grave for weeks to see that no witchdoctor digs up the body. The ghoul might do this with the wicked object of cutting off the tongue, or some other part of the body, turning it into medicine, and converting the dead man into a miniature ghost, which for all time must do his bidding. The Zulu not only firmly believes in these little ghosts, but he will often tell you he has seen them. They are never more than three feet high, and live entirely on the drainings of *kafir* beer; and their vocation is to torture the enemies of the witchdoctor.

Quite recently a native named Sibidhle was victimized at Ndwedwe, where an *umtakati* asked him to sell some cattle. Sibidhle wanted his cattle, and refused to part from them, so the witchdoctor made things particularly unpleasant for him. Sibidhle was found lying outside his hut, very ill indeed beyond all question. He could neither speak nor walk for three weeks, but gradually he recovered and confided in the local sergeant of the police. He was lying in his hut, he explained, when a dozen little men entered and made a fire on the floor. Then they started to throw earth at him. Presently the *umtakati* entered and asked whether they had hurt Sibidhle sufficiently. Some of the little men thought they had not, so they got a fresh supply of earth and bombarded him again.

The witchdoctor meanwhile took all his money and *muti*, and then the little tormentors carried the native out of his hut, and deposited him where he was found next day by his wives. He was still ill when he told the police all about it, and he begged the sergeant not to do anything to the *umtakati*, lest the latter should kill him. The *abatakati* probably produce these hallucinations by means of hypnotism. Nearly every native carries about with him his small *muti* bag, containing little bits of herb or roots which nothing would induce him to part with. Often he is quite unable to tell what effect this *muti* has on his life, but generally it is carried for some definite purpose, such as a love-charm or to ward off evil spirits. Civilized folk scoff at him frequently for this peculiarity, quite forgetting that they themselves probably always carefully carry their own mascot, such as a lucky sixpence or some absurd trinket, with the firm belief that something would go wrong if they left it behind.

When Pondoland warriors are preparing for war they catch a black bull and cut one of its forelegs off by the shoulder while it is alive. *Muti* is made out of the severed member, and with it each fighting man is smeared on the forehead. They would not dream of going into battle without being doctored in this way, and, once doctored, no native must sleep in a hut until after the fight. Their superstition is so profound that if a fight went against them they would not under any circumstances wield an *assegai* against another man until fresh *muti* had been placed on their forehead.

The native's craving for *muti* cost the Natal Police the life of the regimental pet a few years ago. Once day a fine young zebra mare, while running wild, joined a troop of horses on a farm at Vryheid. It grew tame, and was afterwards bought by the police for £25 and christened "Jan." The zebra became a great favourite with every one excepting the two trumpeters, who on parade days had to don their war paint and take charge of her. Jan had no dignity on those dignified occasions. Her chief joy in life seemed to be to wait for the most awkward moment on parade and then kick and bolt. On most other occasions she was docile enough. She had a bosom companion in an old pack pony that shared her stable. The two were inseparable, and if the pack pony were sent out on duty Jan would trot along placidly at her side.

One night Jan took it into her head to roam on her own account, and on this excursion she met her doom. Getting out of her stable at the barracks, she trotted straight off into the country. When she was missed next morning search parties were sent out. One of the police got on to her track, being informed by different natives in which direction she had been seen trotting. He reached the location near Table Mountain, about twenty-five miles from Pietermaritzburg, and then lost trace of her. Hearing that a witchdoctor was putting *muti* on a party of natives, the trooper grew suspicious, and found the *umtakati* holding the severed tail of poor Jan in his hand, dipping it in her blood and smearing the Zulus around with it.

The chief of the tribe had remonstrated with his men for killing the zebra, telling them it was the private property of the police. This, in their eyes, made the *muti* all the better. Such was the feeling of affection on the part of the police towards Jan that if a number of the troopers had arrived on the scene when her blood was being used as medicine there would have been a good deal of human blood shed. As it was, those responsible for her death were taken before the magistrate and fined £5 each.

One of the few other regimental pets the force ever had was a queer old mongrel dog which strolled up to the police and claimed their friendship in 1876 when they were taking part in the annexation of the Transvaal. From the moment he entered the camp the dog took the whole force under his wing, and they called him Transvaal. He had some extraordinary habits. When it got into his canine brain that he ought to inspect the camp at Grey town, nearly fifty miles away, he would start off quietly and drop in amongst his trooper friends there unexpectedly. Perhaps, after he had had a look round there and found everything in good order, he would disappear again and turn up at some other station far away, finally wandering back to headquarters.

Transvaal would go anywhere with any man wearing the Natal Police uniform, as they were all part of his family, and if he happened to follow a man who was going to visit friends in the town he would wait for that particular man on the doorstep even if he had to stop there all night. No other trooper could persuade him to desert that doorstep; he was "on duty," and remained there as faithfully as though the honour of the force depended on it.

On one occasion five horses were lost from the barracks at Pietermaritzburg. When they were traced, about forty miles from the camp, the old dog was found faithfully guarding them. He had been looking after them while they wandered on for three days.

For many years he stuck to his police friends, trekking with them when they were ordered into battle. Transvaal went with the corps through the Zulu War of 1879, the Boer War of 1881, and the Basuto

War. Nobody knows exactly what was his end. Either a bullet got him in one of the skirmishes, or he fell into the hands of the natives, to be used up as their eternal medicine.

Native superstition led to the arrest within forty-eight hours of a Zulu who in 1906 murdered a road party overseer named Waters, six miles from Nkandhla. Waters was *assegaied* at night in his tent by a native known as Maqomankulu. He stole the dead man's carbines, and fired two shots to frighten away other Zulus who came near. With the usual inaccuracy of the excited black, one of them ran to the local police headquarters and reported that a "big *impi* had wiped out the missionary and the white overseer of the road party." The police had the greatest difficulty in reaching the dead man's body on account of Waters' dog, a bull terrier, which stood over the corpse and refused to allow anyone to approach it.

It is one of the firm rules observed by Zulus that nobody who has committed murder sleeps in his hut or on a mat for four days, though he may sleep on a bed of grass in the *ixiba* or outhouse. Sergeant F. L. Wilkinson, who had charge of the case, discovered that Maqomankulu was following this custom. A murderer also kills a goat and makes "medicine," which eases his conscience. This Zulu had also killed a goat, and its body was found. When the police arrived he trekked to a *donga* with eight other rebels. After midnight Wilkinson set out with Trooper de Ros and a couple of native policemen. They found the murderer at a *kraal* close to the scene of the crime. At first he tried to escape, but finding that he was surrounded expressed astonishment when the charge of murder was mentioned. He declared he was actually hunting for the culprit.

Some curious charms, usually worn round the neck, had been found on the man's bed of grass. It was proved that these were the property of Maqomankulu, and attached to them were some scraps of roots which he had bitten and carried about with him "to give him strength in his arms." These were proved to be his, and though he never admitted his guilt he was convicted.

One of the first forms of *muti* a Zulu flies to in case of sickness, real or imaginary, is cutting his flesh. If they fancy they are ill they go to a friend and beg him to apply the knife. As soon as the wound has bled they rub into it a black powder, which smarts horribly, and is supposed to have the power of healing the cut.

The very old doctors, who really have great knowledge of herbs, are nearly invariably wrinkled on the face to an extraordinary degree.

Men who know the Zulu and his ways will tell you this is due to a life-long effort of memory. Certainly they have a memory far excelling that of any white man. If a sheep were lost, and one of those old doctors had examined it casually a couple of months before, he would be able to pick the missing animal out from a flock of two or three hundred with absolute certainty.

He can neither read nor write, and all his learning is stored up in his memory from the moment when, as a boy of twelve or thirteen, he starts out on his travels as assistant to some other doctor. The pair of them go off on a long tour, sometimes lasting six months, and on the way the boy carries his master's smoking horn, mats, blankets, wooden pillow, bags and medicine, the lot often weighing fifty pounds. He studies his master's methods, and picks up his learning in this way alone. The fee of a first-class native doctor who actually can cure his patients, is one beast per patient, and they acquire considerable wealth in this way. Instead of driving the beast along with them they leave it at the patient's *kraal*, where it remains until it is claimed. If a doctor even had half a hundred beasts scattered all over the country he could describe the colours of each animal and its peculiarities with unerring exactness.

Although the witchdoctors as a rule have absolute faith in their own magic, there are a few charlatans amongst them, as in any other business. When Sir Godfrey Langdon was Native Commissioner in Basutoland he took a very great interest in his poultry. So did the local Basutos, with the result that his birds diminished in numbers rapidly. They were clever thieves, and could rarely be caught in the act. One day the Commissioner mentioned his trouble to a chief, who said he would send a witchdoctor—the cleverest man in the land, who made a large income at his work—to put a spell on the chickens, thus rendering them safe from intruders. Sir Godfrey laughed, but the witchdoctor arrived shortly afterwards, clad in a wonderful costume, comprising all the paraphernalia of his kind. He was wrapped round and about with snake skins, and mysterious articles were suspended from his clothing. Bowing and scraping, he begged in the native tongue to be allowed—in consideration of an adequate fee—to work his spell.

More out of curiosity than anything else, the Commissioner told the man to get on with his performance, and he watched the proceeding intently. Gathering together innumerable small white stones, the native put these all round the chicken-run very slowly and with much solemn pantomime, the while chanting an incantation. Sir Godfrey followed him and strained his ears to catch the weird words which were to ensure him keeping his precious chickens.

When the ceremony was concluded the witchdoctor, looking round to see that they were alone, said in perfect English, without even a trace of the Cape-educated black's accent: "Of course, Sir Godfrey, you and I know this is all damned rot, but it will keep the niggers away."

Afterwards Sir Godfrey could not even get a native to go near enough to the chickens to feed them.

CHAPTER 25

Coloured Criminals

As a criminal the Zulu is not a success. He is a cunning, vicious creature, but he is not particularly clever, for he will leave the most glaring traces of his handiwork behind without thinking of the consequences. His crude methods would disgust the finished cracksman of England.

He is a dangerous sort of person to take into custody, for he would readily murder his captors to regain freedom if he could, and he puts very little value on his own life when cornered, although as a general rule the Zulu is particularly fond of life. Once demoralized he becomes very subtle. If he desired to kill any one he would smilingly accept his victim's hospitality for a week or more, the while waiting for an opportunity to murder him.

Even to the native's primitive mind, it is wrong to steal, but the Zulu who has become a criminal steals for the sheer love of stealing, and not because of actual want. No native who is willing to work need go hungry, for he can obtain employment at any time. Most farmers will advance him a sack of *mealies* if he will undertake to remain with them for a month. There are honest natives, but it is an indisputable fact that those who have taken to wearing European clothing can be trusted least, for they want money, and money they will obtain, somehow or other.

The raw native who still wears only his *umutsha*,[1] has practically only one ambition, and that is to obtain wives, so that his progeny may be numerous and work for him, enabling him to "retire" at the age of thirty-five or forty. He is honest, according to his own outlook on life, but the honest native is getting scarce, very largely as a result of the

---

1. The native dress.

influence of "civilization." In recent years the natives have lost their cattle and goats from plagues, and now must work, steal, or fall.

In his raw state a Zulu is admirable in many ways, but as he mixes with white people he picks up all their vices and few of their virtues. Not many years since one would have been able to leave a wagon laden with valuables at a *kraal* for months and find it untouched when one returned. Now not only its contents but the wagon also would probably disappear.

One marked trait in the character of the native criminal is that after he has started to commit one particular sort of offence he will continue with that form of crime.

There was a *kafir* who was as honest as a bishop until he got anywhere near fowls, and then he could not resist the temptation to steal them. On twenty occasions he was sent to prison for this form of misdemeanour, and he was never known to offend in any other manner.

Still more remarkable was the record of an ancient Zulu named Umbuzo. He was a fatherly old soul, with a marvellous memory for faces. His weakness was cattle-stealing, and he spent thirty-five years in prison altogether. Like many more of his kind, he remained faithful to one form of crime.

This old individual was remarkably useful in prison. His *kraal* was in the Camperdown district, and as he never went far from home in pursuit of his misdeeds, he always landed back in the central gaol at Pietermaritzburg. Before the introduction of the finger-print system the police had to depend upon memory to tell whether a man had been through their hands before or not. The old cattle-thief was practically infallible. It was his boast that he never forgot a face, and he was certainly very extraordinary in this respect. He was never taken into court to prove a previous conviction, but whenever there was any doubt about a man the opinion of the antique Zulu was asked, to assist the police in hunting up his record. The cattle-thief must have been fairly happy in prison, for the moment he was released he started stealing other people's beasts again without even taking the trouble to go into another district.

Umbuzo ended his days in prison while serving a sentence of nine years.

A native thief depends upon his own agility to avoid capture instead of using his brains. There are instances of Zulus having been convicted three times as a result of their leaving finger-prints on glass. Even the dullest European criminal would hardly be likely to fall into this trap a third time.

The average Zulu distinctly objects to work, and, when he can, he lives by his wits, though he rarely knows how to do that properly. There is one notable exception in the person of Fayedwa.

Nobody who ever had anything to do with this individual will forget him. He is in prison now, and he has been in prison a dozen times before, but he is one of the most remarkable ventriloquists breathing. Every Zulu has a way of making himself heard at a distance. This is due to the formation of the Zulu words, and the native's clear enunciation, although many people living in the country today, (at time of first publication), ascribe it to a form of ventriloquism. After two natives have met on a country road and exchanged the usual courtesies, which are as likely as not to consist of inquisitive questions, they continue to talk while walking away from one another for a considerable distance, without turning round. A white man, speaking in the same tone, could not make himself heard at half the distance.

This faculty was strongly developed in Fayedwa, and in his early youth he travelled about with a circus, doing an ordinary "boy's"[2] work. A ventriloquist who was amongst the performers interested him greatly, and Fayedwa studied at his feet, eventually becoming far more expert than his master. Perhaps he would have been a good Zulu all the days of his life had he not picked up the trick of ventriloquism, but it ruined him socially and morally; for he is a wily mortal, and soon saw that he could earn a lot of money by frightening his simple, superstitious fellow-beings.

Nobody knows, nor ever will know, what pranks he got up to at first, but he originally came under the notice of the police at Camperdown, where it was discovered that he had secured great influence over a chief. He used to go into a hut and stagger the occupants of the place by making voices appear to come from outside or up in the roof. Addressing the men by name, the voice told them that some appalling calamity would visit them if they did not present Fayedwa with money, cattle, goats, or women. The voice purported to be that of a departed spirit, and the terrified natives hastened to give the ventriloquist anything that he chose to ask for. He found this more amusing, and infinitely more profitable, than being a circus handyman, and he even extracted money from the chief of the local tribe.

These mysterious events came to the ears of the police, who sent native constables to arrest the man. The quick-witted Fayedwa was

2. A native servant, however old he may be, is invariably referred to as a boy.

259

equal to the occasion. As soon as a constable got near him he would be horrified to hear a voice behind him saying, "Touch not this man, or woe betide you, your family, and your friends"—or something equally startling.

Turning round in alarm, and seeing nobody there, the constables were scared. Thinking it was the dreaded voice of an *umtakati*, they dared not arrest the man.

Improbable though this sounds, for the average music-hall ventriloquist could not deceive anyone in the same way, it is officially recorded at the C.I.D. that for years Fayedwa kept the native police from laying hands on him by means of ventriloquism. They looked upon him as something sacred.

After he had been in prison the first time he took a house outside Durban and carried on the same game. Two native constables were sent after the man, and they took him into custody, but let him go and ran in holy horror as soon as they heard the voice explaining what would happen to them if they dared to detain this august person. He was soon afterwards taken into custody, and after a second term of imprisonment took up his abode on the south coast of Natal. He was too clever to go back to his old haunts, for the natives there would not have been so credulous as to satisfy his demands when they knew he had been in prison.

After Fayedwa had been in gaol twice the native constables were not so terrified of him, though they evinced a distinct objection to have anything to do with the gentleman for years afterwards. Sometimes, when sent out to arrest him, they would return and report that he had left the district, or was not to be found. In these cases he had frightened them away, as a rule, and they did not like to admit it.

Even now some of the native police are very frightened of him. Fayedwa amused himself at the expense of the native warders when he was first put into prison. They were in a state of alarm, and the authorities were even afraid that he would induce some native to let him get away. The guards heard the voices of their grandmothers and other people promising death and destruction if they did not see that the prisoner got away, but extra care was taken of the man, and he has never succeeded in escaping so far.

For the last seventeen years, (at time of first publication), Fayedwa has thriven on his ventriloquism. He could make an excellent living on the stage, for there are few so skilled as he, but he makes a better one out of the raw natives in different places.

A native of a very different stamp walked into the Umgeni police station in 1908 and said he wished to be properly punished for stealing a horse at Ladysmith some years previously. The police, perhaps naturally, were unsympathetic, and as he persisted, came to the conclusion that he was insane.

Quite hurt, the native walked to the C.I.D. office in Pietermaritzburg and repeated his story there. The officials were not much inclined to believe him, as the request was such an extraordinary one for a black to make, particularly after such a length of time had elapsed, but on looking up the records they found that there had been a horse theft on the day he mentioned, and the circumstances were exactly as he described them.

The most remarkable part of the affair was the reason he gave for making the confession. He said he had had a vision, in which he walked through a very beautiful country which was strange to him. Suddenly he was confronted by a being who he saw was not human. This being held out a book in which the *kafir* saw entered his first crime. He looked at the opposite page and saw that he had atoned, by going to prison, for this offence, and when he looked again at the first page the entry had disappeared.

This went on with each of his offences until he was shown the one for which he gave himself up. This refused to vanish from the page, but instead grew blacker and blacker. The being informed him that the book was his heart, that he must report himself to the police without delay, and that he must go to prison to atone for the theft of the horse.

He was tried and found guilty; and it is a pity nobody knows whether the sentence did him any good afterwards, for he got twenty lashes, followed by a year's hard labour.

The Indians in Natal and Zululand are much more law-abiding than the Zulus. There are not nearly so many of them—about 150,000 Indians to 1,000,000 Zulus—and the chief offences for which they have to be watched are such as refusing to work for the employer to whom they are indentured. There is comparatively little crime amongst them, and, unlike the Zulus, they commit offences chiefly amongst their own people.

About four years ago there was a curious case at Cramond, on the Clan Wattle Syndicate's estate, near New Hanover. Groans were heard coming from the direction of a small building near the barracks, and an Indian, who had only been in the country ten days, was found on the ground with both his feet and his right hand cut off. In this mangled condition he had crawled part of the way round the building.

He declared that someone had attacked him, but there were one or two circumstances which cast doubt on his statement. In the first place, he had declared he would rather do anything than work; nobody could discover that he had a single enemy; he could not say who had attacked him; and in view of the fact that his right hand was severed it was significant that he was left-handed. He was not found until twelve hours after the maiming had been done, and although in a fainting condition he was far from dying. The Indian was not insane; but Indians are peculiarly obstinate when they decide not to continue work. The probability is that he cut off his own feet and hand to make certain that his employer would not be able to compel him to rejoin the labour gang.

The Zulu who for generations has taken *kafir* beer in considerable quantities when he felt so inclined, is predisposed to alcohol, and this has been the cause of a problem which is constantly in front of the police. The native beer (called *utshwala*) is a concoction made from millet (known as *amabele*), and induces heaviness rather than inebriation. This liquid he is permitted to imbibe, but it is a criminal offence for him to take other forms of alcohol, and it is also a criminal offence for white men to give or sell liquor to the natives, who, having little or no restraint, would drink to excess whenever they snatched the opportunity. It demoralises them completely, and there is no knowing what they will do when under its influence.

And yet the Zulus are constantly found to be obtaining drink, particularly those who have lived in the neighbourhood of Johannesburg, where they have acquired the craving as a result of the extensive scale on which the illicit drink trade is carried on there. The trouble exists largely in the remote Natal and Zululand districts, where the publican retails liquor at exorbitant prices to the Zulus whom he knows. These publicans will rarely supply a native whom they do not know, dreading the danger of police traps. So far these traps have been the only way in which the culprits could be caught. Nobody likes employing traps in police work, but it is a case of necessity in regard to selling liquor to natives.

In order to get a conviction, the police have to obtain a perfectly clear case against the publican, and must produce in court the identical liquor sold to the native. When it becomes evident that some licence-holder is carrying on this illicit trade, a European member of the force takes with him two native constables, and, after searching them to see that they have no other money in their possession, gives them certain marked coins and sends them into the suspected house. He must make certain that they do not go elsewhere, and in order to be able to swear to their movements sometimes lies for a long time in the grass or behind other suitable cover awaiting their return.

Before going into the house they are provided with a bottle, and they have to resort to all sorts of tricks to get the liquor. Sometimes they put a sponge in their mouth and, after emptying the glass, squeeze the drink into the bottle. But even there the difficulties of the police do not end. The native constables occasionally have to wait a long time before Boniface will serve them, and the officer outside has to be patient.

Experience has shown that if two natives do not give identically the same version of what happened, the licence-holder gets the benefit of the doubt. The cases are always defended by a smart lawyer, and as it is not difficult to make a native tie himself into a knot during cross-examination, the task of the police is peculiarly difficult and disagreeable.

Sometimes a native will boldly sell extremely bad whisky or gin— with which he has been supplied at an enormous profit by a low-class white man—in a shanty of his own, but these drinking dens are soon closed down, for their existence rapidly becomes obvious and the police have power to walk straight in and search the place.

Two formidable Zulus, Hlobana and Somtshali, created a reign of terror in the neighbourhood of Colenso a few years ago. They began with holding up a number of Italian railway contractors at Colenso, and sometime after this they held up a native store at Chieveley, having rigged themselves out in some old native police uniforms. A volunteer had left his rifle at the Chieveley railway station, and while the night guard was attending to a train, they entered the office by a back window and stole the weapon.

A couple of nights later they broke into the goods shed, and got away with property worth about £15; and then, having travelled about sixty miles during the night, probably on stolen horses, they held up a store on the banks of the Tugela, threatening the Indian who kept it until he handed over a quantity of jewellery and some watches. From there they made a rapid move to a mission station near Chieveley. Pointing the gun at the missionary, they demanded money. He gave them all he had and invited them to join in prayer. They gravely promised to return for that purpose another day.

Two nights after they again held up an Arab store in Chieveley, securing a considerable quantity of property, after which they took jewellery worth £16 from an Indian storekeeper at Frere.

After having stolen a night lamp at Colenso railway station, they returned a little while later and broke into the goods store, where they secured some boxes of soap, and sweets, thinking they contained liquor. After carrying these out on to the *veldt*, and discovering their mistake, they destroyed them, and, returning to Colenso, broke into a store. From there they went to Ladysmith, and, having ransacked a store, burnt it to the ground.

The pair were arrested by a C.I.D. detective at Colenso, Hlobana being imprisoned for ten years, and Somtshali for seven.

While serving their sentences at Pietermaritzburg they escaped, together with another thief named Gogogo, who had been closely associated with them in many of their misdeeds. The trio got away from the labour gang about a couple of years ago; Somtshali was recaptured the same day, Gogogo was taken at his *kraal*, and Hlobana has not been heard of since, though there is not the slightest doubt that, unless he happens to have died, he will be arrested for a repetition of his own particular form of offence, when his finger-prints will give him away.

A sable gentleman named Badhlu some years ago spent a long time worrying the life out of the police. He was an inveterate sheep-stealer, and at times he varied the monotony by annexing horses.

Badhlu was a tall Zulu of magnificent physique, and generally wore just the native *umutsha*. He was as quick as a lizard, strong as a bull, and had much more intelligence than most of his kind. His keen, brown eyes could detect danger where none else could see it, and for months he defied not only the police, but also two native tribes which joined in the hunt.

His *kraal* was at Hella Hella, near Richmond, and once he had learnt the art of stealing, his audacity knew no bounds. Farmers all over the district complained bitterly of missing animals. Generally he skinned the sheep where he killed it, and disappeared with his booty into the dense bush that covers that part of the country. The police soon discovered who the culprit was. That was simple enough, because other natives, fearful of being accused themselves, admitted that Badhlu was constantly making mysterious nocturnal excursions, disappearing into the great Enon bush at dusk, although superstition prevented other natives from entering it at nightfall.

There were traces, too, of Badhlu's handiwork in many cases of horse theft. These animals were found at different *kraals*, where they had been sold by a tall Zulu who was glad to part with them for a nominal price. The trouble was to catch, or even see the wily thief.

Rumours would reach the police camp at times that Badhlu had come back to the neighbourhood, and on these occasions the whole available force would turn out for a grand hunt. This occurred several times at night, and the men scoured the district for miles. Badhlu could run like a hare, and as he knew every inch of the country it was almost impossible to run him to earth amongst the hills and deep gullies. Of course, his *kraal* was watched closely, whenever the necessary men could be spared, but that had little effect, for Badhlu was the last man in the world to walk into a trap, so his wife rarely saw him. She did once, however, and never forgot it. She told the story to the police, full of indignation.

One pitch dark night, when the rain was falling as it only can rain in that climate, someone knocked at the door of her *kraal*, and she found her husband outside securely bound on the back of a pony. Two mounted men told her curtly that they were detectives, that they had arrested Badhlu, and had orders to convey her with him to the magistracy.

With somewhat mixed feelings, for the horse thief was not a model husband, she obeyed, and trudged through the rain for some miles. To her surprise, however, Badhlu was then set free and the horses were abandoned. She was coolly informed that the whole thing was a ruse to get her to accompany him to another state, as that district was getting too hot to hold him. The astonished woman became angry instead of falling on the neck of her spouse and congratulating him on not being captured. Moreover, she declined to go another step, and declared she was going to return to her home and friends.

Badhlu was an awkward person to thwart, and he gave her such a thrashing, aided by the two "detectives," that she feigned submission and walked on with the party. For three nights she kept up with them, and at last escaped in the darkness.

Her first action was to report to the police what her husband had done—she was bruised and starving—and where he was. The pseudo-detectives she described so minutely that they were arrested within a week and imprisoned for impersonating the police. But the slim sheep-stealer had vanished, and his two colleagues denied all knowledge of his movements. For a while no sheep were missed, Badhlu either being away or lying low.

Once his easily distinguished figure was seen by a band of native police who were armed with *knobkerries* and *assegais*. He shot off like an antelope, but they kept on his track till he came to a small precipice. Here his pursuers opened out with the object of hemming him in, but the fearless Zulu leaped into the scrub below, a drop of quite ten yards. Expecting to find their quarry mangled or dead, they hurried down—to find nothing but a small pool of blood. Once again the native had made good his escape.

The sheep-stealing became so bad that the Government called upon the chiefs of a couple of tribes to assist the police. He heard of this, but appeared to view the fresh danger as an added fascination, and for over three months continued his operations, avoiding capture with amazing skill, and declaring to his friends that he would never be taken alive. As he invariably carried an *assegai* and an axe, this possibly damped the ardour of the two native tribes that had been requested to capture him.

Some of the farmers, highly incensed at losing sheep continually, declared their intention of shooting Badhlu on sight if they got the chance, and the man lived the life of a hunted animal apparently with the greatest of pleasure.

His downfall was positively prosaic after all his exciting adventures. One afternoon, when the sun was blazing down in all its fury, he was found by four natives, snoring under a mimosa bush, probably as the sequel to an orgy of *kafir* beer and meat. His weapons were lying by his side, so these were quietly removed, and he awoke to find himself a captive.

Badhlu was not an ordinary being, and he should have been very securely tied up to make things doubly certain, but the four proud natives who had taken him did not think of that, and Badhlu did exactly what one might have expected. On the way to the village he dived out of their reach and began to run as he had never run before. Again he would undoubtedly have got clean away had not Sergeant Lempriere and the clerk of the magistrate's court happened to be riding not far away. They saw the man bolt, and galloped after him. The exciting chase went on over exceedingly rough country, and Badhlu made for the river, which was difficult to cross.

Over this the thief and two horsemen went at a great pace, but the native eventually got into difficulties with a barbed-wire fence. He had only a few precious seconds in which to negotiate it, and had he once passed it it would have saved him, but his pursuers swooped down on him. Neither of them was armed, but with a stirrup iron swinging on the end of a leather they persuaded him to see the folly of further resistance.

Then for the first time the sergeant saw whom he had caught, and Badhlu was bound, with almost loving care, with spare reins about his arms. Another strap was put about his neck, and so he was led to a safe place where sheep-stealing does not occur.

Badhlu, in the course of his brief but thrilling career of lawlessness, had reverted to a state of primitive wildness. Even in court he had to be watched very carefully. He was not so interested in the formal proceedings as he was in the possibility of getting away; but being far from the fastnesses of his natural haunts he had to submit, and in the end he did his share of building a new dock at Cape Town under the watchful eyes of warders.

One of the most puzzling cases that ever came into the hands of the police of Natal was the treacherous murder of Mr. H. M. Stainbank, magistrate of the Mahlabatini district of Zululand. He was killed on the 3rd May 1906, and it was six years afterwards when the case was finally settled. It was a political murder, and as the man was not caught in the act the case bristled with difficulties, for those natives who knew anything about it would not, or dared not, speak.

Mr. Stainbank had been collecting from the chief Mgobozane, whose people showed little inclination to pay the poll-tax. With the magistrate were his wife, child, and governess, two troopers of the police, and half a dozen native constables. They were camped on the bank of the White Umfolosi River, about four miles from the scene of the Battle of Ulundi, in a district covered with bush, and sparsely populated owing to the prevalence of malaria.

In the evening Mr. Stainbank wished to speak to Mr. Saunders, the Commissioner for Native Affairs, at Nkandhla, and, accompanied by Troopers A. J. Sells and Martin, left the camp and went about a hundred yards away to tap the wire with a field telephone.

He was just putting the receiver to his ear when a shot was fired somewhere near in the bush, and the magistrate fell back wounded. In quick succession three other shots followed, two of them hitting Sells. Mr. Stainbank's knee was smashed, the main artery being severed, and he died soon afterwards. Sells received one bullet in the arm and another in his side. Martin escaped injury.

The nearest assistance was at the magistracy, nine miles away. One of the native constables set out on foot, and just an hour later told Sergeant A. H. Smith, in a state of wild excitement, that the *inkosi* [4] "and everybody else" had been murdered. The white people in those troublous days were all living on the edge of a volcano, and Sergeant Smith naturally feared that an *impi* had begun a massacre. He found three troopers at the Mahlabatini station, and decided to make for the scene of the murder on foot, as they would have a better chance of getting there undetected that way than if they rode. By the time they got as far as the magistracy, however, Martin had arrived there with the body of Mr. Stainbank and the rest of the party in a wagon. He had left the camp just as it was, with the money that had been collected there.

Having telephoned to Mr. Saunders and Mr. Armstrong, the Nongoma magistrate, reporting on the seriousness of the situation, Sergeant Smith formed a *laager* of one of the gaol rooms and sandbagged the windows in anticipation of an attack; and the loyal chief Nqodi was called upon to assist in defending the magistracy. Nqodi's warriors turned out, and were posted in groups of fifty on the surrounding hills. A trooper was also sent to warn the white residents in the district to take shelter in the *laager*, as a rising was feared.

Throughout the night an anxious watch was kept, although it was not expected that the natives would attack the *laager*, if they were going to attack at all, until dawn, in accordance with their usual practice. There was a lonely station at Nhlatze, about twenty-five miles away, and in the light of a flickering candle Sergeant Smith wrote the following report to Trooper Dumphreys there, warning him to get ready for a possible attack, the letter being carried to Nhlatze by a native constable:—

I have to report to you that Mr. Stainbank and family, accompanied by Troopers Sells and Martin, while on hut and dog-tax inspection at the White Umfolosi Drift, were molested. Mr Stainbank had attached a telephone about a hundred yards from his camp at 7 p.m. last night. He was accompanied by Trooper Sells, and was fired on by natives in the bush, one bullet piercing Mr. Stainbank's knee and evidently smashing it. Trooper Sells received a wound through the arm and ribs. The party managed to reach the magistracy without further molestation. I regret that Mr. Stainbank has since expired. We are now in

4. Magistrate.

laager.

I have warned Chief Nqodi to arm his men and send them up here to protect us. I cannot express an opinion whether there was an *impi* at the White Umfolosi Drift or not, but the magistrate's party were allowed to in-span and drive away. However, you must take all precautionary measures. I have communicated with Mr. Saunders and Mr. Armstrong, and there is a probability of an armed force being sent here. I will endeavour to get further information through to you. You had better report this to Vryheid immediately in case the information cannot be sent *via* Melmoth or Eshowe.

Daybreak came, and there was no sign of violence, much to the relief of the little party. All the chiefs of the division came in, however, to express their regret at the murder, and three days later the *laager* was broken up, it being evident that there was no *impi* abroad. Four empty cartridge cases were found near the place where Mr. Stainbank had been shot, showing that the crime had been committed with a .303 rifle; and that was the sum total of available evidence. Not a single Zulu would admit the slightest knowledge of anything concerning the murder.

In the olden days the chief of a tribe was held responsible for a murder unless he could find the culprit, and if he failed he was sometimes wiped out by his black brethren. Civilization, however, has killed this custom, but a chief is still expected to assist in tracing a murderer. A consultation was held with Ngobozane, in whose district the magistrate was shot, and though very little definite information was secured, the name of a native named Mpeta was mentioned. The old saying that *murder will out* is infinitely truer in Zululand than it ever was in Whitechapel, but as the police found themselves up against a blank wall they decided to appear to let the matter rest for a while. Eventually incriminating statements were made against Mpeta, and about six months after the shooting, he, with three others, was charged with the murder of Mr. Stainbank, but they were acquitted.

The ingenuity of the Criminal Investigation Department and the magistrates in the district was sorely taxed in the years that followed, and it was more than suspected that many of the natives knew all about the affair but dared not speak. With that grim persistence which characterizes the Natal Police authorities in cases of murder, they continued their inquiries for six years, and though many individuals put in a great deal of work and wits, it was chiefly due to the efforts of Mr.

A. D. Graham, the magistrate at Mahlabatini, ably assisted by Sergeants Ker, Campbell, Wilkinson, and Smith, that a native named Mayatana was eventually charged. He was convicted solely on evidence given by Zulus after certain influential natives had been removed from the district.

It was proved that Mayatana had been carrying a .303 pattern Lee-Metford rifle near the camp where the shooting took place. There was no difficulty in finding Mayatana, for he was already in prison at Pietermaritzburg, having killed someone else. Once the Zulus began to talk there was not much trouble in proving the man's guilt, although the natives have a curious trick of keeping things to themselves on occasions. After one of them has made a statement of vital importance, he may say, on being asked why on earth he never volunteered the information before, "Oh, it was not my business."

Mayatana was at last tried, and sentenced to death, but even then the case was not finished. An appeal was made, and his sentence was commuted to one of penal servitude for life.

Mpeta was again placed in the dock, this time charged with attempting to murder Sells. He was sent to ten years' penal servitude, but, on appeal, was released.

CHAPTER 26

The Brigands of De Jager's Drift

In the annals of crime committed in Natal and Zululand there is one episode which will always stand out prominently, and that is the mad debauch of lawlessness which ended in the undoing of Beni Mhlanga and Mzwangedwa, Beni being known more generally as Ben.

The whole amazing business began in the dingy interior of Dundee prison, where the villainous couple found themselves resting, preparatory to trial, with three kindred spirits, Samu Xulu, Velapi Nculwane, and Nkulu Zulu. The five men had been stealing horses and cattle, and as the period of waiting became irksome they killed time by planning an escape from prison, to be followed by an unrestrained bout of crime. Samu, otherwise referred to as Sam, had incidentally been employed by Inspector Lyttle, of the Natal Police, for a long time, having served him all over the country.

The escape was frustrated owing to a gaoler hearing a little of their private conversation, but the only one convicted was Ben. He was awarded two years' hard labour for his sins. Both Mr. A. A. Smith, the lawyer who defended the men, and Ben considered the sentence was unjustified, therefore Mr. Smith lodged an appeal and gave bail to the extent of £50, ensuring the appearance of Ben when the case came on again. The Zulu was accordingly released, and he promptly joined the acquitted quartette, their band being made up to six by the addition of Jakobe Dhladhla, a promising ruffian who had been the principal witness for the defence.

There was something sublime about the first thing Ben did when he got free from the fetters of imprisonment. He wished, apparently, to show Mr. Smith that he was a trustworthy boy, and not desiring to remain in the debt of the lawyer he broke into the house occupied by Mr. Smith's clerk, stole the keys, walked along to Mr. Smith's office and opened the safe. He took all the money he could lay his hands on, obligingly relocked the safe, and walked out.

Here his good intentions broke down: he omitted to hand the £50 to Mr. Smith. He took with him, however, the stolen keys, and fell into the error of keeping them, for when, long afterwards, they were found in his possession, he was quite unable to explain them away.

Feeling easier in his mind, he trekked for De Jager's Drift, where Jakobe had a *kraal*, the gang having decided to make this their headquarters. There, free from interference, they drew up a campaign of robbery and plunder, nor were they long in getting to work.

On the night of the 9th June 1903, they put in a quiet appearance at Redmond's store in the Ntabankulu district, forty miles from their stronghold, having stolen a couple of horses *en route*. They intended to break into the place, but finding, on inquiry, that the proprietor had banked his money they abandoned the idea.

Several of them went to Vant's Drift, and Ben, Jakobe, and Velapi, seeking to spend the time profitably, planned an attack on Codd's store. The first two went in and innocently bought a loaf of bread, casually making a few inquiries about the takings. At nightfall Codd was having dinner when he was informed that two natives were at the bar-room door. Codd let them in, and they bought a couple of pairs of boots. They asked him to throw in a pair of socks, which he obligingly did, but when he mentioned the subject of money Jakobe suddenly pulled out a revolver and without the slightest hesitation fired point-blank at the storekeeper's head.

The shot missed, and Codd vaulted over the counter to close with Jakobe, who was too quick for him and rushed into the house, through the dining-room and through the sitting-room, Codd on his heels. While running Jakobe again tried to shoot his pursuer, but the bullet hit the ceiling, and he ran out of the door. As soon as the firing began Ben dived through the plate-glass window into the road. Both men disappeared, and Codd was unable to trace them. The nearest police station was at Nqutu, fourteen miles away. All that was found was a stick, a mackintosh, and some *muti* on a hillock where the men had been hiding all day.

So far the brigands had not had any notable success, and after a consultation at headquarters they proposed to rifle the Umvun-yana store, at which Ben and Mzwangedwa arrived on the 14th June. Mzwangedwa, thinking to hide his identity, adopted the Basuto custom of shaving his head, and in the afternoon asked for a drink of water at the store, with the object of seeing what the position was there. They tethered their horses near the river, where they were seen by a woman who had been engaged to Ben. Unfortunately for them she was able to identify them subsequently.

The storekeeper was an Englishman named Hunt. As he was having his evening meal, sitting sideways on the table, there came a knock at the door. Hunt, without getting up, leaned forward and turned the handle. A revolver was thrust through the half-opened door and a shot was fired, the storekeeper collapsing. There were two natives, the store boy and the post boy, in the building. Not wanting these to escape, the attacking party bombarded the place with shots, but one of the natives got through a window. Ben and Mzwangedwa then went into the place and, after severely ill-treating the other boy, took the money from the till, a revolver, and a key from the dead man's breast pocket. This key, when found on Mzwangedwa afterwards, and produced as evidence of his guilt, still bore the stain of Hunt's life's blood.

One native, on getting out of the store, jumped on a horse and rode to Nondweni, nine miles away, where he informed the police of what had happened, adding that the murderers were holding up the place with firearms. Troopers A. H. Smith and L. Smith galloped over to Umvunyana, deciding to rush the place in the dark. When they arrived A. H. Smith saw a native running from the kitchen to the store, so he rode straight up to him, put the barrel of his revolver almost against the Zulu's neck and pressed the trigger.

No native was ever much nearer going to his grave than this one was. Fortunately for him, he saluted in the nick of time, and Smith discovered he had nearly killed the *induna* of Chief Mpiyake who, having heard of the murder, had called out his men. Afterwards Smith found that there was actually a dent on the cartridge in his revolver where the hammer had pressed on to it, showing what a narrow escape the *induna* had had.

Ben and Mzwangedwa had cleared off, and Hunt was found dying on the floor of the store. He did not regain consciousness, and expired the next morning. Mpiyake was subsequently rewarded by the Government with a shot gun in recognition of his services.

Ultimately it was found that the two ruffians rode away from the store on stolen horses at such a pace that one of the animals died on the banks of the Blood River. The two men then made their way back to De Jager's Drift. By this time the scattered inhabitants of the district had become thoroughly alarmed. Nobody had the slightest idea who the culprits were, and every storekeeper was prepared to shoot on sight when there was promise of trouble. It was never suspected for a moment that a desperate gang was working, and Ben, in between robberies, was apparently living a virtuous life awaiting the hearing of his appeal. Mr. Smith was blissfully unconscious of the fact that it was Ben who had rifled his safe.

On the night of the 17th June, Sam, Ben, and Mzwangedwa left their headquarters and turned up at Laffnie's Drift store, where a scared native, who had been left in charge, refused to open the door. He sold them some bread through the window, but on the plea that they could not see their money they persuaded him to light a lantern and let them in. Then the terrified native saw that their faces were stained with burnt grass and that they were robbers. They kept him there while they took what they wanted, and afterwards made him kneel down and say a prayer to his forefathers, telling him to go home and kill a white goat to appease his ancestral spirits. At Mr. Laffnie's stable, a few hundred yards away, they stole a black stallion which had a slight lump on its neck. This mark on the animal had due significance when the trial came on later.

With astonishing impudence they rode straight to Vant's Drift and broke into Matterson's store, right opposite the store where Codd had narrowly escaped being murdered. Here they appropriated tinned meat and some concertinas. This was followed by a quick ride to Wessel's Nek, about thirty-five miles away, where they were seen passing down the Amanzimnyama stream early in the morning. They ate tinned meat there, and were traced by the tins, which bore Matterson's private mark. The next day they had the audacity to return to Wessel's Nek and break into a house, eating a meal which lay on the table while its rightful owners, a number of miners, were away at work.

A visit of Sam, with Ben and another of the gang on his heels, to the *kraal* of his *fiancée* at Meran, nearly led to his premature downfall. Trooper Leyman, of the Natal Police, met the trio, whose guilty consciences caused them to bolt. They dodged the trooper, who got assistance and went to the woman's *kraal*. The Zulus, however, slept in an old, disused cattle *kraal* and eluded the police. At dawn they made a hasty exit, leaving their horses, saddles, and arms. Sam "jumped" a train bound for Glencoe Junction, and on his way from there stole a stallion out of a private stable at Dundee, to simplify the journey to De Jager's Drift. There was a Basuto's horse and wagon on the outskirts of Dundee, and Sam found it impossible to resist the temptation to annex this animal also. Ben, meanwhile, boarded another train, bound for Hatting Spruit, in the same way.

For a day or two the gang went off in different directions on horse-stealing expeditions, and then the six held a council of war at De Jager's Drift.

By now they had a good deal of valuable property hidden away at their stronghold, having dug large holes in the banks of the river and buried their booty. They also used an old *kraal* at the top of the Doornberg as a stable, the *kraal* being so situated that had the police swooped down on them they could easily have secured their horses and ridden off.

A dance was being held at the Victoria Hotel in Dundee, and it was decided to make a raid on the establishment while the festivities were in full swing. Sam, Ben, Mzwangedwa, and Jakobe strolled up to the place, leaving the others to hold the horses. They walked straight in and, as nobody knew who they were, calmly rifled the place, getting away with money and anything else of value that they could lay their hands on. Part of their haul consisted of spoons and forks, which they sold to an Arab outside. Triumphantly they went on to a butcher's shop, and amongst the assortment of keys which they had acquired in various parts of the country they found one with which the door could be opened. The till there was promptly emptied.

The same day they ascertained where Mr. Curtis, the manager of Mortimer's store, lived. In his absence they broke into the house, stole his keys, and then plundered the store. Finding their campaign of robbery so successful, they grew more and more reckless, and rapidly cultivated a love of sheer, wanton destruction, stealing many things for the sake of stealing, and throwing them away later on because they were of no practical use.

After another consultation at De Jager's Drift they made a move to Mbabane, where with revolvers they held up Arabs who kept three different stores; and by threatening summary destruction extorted money and a number of watches. Two of these stores they burnt down. On their return journey they passed Farm Elizabeth, the home of Mr. H. Wiltshire, a member of the Legislative Assembly, where they stole his carriage horses. When, however, they got within a few miles of their headquarters they began to feel uneasy. Mr. Wiltshire, they remembered, was "a big white man" who might feel so annoyed about having his horses stolen that he would create trouble. With this fear in their hearts they abandoned the animals on the roadside.

With hardly a rest after their exertions, Sam, Ben, Jakobe, and Mzwangedwa set out again, but, finding things dull, killed seventeen sheep at Blood River Poort, just for something to do and to show that they had been there. Wandering on, they came to a bridge over the Pivaan River, which was being repaired. Apparently a *quartette* of footsore, weary, but honest pedestrians, bound for work, the rascals begged the native labourers to give them shelter for the night. This was readily granted—and next morning there was consternation in the camp when the white men awoke. Half their kit was missing and the native labourers had also been robbed; the four wayfarers had crept silently away.

The time came when the virtuous Ben was due to appear before the Court of Appeal, and with strange inconsistency he turned up; but though the case went against him, the sentence of two years' hard labour being confirmed, the occasion must have been a colossal jest to the Zulu. At the moment when everything seemed blackest for him, and there was no prospect of looting, or *kafir* beer, for a couple of years, he was handed over to a native court messenger, who politely invited him to sit down in a corridor. This suited the wily Ben excellently, and a few moments later he strolled casually out of the building, nobody being aware of his escape until he was well on his way. Before he had been free more than a minute or two he snatched a pair of shoes from an Arab's shop.

Once free and knowing that recapture meant two years behind prison bars, Ben exercised much discretion. The first thing he had to do was to put as great a distance as possible between himself and the court-house that day, so he went up to Kettlefontein, where there is a steep gradient on the railway and where he knew the trains had to climb very slowly. Here he scrambled on to a passing goods train, dropping off it at Dannhauser, about 150 miles away. He rejoined his friends at De Jager's Drift, and as they were short of horses they trekked to Spies' farm, near Blood River Poort, where they secured remounts, saddles and bridles, in their own cheerful way. Feeling secure with good animals under them once more, they broke into the Blood River Hotel, where they stole a number of bottles of whisky, and actually took the blankets off a married couple who were asleep.

The next move was almost as impudent as any they had made. In the magistrate's room at the Vryheid court-house there were several rifles which had been confiscated, and the gang set their hearts on these weapons. They rode over to Vryheid, a distance of about thirty miles, and put their horses in the cemetery. Leaving a man to guard them, three of the Zulus went into the town. After dark had fallen Sam went boldly up to the court-house, and was in the act of forcing his way in when a native constable interrupted him. Not in the least perturbed, Sam smiled blandly and explained that he was looking for the sergeant. He acted the part so well in extremely trying circumstances, that the constable believed him. But Sam omitted to wait for that interview with the sergeant, and went out to rejoin his associates.

He met another constable, who informed him that he looked suspiciously like one of the wanted Zulus. The culprit took to his heels very quickly and got back to the cemetery safely.

Their next *coup* was to have been at the bank, the door of which they had intended to blow open with the rifles, but owing to Sam having been frustrated at the court-house door they had to drop that ambitious scheme.

Even the smartest of criminals cannot hope to go undetected for ever, and the episode which followed proved painfully unlucky. Ben and Mzwangedwa walked into the President Hotel and began to steal when the 9 p.m. bell rang, indicating that all natives must be in their homes. The two boys hid under the floor of a bedroom that was raised from the ground. A little later they crept out, and Ben escaped, but Mzwangedwa, the murderer, cattle-stealer, and burglar, fell into the arms of the law, two native constables taking him to the police camp on the charge of being out of doors after hours.

The whole country was being searched for a Zulu with a revolver as a result of the murder of Hunt, and the police were surprised to find Mzwangedwa was armed with one. A sergeant was taking the ammunition out of it, when Mzwangedwa, as slippery as his fellow-sinner Ben, dodged away and ran for his life. Even this experience did not deter him from carrying on his career of crime. He went straight to the rest of the gang, and they again broke into the Blood River Hotel, stealing, amongst other things, a bicycle, which they threw into the Buffalo River. But the revolver found on Mzwangedwa indirectly threw a light on the situation.

Sometime after the murder of Hunt, one of the most skilled and persevering officers in the Criminal Investigation Department at Pietermaritzburg, Detective-Sergeant Ker, was hastily sent to the district, but as the murderers had left no clue to their identity behind them he was faced with a baffling task. The complication of all the other outrages did not make matters any simpler for him, because the gang moved about the country with extraordinary rapidity, riding their stolen horses till the beasts were ready to drop and securing remounts at the handiest stable without asking permission.

So wide apart were the different robberies, and within such a short time of one another, that the theory that one gang accomplished them all did not seem credible. Although fifty-two crimes had been perpetrated by the gang of six Zulus all over the northern portion of the colony between the 9th June and the 26th July, there was still no reason to suspect that Hunt's murderer had anything to do with them.

The police were also searching for Ben after he walked out of the court instead of doing two years' hard labour, and he met his fate while dreaming peacefully on the banks of the Buffalo River. He awoke to find himself in custody once more, and on him was found the key of Mr. Smith's safe. At first Ben was suspected of no more serious crime than that for which he had been convicted, but the Criminal Investigation Department, considering that he had been arrested in the neighbourhood of all these robberies, began to take a different view. Although closely questioned, however, he gave nothing away.

When Sam and Ben were surprised, prior to this, by Trooper Leyman at Meran, where Sam had gone to see one of his prospective brides, and left their horses in the scramble to get away, the trooper found the animals, and noticed that one of them had a slight lump on its neck. When Sam's *fiancée* was indiscreet enough to mention that she had seen him there, it became clear that he was one of the men who had bolted. By judicious questioning it also was ascertained that Sam had a friend named Ben. A search warrant was obtained, and in Sam's *kraal* the police found a great deal of property that had been stolen before the merry band of six began their concerted operations.

The outlook began to look blacker for both Sam and Ben, and a circular was issued giving a minute description of the missing Sam, Soon after this was read to the native constables in Newcastle one of them reported to Inspector Marshall that in a local shop there was a native who answered the description. The net was fast closing on the Zulu. The shopman said Sam had arrived very footsore only that morning. The culprit was promptly put into gaol, and three days later, when at Dundee, he began a confession which proved to the police that his accomplice Ben was in their hands at Pietermaritzburg.

Mzwangedwa, with detectives now hot on his trail, fled from the district to Nongoma, in the north of Zululand, but the police got on to his track, and he made for Swaziland, where he was eventually traced. "I am a dead man," he said in a matter-of-fact tone when arrested; and he threw his *assegais* down to the ground.

The remainder of the gang were arrested at De Jager's Drift, and placed in Dundee gaol, where, bit by bit, Detective-Sergeant Ker extracted from them the full story of their misdeeds. Ben and Mzwangedwa were hanged for the murder of Hunt. The two men died as they had lived, utterly without emotion. On the scaffold they appeared to put no greater value on their own lives than they had done on that of the storekeeper as he was shot. Sam, Jakobe, and Nkulu were sentenced to long terms of imprisonment, Sam dying about a couple of years after he was incarcerated; and Velapi was acquitted on a technical point.

The greatest credit was due to Detective-Sergeant Ker for the way in which he pieced together the tangled evidence of a very complex case in spite of all manner of difficulties, not the least of which was the fact that at that time little assistance could be got from the natives, as there was a seething undercurrent of unrest amongst them which culminated three years later in the rebellion of 1906.

CHAPTER 27

The Zululand Police

No record of police work amongst the Zulus would be complete without a reference to the Zululand Native Police, which, though now disbanded, was a magnificent support to the Natal Police for twenty-one years.

The corps, known at first as the Reserve Territory Carbineers, was raised in 1883 by Inspector Mansel (subsequently Chief Commissioner of the Natal Police) to act as body-guard to the late Sir Melmoth Osborn, the Zululand Resident Commissioner, the second-in-command being Mr. R. H. Addison. Just over a score of men were recruited in Pietermaritzburg, and these were marched up to Eshowe in Zululand, where the force was brought up to 50 native non-commissioned officers and men, the first sergeant-major being Nobadula, or "Lanky Boy."

The force was about a year old, and 60 strong, when it received its baptism of fire at Inogonga, where an Usutu *impi*, under Dabulamanzi, attacked the Resident Commissioner's camp at about 3 a.m. There was a native contingent with the commissioner, but as soon as the *impi* appeared the contingent bolted, and their mat-carriers rushed into the camp screaming with terror and mobbing the Reserve Territory Carbineers, who had taken up a somewhat strong position behind some stones.

Commandant Mansel decided to march his men straight out to meet the Usutus face to face, and as they got clear of the camp a dense mass of Zulus came over the brow of a hill not far away.

It was a bright, moonlight night, and the native *carbineers*, though opposed to a force far exceeding their own in strength, did not show the slightest sign of wavering. They were perfectly steady, and obeyed every order. When the *impi* was within 120 yards the commandant gave the order "Ready—Present—Fire." The marksmen acted as though they were on parade, and when told to fire independently they kept up a tremendous fusillade, discharging their weapons with the utmost rapidity and telling effect.

The war-cry of "Usutu" was raised by the *impi*, which rushed on and tried to get to close quarters. Very few of them, however, succeeded, for the *carbineers* kept firing steadily. The *impi*, too, discharged their weapons, but their shooting was so ineffective that only one man was killed and a few were wounded.

Wavering under the stream of lead, the *impi* turned back over the hill and left a hundred men dead.

Just before the *carbineers* made this magnificent stand the statement had been made to Sir Melmoth Osborn that they could not be trusted and would turn on him at the first opportunity. Dabulamanzi had also sent a message to the *carbineers* themselves to the effect that they were a lot of boys, and that he and his men were coming to give them a lesson they would never forget.

They did not take part in any further fighting until the 2nd June 1888, by which time their name had been changed to the Zululand Police.

Commandant Mansel left the camp at Nkonjeni with about a hundred members of his force, with the object of arresting Dinuzulu, who was at the Ceza Bush, about twenty-five miles away, with a large *impi*. The police were supported by two troops of the Inniskilling Dragoons, under Captain Pennefather, and a company of mounted infantry, under Captain Purdon.

At the other side of the Black Umfolosi the force was joined by Mnyamana, with about five hundred of his warriors. It was early on the morning of the 2nd, when a large *impi* was sighted formed up in an opening of the Ceza Bush. It appeared to consist of between two and three thousand men; and as soon as the troops were seen the Zulus began streaming up through the bush. They established themselves on the top of a hill; and after a consultation between the commandant and Captain Pennefather it was agreed that the Zululand Police, who were mounted, and numbered twenty, were to push on ahead, the foot police and Mnyamana's men following as quickly as possible.

When the Usutus saw what was happening they all came down from the hill, and formed up again in an opening of the bush. As soon as Mnyamana's braves saw the *impi* do this they turned tail and did not stop running until they were safe at the other side of the Black

281

Umfolosi River.

The mounted *Zululand* Police rode straight on until they were within four hundred yards of the enemy. They then got off their horses, linked the animals together, and established themselves on the top of a small *kopje*.

A shot was fired and suddenly about five hundred Zulus detached themselves from the main body of the *impi*. They extended in skirmishing order and rushed straight on, this being the Falazi Regiment (Dinuzulu's Own). They were a magnificent body of young men, armed with *assegais* and shields. At the same time, the main *impi* opened a heavy fire, killing more than half a dozen of the police horses, including that upon which the commandant was sitting. The Falazi Regiment rushed straight on and got within twenty yards of the Zululand Police, but they were unable to reach the crest before being shot down. The firing on the part of the Zululand Police force was fast and furious, but a mounted orderly galloped up to the commandant, saying, "Captain Pennefather sends his compliments, and says you had better retire, as the enemy are working round his flanks, and that he cannot hold his own."

"Go back to Captain Pennefather and tell him to come on, as we have beaten the enemy here and should go for the main *impi*" replied the commandant; but the same orderly returned soon afterwards.

"Captain Pennefather says he must leave you, if you won't come back, as he is being surrounded," was his message.

Commandant Mansel tied a handkerchief to the muzzle of his carbine and went back towards the mounted infantry, who were between him and the Inniskillings. He waved to them to join him, but they began to retire, as did also the cavalry beyond them. A Zulu followed the commandant while he was engaged in this way, having several shots at him. Mr. Mansel fired in return, missing the man once as he went over a big boulder, and laying him out with the second shot.

It was now high time for the police to abandon the *kopje*, so they took possession of such horses as remained, and retired leading the animals. The Falazi Regiment had been lying in a bush after being repulsed, and when the police began to retire they got up to follow them. This the police soon checked, Dinuzulu's Own having had about enough of it; and the police safely rejoined the rest of the force which had gone to an open ridge.

There Commandant Mansel found the rest of the police, who had been stopped by Captain Grey of the Inniskillings and put into a position to check the Zulus working round the right flank.

The Usutus made their way down to the open, and there a splendid charge was made upon them by Captain Pennefather with the Dragoons. The enemy did not appear to realize what was taking place, and they stood still until the Dragoons were almost on top of them. Then they broke and scattered like rabbits in every direction.

The Dragoons rode down a number of the blacks, galloping over them, and some they cut down, but one of their own men was killed in the charge and another badly wounded. During the day the mounted infantry had one man killed and one badly wounded, there also being three or four of the police in the list of injured. When asked long afterwards how many of the Falazi Regiment were lost at Ceza, Dinuzulu would not answer at first, but on being pressed he admitted that forty of them were killed and so many were wounded that he "could not count them."

After the fighting the troops recrossed the Black Umfolosi, the Zulus following them at a discreet distance until they reached the river. During the day the whole of the attacking force, both black and white, behaved magnificently, but one of the features of the fight was the determined way in which the twenty Zululand Police held their ground and beat off the Falazi Regiment as it charged up the *kopje*. Commandant Mansel regarded the situation as desperate at that moment, but his men never showed the slightest sign of wavering.

A little while after the fight at the Ceza Bush the Usutus attacked the chief Sibepu, who was encamped with an *impi* close to the magistracy at Nongoma, where a small fort had been put up by the police. The magistrate, Mr. Addison, was in the fort, together with a few white refugees, the defending force consisting of thirty members of the Zululand Police and three dragoons who were acting as signallers. The Usutus rushed down in overwhelming force, killing over four hundred of Sibepu's men, and the rest fled past the fort, from which a steady fire was opened on the Usutus. The pursuers were thus checked to some extent, and this enabled Sibepu and many of his followers to take refuge.

The Usutus had a large number killed by the fire from the fort, which it was feared for some time they were going to rush. This, however, they did not do, and contented themselves by firing at it for some time from a distance.

At about the same time the magistracy at Lower Umfolosi was attacked by a strong body of Usutus. A detachment of the native police was stationed there in a small fort, under Sub-Inspector Marshall, and they easily repulsed the attack.

The next fight of any consequence in which the Zululand Police took part was at Hlopekulu, on the 2nd July 1888. Shingana Mpande, one of Cetewayo's brothers, who had over two thousand men with him, took up a very strong position in the valley of the White Umfolosi, near Ulundi, and from there kept sending threatening and insulting messages to the force at Nkonjeni, so it was decided to attack them. The force that set out consisted of the Inniskilling Dragoons, a company of mounted infantry under Colonel Spark Stabb, 250 of Hlubi's Mounted Basutos, under Major M'Kean, 103 Zululand Police, under the Commandant and Sub-Inspector Osborn, besides about 2000 of the native contingent, under Mr. Trent.

It was soon seen, as Hlopekulu was approached, towards midday, that the enemy meant to fight. After a consultation it was decided that the Basutos were to attack the left of the position. The native contingent were sent to work round the right of the enemy, and Commandant Mansel went straight on to attack the centre of the *impi* with the police. As Mr. Mansel was moving forward, encountering very little opposition, a message reached him to the effect that the advance of the Basutos was checked, and numbers of the enemy began to appear on a ridge that ran out of the bush near the top of the hill. They appeared to be wildly excited, brandishing their *assegais* and shouting defiance at the police.

Commandant Mansel dispatched Sub-Inspector Osborn with a few mounted men to see what had become of the Basutos, but they did not get far before a heavy fire was opened on them by a number of the enemy who were entrenched behind a stone wall. One of the police reeled from his horse, whereupon Sub-Inspector Osborn placed his men under the shelter of a hill, and then dismounted. Taking two men with him, he ran up to the wall and carried the fallen man (who proved to be dead) away while bullets were flying through the air. Subsequently the sub-inspector was recommended for the V.C., but the cherished medal was not awarded.

Commandant Mansel moved off to attack the ridge at the top of the bush, and as soon as they came within sight of the Zulus behind the wall the police were fired on. The men were got into line, slightly extended, and advanced steadily up the hill towards the wall, from behind which a galling fire was poured, bullets also coming from some bush.

When the police were within a score yards of the wall the commandant gave the order to charge. The men cheered and dashed forward. The commandant's horse cleared the wall, and the police scrambled over after him, whereupon the enemy bolted along the ridge up to the bush, at the edge of which they had constructed a sort of stone fort. Here they made a momentary stand, until the police rushed it with fixed bayonets.

Over the edge of the fort the attackers climbed, their old fighting spirit thoroughly roused, and a moment later they had turned the little place into a veritable shambles. The enemy made an attempt at resistance, but were literally pitchforked out of the place on the end of the bayonets, the police shouting wildly all the time. As the remnants of the *impi* ran away the police followed, still jabbing at them with their bayonets, which were afterwards found to be bent and twisted into all sorts of shapes, the majority of them having to be thrown away as useless.

The police, warmed up to their work, got entirely out of hand, and the commandant found himself alone, with no supports near. When a native sergeant and half a dozen troopers ran past, Mr. Mansel had the greatest difficulty in restraining their ardour, and persuading them to remain behind their colleagues. Shortly afterwards he was joined by Sub-Inspector Osborn and the mounted police, whose horses, owing to the very rough nature of the country, had not been able to keep up to the front.

From the position where they stood they got a remarkable view of a terrible conflict between Mr. Trent's native contingent and the enemy. Stretching out in front of them was the bed of the White Umfolosi River, which is very broad at that point. Coming down the white sand in the bed of the stream, far away, was a force of the enemy, and walking up to them was the native contingent, which could be plainly distinguished, as the men were wearing red *pugarees*. They were half a mile from the place where Commandant Mansel and his men were standing, but were plainly visible through field-glasses.

The two forces met in mid-stream, and a terrific encounter it was. They were all fighting with *assegais*, and for two or three minutes the struggle was enveloped in a cloud of spray.

Suddenly the splashing almost ceased. The native contingent had given way, and was racing for the bank. Mr. Trent's men lost more than 70 killed, besides many wounded, and he himself died while climbing from the bed of the river, probably from heart failure.

Large herds of cattle could be seen from the position where the commandant stood, and he sent a note to Colonel Stabb by a mounted native, saying, "We have carried the position here. The cattle are down below, and we are going to send for them. Please send on supports."

No supports arrived, and soon the police could be seen making for the cattle. The Zulus who had been victorious in the river now hastened to defend the animals, and another tremendous fight took place, but as the police were armed with guns the *impi* could not stand against them. There were 92 dead men near the place when the cattle were finally driven off by the native police, and the enemy were hiding in some caves.

Towards evening, when the commandant got his men together, he was astonished to find that only three of them had been killed, though several had been slightly wounded. They started out with 90 rounds of ammunition each, and they had fired nearly every cartridge, having killed between 400 and 450 of the enemy. Some of them had been wonderfully brave, and the Government afterwards recognized their valour by making them a grant of £2 each. The Imperial troops took no part in the action, and several of their officers who had served in India stated that the best Indian troops would not have stood much chance against the trained Zululand Police.

After this the strength of the force was raised to 250 non-commissioned officers and men, but the Zulus saw no further fighting until the last Boer War, when more were taken on, bringing the total to 8 European officers and 600 non-commissioned officers and men. They were employed chiefly in and about Melmoth during the war. They put the place into a state of defence by building forts and digging trenches, and were also useful in providing escorts for convoys to Nkandhla . One of these escorts comprised 40 men when a Boer force made an attack. The native police did not show the least trace of fear, but beat the enemy off.

A score of the Zululand Police also acquitted themselves in an admirable manner when General Botha attacked Fort Prospect.

On one occasion the majority of the men left Eshowe for Nqutu, making a march which was remarkably quick for infantry. In five days and five hours they covered the rough country from Eshowe to Melmoth and from there to Nqutu, a distance of 120 miles.

A great deal of police work was done continually, and many small patrols were sent out. The Zululand Police were used as guards when the first Chinese landed at Durban, being employed for about three months on this work. This was the first time that any large bodies of the Natal Police and the native corps were camped together.

For some time the Zulus were on quarantine duty at Charlestown. While there they went to a circus at Volksrust, and when the band played "God save the King" the old native sergeant in charge rose to the occasion. He called his men to attention, which attitude they maintained like statues, to the amusement of the rest of the audience, many of whom were not aware of the great loyalty of the Zululand Police.

The diaries kept at the headquarters of the Zululand Police show that many eminent soldiers inspected the force at various times, and spoke very highly of their efficiency.

While General Dartnell was with the force besieged at Ladysmith, Mr. Mansel returned to Pietermaritzburg to act as Chief Commissioner of the Natal Police. The latter force absorbed the native police when Zululand was annexed, and Sub-Inspector C. E. Fairlie (afterwards inspector) took charge of the natives, having Sub-Inspector Lindsay as second-in-command. The Zululand Police maintained a highly efficient state, but had to be abandoned in 1904 by order of the Natal Government. The natives, who had always taken the keenest delight in their work, were sorely disappointed when this step was taken, but when the rebellion of 1906 broke out they refused to rejoin unless they were to serve under their old officers.

The officers who served with them prior to the disbandment in 1904 were:

Commandant, George Mansel, C.M.G.
Inspector C. E. Fairlie (of the Natal Police).
Inspector R. S. Maxwell (who served during 1901-2 at Melmoth and Nkandhla).
Sub-Inspector R. H. Addison (now District Native Commissioner, Zululand).
Sub-Inspector J. H. Osborn.
Sub-Inspector C. E. Pearse.
Sub-Inspector C. C. Foxon (afterwards magistrate in Zululand).
Sub-Inspector F. Evans (of the Natal Police: retired).
Sub-Inspector J. E. Marshall (afterwards Inspector of Natal Police).
Sub-Inspector C. F. Hignett (afterwards magistrate of Umzinto).

Sub-Inspector Lindsay (of the Natal Police: retired).
Sub-Inspector Fothergill (of the Natal Police).
Sub-Inspector Hellet (of the Natal Police).
Sub-Inspector J. Hamilton (of the Natal Police).
Sub-Inspector Ottley (of the Natal Police: retired).

The Zululand Police acquitted themselves magnificently during the rebellion of 1906, at the Bobe Ridge fight, and again at the Home Gorge. During the march to the Bobe Ridge the natives provided the advance guard, and did all the scouting through the bush; and when the enemy charged at the British column, as stated elsewhere, they repelled the attack. No troops could have been cooler or more steady.

After the Bobe Ridge fight a member of the Natal Police and a native policeman, having been wounded, were sent down to Eshowe for treatment, being put side by side in the bottom of an ambulance. The Zulu had been provided with several small luxuries by his officers, and the wounded white man had also been given certain delicacies for consumption on the journey. They were both very sick, but while being driven to Eshowe the Zulu was noticed offering what he had to the white man, who in his turn shared his luxuries with the native, there being a mutual recognition of affliction.

On the morning of the Mome fight the Zululand Police marched with Colonel Barker's column to the scene of the conflict, where they were ordered, with the native levies, to close the head of the gorge. This was done, and they opened fire with the rest of the troops when that deadly hail of lead was poured upon Bambata's sleeping men. After daylight they had a hand-to-hand encounter with some of the enemy.

Later in the day the Zululand Police were sent into a bush to drive it, and did considerable execution amongst the enemy, who in some cases were up in the trees firing on them, but were soon picked out and fell.

Owing to some misunderstanding the troops flanking the bush were firing on the native police, and Inspector Fairlie was forced to take his men cut before the work was quite completed.

In his dispatch after the action Colonel Barker wrote:

I have much pleasure in bringing to your notice the keen manner in which the Zululand Native Police carried out their part of the operations under Inspector Fairlie.

In July 1906 there was a big drive on the Natal side of the Tugela, when the Zululand Police shot and captured a number of rebels. After this the corps was occupied for some time in preventing the natives in Natal, who were inclined to cause trouble, from crossing the border into Zululand. The rebellion was virtually over, but there still remained a great deal of hard work to do. Fifty of the Natal Police, with the native corps, and a party of Dunn's scouts, were sent into the Stanger district to maintain order, and it was in this part of the country that the last shots in the rebellion were fired by a patrol of the Zululand Police, when four much-wanted natives were captured and two were killed on the 22nd August. Thus the work of clearing up went on until the districts of Stanger and Mapumulo were quiet.

Not long after this the contingent of Natal Police returned to Pietermaritzburg, and the conclusion of the year saw the final disbandment of the Zululand Police. Much has been written and said on the debated point as to whether Zulus should be allowed to constitute a trained and armed force, some people pointing out instances where similar bodies have proved a very formidable foe to those who trained them. The opinion of the European officers who had charge of the Zululand Police should have considerable weight. Inspector Fairlie assured the writer that he always trusted the Zululand Police and felt he could depend on them.

"I should like to lay stress on the moral influence the Zululand Police had on the rest of the natives during the rebellion of '06," he added. "Many more Zulus would undoubtedly have fought with the rebels had it not been for our trained force of natives."

Commandant Mansel speaks very highly of them, and bears full testimony to their value as soldiers. Their instincts are wholly military, he declares, and a Zulu recruit is a ready-made soldier. All that is necessary is to teach him to handle a rifle, and this can be done in three or four months. He is then as good a soldier as ever he will become. He is easily managed, good tempered, understands discipline by instinct, is docile and plucky, and is proud of himself and his corps. The Zulu soldier is kindly disposed towards his officers, is full of metal, and is capable of enduring the extremes of marching and hunger.

"The trained Zulu," says Mr. Mansel, "works splendidly with white men in the field, though I think they should be kept entirely apart in quarters. The Imperial troops and the Zululand Police got on wonderfully well during the operations in Zululand, and were always the best of friends.

"I always had the feeling that with 500 Natal Police and 1000 Zulus, one could go anywhere, and do anything; and I think that everyone in the Natal Police shares that opinion.

"It is a noteworthy fact that though the Zululand Police were often fighting against their own kith and kin, not a single case of treachery or breach of faith ever occurred."

CHAPTER 28

The Water Police

There is probably no shipping port in the world at which vessels get better and quicker attention from the police than is the case at Durban, where the Water Police have formed an interesting branch of the Natal Police since the force was taken over in 1894. At that time it consisted of two sergeants, eight European constables, and twenty-two natives, these being under the control of Superintendent G. E. Tatum.

A dilapidated old building constituted the headquarters, and as Durban was at that time almost in its infancy, there was comparatively little work to do, though the task of the police has steadily increased as the Durban wharves have extended. It was not until 1898 that members of the Natal Police were drafted into this force, and then three troopers were sent to Durban, and a sergeant became boarding officer under the immigration regulations. It became necessary to increase the force in strength in 1901, owing to the number of restricted immigrants that were taken to Natal, principally from India.

There were twenty-seven constables employed boarding ships, and dealing with the immigrants, until 1905, when a wave of depression swept over the colony, and all these men were transferred to headquarters at Pietermaritzburg and Zululand, just in time for them to take part in the fighting during the last rebellion.

Superintendent Tatum retired on a pension in 1905, being succeeded by Inspector Fairlie, who supervised the work of the Water Police until he returned to Zululand as Commandant of the Zululand Native Police.

Today, (as at time of first publication), Superintendent J. McCarthy, who is at the head of the Water Police, has under him four sergeants, twenty-two European constables, and sixty-four natives. There are seven miles of wharves to be patrolled, and as the trade of the port in-

291

THE WATER POLICE

creased a force of twenty-six special European constables was engaged at the request of the various shipping agents in 1908. They are not members of the Water Police, but work under the supervision of that body in protecting the various ships that enter Durban.

The Water Police now work eight hours a day, though from 1894 to 1901 they each worked for a nominal twelve, but an actual thirteen, hours a day, for three hundred and sixty-five days a year, it being impossible to grant half-day holidays. The men generally reserved their annual fourteen days' leave until they had a month or two to fall back upon. This continued until just over ten years ago, when three watches a day were instituted.

Mr. Tatum was in command of the Natal Volunteers as well as Superintendent of the Water Police. When the last Boer War broke out he went to the front with the first of the Natal Volunteers that were called out, Sergeant McCarthy being left in charge of the Water Police, who had a great deal of hard work during that time. Only half a dozen of them were Europeans, and the idea of regular watches had to be abandoned. They mustered at five a.m., and did not leave duty until the last of the trains containing troops had gone upcountry. There were crowds of refugees in Durban, and the whole of the work of regulating the traffic at the congested wharves devolved upon the Water Police, who had to erect barriers round the troop-ships and keep the crowds back.

Whenever an accident occurs in the bay the Water Police are expected to put off in their small rowing-boat to render assistance, and there is often grave risk of the little craft being capsized. A decked-in steam or motor launch is badly required, but apparently the authorities do not recognize this.

In addition to their other duties, the Water Police carry out instructions received from the captain of the port, the port manager, and the harbour engineer, the force working in conjunction with these officials. The Water Police also act as Customs officials. Until recently there was only one preventive officer on watch at night, the Water Police being recognized as the men responsible for the detection of smuggling. The principal delinquents are sailors who, having been refused an advance of money by their captain, take ashore plugs of tobacco in the hope of being able to sell it, preparatory to a burst of intemperance.

Whenever there is serious trouble with a drunken crew the Water Police are looked to to preserve order. There was one particularly exciting night in 1901, when the crew of the British troop-ship *Columbian* set the captain at defiance. The *Columbian* was moored at the quay, and she had about thirty men on board. Inspired with the all-prevailing spirit of warfare, the sailors were a dangerous gang to handle. There were only six members of the Water Police available for duty, but they tackled the mutinous crew. It was pitch dark when they went up the gangway to the vessel with drawn batons, and there was every appearance of their having a rough time, but under the direction of Sergeant McCarthy they advanced boldly.

At first the mutineers showed defiance, and the police deemed it wise to retire, so they secured the assistance of two of the Borough Police and returned to the attack. This time they went up the gangway at a run.

"They're coming!" yelled one of the crew.

"Yes, and there's a regiment of us this time," shouted back one of the police. Without a moment's hesitation they rushed straight on, and began to hit out at every one who resisted, with their batons.

The fighting lasted for several minutes, and then the crew bolted into the fo'castle, where nineteen of them were arrested and taken to gaol by the eight policemen.

While the British sailing-ship *Loch Garve* was making her way towards Durban in 1904, the crew mutinied on the high seas, got at the whisky and gin, and refused point-blank to do any work. One or two apprentices remained loyal to the captain, and helped him to work the ship into Durban.

As the vessel approached the shore she signalled for the police, and four men went off in a small boat. They found twenty-three members of the crew intoxicated, and mutinous; and arrested them all. The small boat used by the police was not nearly large enough to take the prisoners ashore, so a motor boat had to be sent for. The men were sentenced to terms of imprisonment varying from three to nine months.

On another occasion a number of the crew of a large liner had broached six cases of gin while the vessel was lying at anchor off the wharf. They be came utterly unmanageable, and when the vessel was moored at the side of the quay Sergeant Lynch and two other members of the Water Police boarded the liner, tackled the offenders unaided, and arrested eleven of them.

Some years ago one of the duties of the Water Police was the rounding up of all the firemen from the public-houses for the ships that sailed on Saturdays. This was very dangerous work, because the firemen, half-demented by bad liquor, often refused stubbornly to go back to their ship, and displayed murderous tendencies when urged to do so. *Jiu-jitsu* was, and still is, (at time of first publication), a very necessary part of the training of the Water Police, and it was exceedingly useful when the firemen had to be driven on board. In the majority of cases they had to be frog-marched through the streets, and the shipping companies were charged a revenue fee of five shillings for each fireman taken to the boat by the police.

When the supervision of the fisheries was in the hands of the Water Police, the men had many thrilling adventures with the poachers who put out their nets at midnight in the prohibited portions of the river. Several men still in the corps had narrow escapes from death.

One night Sergeant McCarthy and Sergeant Edwards went out on foot to patrol the head of the bay, reaching Congella at twelve o'clock. They half stripped, and, with most of their clothes fastened on their shoulders, waded into the water to cross the channel. It had been a fine, moonlight night at first, but at about two o'clock the weather changed and the moon was obscured by a mist. Some little distance away they had seen a number of Indians poaching, and with great caution they approached them. The two Europeans captured the whole party, numbering nine, illicitly using small-mesh nets in prohibited water. Then the moon vanished altogether, and when the police tried to wade to the shore they lost their bearings.

The water came up to their hips, and whichever way they went it was deeper. They floundered about hopelessly for a while, and as the position became desperate the two Europeans decided to release their prisoners, thinking the latter would probably know the safest way back to the shore. This they accordingly did, but the Indians began to howl, for they were no better off than the Europeans. The water seemed to be steadily rising with the tide, and all the eleven men would probably have been drowned had not the mist lifted slightly and revealed the Bluff light dimly shining in the distance.

Taking his bearings from that point, Sergeant McCarthy decided that the Congella beach must be in a certain direction, so he determined to swim for it or drown. He waded on until the water was up to his neck—and then found himself on rising ground. Although the situation was still critical the police again made prisoners of the Indians, who were with great difficulty taken ashore. It was after four o'clock in the morning when they arrived at the police station, wet through, with the nine poachers.

CHAPTER 29

The Railway Police

When the Railway Police force was amalgamated with the other branches of the Natal Police in 1894, its staff consisted of two Europeans—one at Durban and one at Pietermaritzburg—and about thirty coloured constables. No change was made until May 1895, when Trooper Mackay was sent down to Durban to relieve a man for fourteen days. Mention was made to him of a police office, and after a careful search he found it in a corner of the railway yard. The size of this establishment was 8 ft. by 8 ft. and its furniture consisted of a press, table, chair, and a drawer full of old correspondence and cockroaches.

The only document handed over to Mackay was the report book. The man whom he had relieved never returned, and the Natal policeman's duty there extended to thirteen weeks, in spite of his efforts to get back to headquarters. After the novelty of the change had worn off he chafed at walking about the yard week after week in "mounted" uniform. He only took part in one really interesting event, and that consisted of arresting 225 Indians. In sheer desperation Mackay applied for his discharge, and Sergeant Bousfield was permanently transferred to the Railway Police, but Mackay was persuaded to remain on the staff on condition that he was allowed to marry. Towards the close of the year Trooper Lightening was also transferred to this branch of the force, and the men's duties were reduced to night and day shifts of twelve hours each.

A busy time began in 1896, when there was a rush of refugees from Johannesburg. On the 21st January the police attended the arrival and embarkation of Dr. Jameson and his officers, this being done very quietly, early in the morning. Far more trouble was experienced three days later when Dr. Jameson's men embarked, for the trains were late, and great care had to be exercised in preventing the prisoners, who were in *mufti*, from mixing with the crowd. Several of the prisoners, by the way, were ex-members of the Natal Police, and one of the wounded, who were met by Sergeant Bousfield on 7th February, was ex-Sergeant Fyvie. He had joined the Natal Police in 1882, and served in it for fourteen years.

Some months afterwards, the staff of the Railway Police was further added to, and the men's work at Durban was reduced to eight hours a day, though the other sections had to get along as well as they could, without counting too carefully the hours they had to work. The operations of the force gradually extended. In 1899, when there was friction in the Transvaal, and large numbers of refugees began to move down-country, members of the Railway Police were sent up the line. When war broke out Sergeant Whitehead and his native police were driven to Dundee. He was left behind when the British troops left the town, and was captured by the Boers.

All his natives escaped excepting one, who refused to leave without orders. This man got away soon afterwards, made for his *kraal* at Nkandhla, buried his uniform, walked back to Pietermaritzburg and reported himself. As the tide of war rolled on, Sergeant Mackay and Trooper Abrams narrowly escaped being shut into Ladysmith. They were in the town on escort duty the night before the siege began. Several of the Railway Police, however, were fastened up in Ladysmith during that long and trying ordeal.

During the war a wave of lawlessness swept over the country, and a large quantity of goods sent by rail failed to reach their destination. It was suspected that an organized gang was at work, and some of the police were told off to make a special investigation. Five Europeans were arrested at one time, and five more a little later, eight of them being railway servants. Tons of stolen property were recovered.

There was a very exciting incident in October 1902. A Durban gang of ruffians discovered that *specie* was to be sent by train, and they boldly approached a guard with the object of getting his assistance in securing it. The guard answered warily, but informed the authorities, with the result that a trap was arranged by Superintendent Bousfield. A quantity of old iron was put into a safe, and the gang was informed by the guard that it was going on a certain train. In the same van there was placed a large case, in which a number of observation holes had been drilled. Stowed away in this case were Detective-Sergeant Lees-Smith, of the C.I.D., and Detective Wevell, of the Railway Police. Meanwhile Sergeant Sherrell and Detective Kinsey, of the Railway

Police, Detective Tuffs, of the C.I.D., and two other officers, had gone ahead on another train, and were waiting at a place beyond Pinetown bridge, where the members of the gang had been seen loitering about, and where it was assumed the safe would probably be thrown off the train.

When the train containing the supposed *specie* left Durban, three members of the gang jumped into the van with the guard who had given them away. On the journey the men, under the gaze of the detectives in the case, plugged the keyhole of the safe with dynamite, and prepared a fuse. Just after Pinetown bridge was passed they gagged the obliging guard, and moved the safe to the door of the van. As the train was going slowly up a steep incline they pushed the safe out on to the embankment.

At that moment the lid of the case was lifted, and the detectives leaped out with their revolvers, crying, "Hands up!" Two of the gang jumped out of the van, followed by Lees-Smith, but were soon captured. Wevell got the third man as he was trying to climb through the window; and then he stopped the train by applying the vacuum brake.

Two accomplices, one of whom had financed the affair while the other had secured the dynamite and fuse, were also captured; and all five men were sentenced to five years' hard labour.

A couple of years afterwards some smart work was done in connection with an audacious train robbery, carried out by an individual who had some of the self-assurance of Voigt, the Koepenick cobbler, at whose doings half Europe laughed a few years ago.

Just over £900 in gold—consisting of railway *employés'* pay—was in a train, and at Leigh station the robber, dressed as a sergeant of the Natal Police, walked up to the reserved compartment containing the specie and, armed with an "official" telegram, gave instructions that the escort was to return to Pietermaritzburg with the pay-clerk under arrest. Never dreaming that anything was wrong, the escort obeyed, taking the puzzled pay-clerk with him; and he handed the key and safe containing the cash to the bogus sergeant, who disappeared with the money before the train arrived at Estcourt.

The police were baffled until a free railway pass was picked up on the line some days afterwards. It bore a wrong number, and it was soon discovered that it had been issued to an Estcourt man. He was arrested on suspicion, and his house was turned inside out for the missing money, but without success. Doggedly, the police went on searching, and at last Detective Cuff dug up £718 in the culprit's fowl-house. The train robber was sent to hard labour for three years.

Thefts from trains grew very numerous prior to 1905, and many arrests were made, six European railway hands being taken into custody in one place, and still cases were continually reported. A dozen railway *employés* were arrested at Pietermaritzburg, but as certain documents were missing only one of these men was convicted, some of the others being dismissed from the service. The chief clerk absconded with £190 from the Durban goods office in 1906, and he was traced to Charlestown, where he attempted to commit suicide. On being taken back to Durban he was imprisoned for twelve months.

The total number of arrests made by the Railway Police up to July 1910 was 33,350, which indicates how greatly the work increased from 1895, when the Natal Police first took an active part in it.

In 1912 the Railway Police force was abolished, its members being absorbed by the Natal Police, and the work has since been carried on by railway officials.

CHAPTER 30

Many Uniforms

If only samples of the many and varied articles of uniform that have adorned and disfigured the forms of the members of the Natal Police from the day the corps was inaugurated to the present time had been preserved, they would have furnished a quaint museum.

It was exceedingly difficult to obtain anything at all in the way of uniform when Major Dartnell was engaged in his early struggle to keep the force going, and the tailor—known universally as "Billy" Hall—who had to adjust the slop-shop garments to the men, is still living. The first grotesque uniform of corduroy was used for some time.

In 1879 the regulation helmet was white, rather high, and had a brass spike with a chain and monogram. There was one trooper who firmly believed in wearing out his old uniform before buying new, so he stuck faithfully to a helmet of an earlier period—a bright blue affair with brass mounts—until the sergeant-major had a brief but decisive chat with him on the subject; and the blue helmet was seen no more.

After a considerable time the white helmet was succeeded by a black one, with black mounts—a distinctly funereal affair; but this was changed before long for a white helmet of the old army pattern, without either spike or chain. The authorities remained faithful to this form of headgear, until the khaki polo helmet was introduced in the year 1898.

A round forage cap was in use for undress purposes until 1883, when a black *kepi* cap was introduced. This was regarded with disfavour by the men for some time.

For a short period a grey cloth patrol hat with a fore-and-aft peak—a most unsightly construction—with the letters "N.M.P."

worked in worsted in front, became part of the uniform, but fortunately for the force it soon disappeared, and was followed by a grey smasher hat, with a spotted blue *pugaree*. A black smasher hat was also tried, but it was not a success, for smasher hats even when new never looked smart; after a few months' wear on the *veldt* they are calculated to spoil the appearance of the smartest of men.

The black tunic and pants which were in use for many years in the early days, fitted skin tight. They were painfully thick, and the men stationed on the coast, where the weather is most oppressive in the summer, found them very uncomfortable. No such things as slacks and overalls were known in those days.

For riding school and fatigue use, a second pair of grey-coloured cord pants was issued. They were very unserviceable, and as likely as not split the first time the wearer tried to mount his horse. They all appeared to be one size when they were issued from the store, and sometimes looked like overalls on a man before "Billy "Hall got to work on them, and made them fit like a glove.

Today, (as at time of first publication), all the uniforms are of a drab khaki. There is no regiment in the world to beat the Natal Police for smartness in khaki kit, and the men who served in the old days tell the modern troopers they are "lucky dogs" to have such comfortable clothes. It was sometimes a heart-breaking task to march from one end of the colony to the other, as the men had to do many a time, clad in the old tight-fitting cord.

After the earliest days, in which any man was only too glad to get any sort of boot, the regulation foot-gear came up to the knee, having half a dozen buckles down the outside of the leg, which were constantly getting torn off in the ranks. A black field boot then came into use, and was succeeded by a brown leather field boot which was introduced at the same time as the khaki uniform. This was followed by the brown boots and leggings which are in use at the present time, and which for comfort, appearance, and serviceable use would be difficult to improve upon.

When mackintosh coats became part of the uniform they were received as a great blessing. Prior to that a grey cloth overcoat, which was exceedingly heavy, had to answer the purpose. It was awkward when strapped in front of the saddle, and the men often rode on through the rain, getting thoroughly wet, in preference to wearing such a heavy garment.

One extraordinary experiment tried was the *poncho*. This was a

UNIFORM AND KIT OF THE NATAL MOUNTED POLICE IN
THE EARLY EIGHTIES.

great, black mackintosh, seven feet square, with a hole in the middle, through which the men put their heads. A very similar garment is used today, (as at time of first publication), by some of the regiments in England, but there the men do not have to contend with the high winds which sweep violently over Natal on occasions. After it was found that the troopers had the *poncho* blown over their heads some-times, and had a good deal of difficulty in getting disentangled, this combined garment for man and horse was abandoned.

The original police saddle was the old artillery driver's pattern, with a solid leather seat. It was as hard as granite when new, but it was almost everlasting, and for rough work was hard to beat.

During the first twenty years of the corps' existence, cleaning and burnishing occupied much of the day, for there was a great deal of steel amongst the accoutrements. No man who had passed riding school ever dreamed of appearing mounted without a *bridoon* and a big steel bit with brass bosses. Trooper Pearce, who served during the Zulu War of 1879, and was at Isandhlwana when the camp was attacked, was one of the few police who got away before the Zulu *impi* finally closed in and crushed every man there. He was galloping away, but before he had gone far, he discovered that he had left his "big bit" in the camp.

Remarking to a comrade who was escaping with him that "the sergeant-major would be on his track if he were seen without it," he galloped back. This cost him his life, for before he could get away again the black circle was completed.

In the days when the Government were not so liberal with trans-port as they are now, the troopers had saddle-bags which, together with the wallets, contained all the kit that a policeman was supposed to have when trekking. These bags were connected with a strip of leather that lay across the seat of the saddle and hung just behind the leg. The saddle, bridle, and other equipment at that time weighed six stones; and both horses and men were hampered and worn out when they had to carry such a weight.

When the bush fighting started in the rebellion of 1906 an effort was made to get some sort of shirt of chain mail that would be proof against the terrible *assegai*. After considerable trouble a specimen was procured, but it was found to be quite unsuitable on account of its weight and other drawbacks.

It was certainly *assegai* proof, but was quite hopeless as part of the equipment of men who had to move about continuously and quickly by day and by night. The specimen was stuffed with cushions, and several of the troopers made an effort at stabbing at it with an *assegai* in the Chief Commissioner's house. They could not force the point of the weapon through the steel chain, but did considerable damage to the furniture

OFFICERS OF THE NATAL POLICE

Appendix

PAST AND PRESENT OFFICERS OF THE NATAL POLICE
(AT TIME OF FIRST PUBLICATION)

NAME.	DATE APPOINTED.	
Inspector A. G. Abrahams .	1886	Retired, 1906.
Sub-Inspector A. Banister .	1889	
Sub-Inspector W. Barry .	1890	Died at Ingwavuma in 1910.
Superintendent A. C. Bell .	1894	Gaols Department.
Sub-Inspector R. A. Bell .	1886	Retired, 1908.
Inspector E. P. Blake . .	1895	Paymaster ; retired, medically unfit, 1911.
Sub-Inspector A. H. Borgnis	1895	Seconded to Natal Border Police as Lieutenant, 1902 to 1903.
Inspector W. H. Bousfield .	1885	Superintendent Railway Police, 1896 ; relative rank of Inspector in 1904.
Sub-Inspector H. R. Brown	1899	Staff Surgeon.
Sub-Inspector L. Caminada .	1891	Seconded to Natal Border Police as Lieutenant, 1902 to 1903.
Inspector F. A. Campbell .	1874	Retired, 1905 ; died in 1910.
Sub-Inspector W.D.Campbell	1879	Quartermaster ; died in 1902.
Colonel W. J. Clarke . .	1878	Chief Commissioner.
Sub-Inspector A. S. Clifton .	1883	
Inspector J. B. Collyer .	1901	Staff Veterinary Surgeon.
Sub-Inspector E. C. Crallan.	1874	Retired in 1888 ; killed in Boer War, 1899–1902.
Major-General Sir J. G. Dartnell, K.C.B., C.M.G..	1874	Retired.
Inspector D. Deane . .	1894	Governor Gaols Department. Transferred to Gaols Department in 1911.
Inspector O. Dimmick .	1883	Adjutant.

Inspector W. V. Dorehill .	1878	Retired, 1905.
Inspector W. E. Earle .	1889	Head of the C.I.D.
Superintendent A. J. B. Elliot	1883	Superintendent Gaols Dept.
Sub-Inspector F. Evans .	1897	Appointed Sub-Inspector in Zululand Police, 1896; and transferred to Natal Police, 1897, on annexation. Previously served in Natal Police. First enlisted, 1879; retired, 1886.
Sub-Inspector J. H. Evans .	1891	Retired, 1904.
Inspector C. E. Fairlie. .	1890	
Inspector W. F. Fairlie .	1883	Rank of Inspector on appointment to Natal Mounted Police, 1883. Seconded to Natal Border Police as Lieut.-Col., 1902; retired, 1904.
Sub-Inspector B. Fothergill.	1889	
Sub-Inspector F. A. Fynney	1897	Appointed Sub-Inspector in Zululand Police, 1897; transferred to Natal Police, with rank of Sub-Inspector, 1897; resigned 1900.
Inspector W. C. H. George .	1880	Retired, 1911.
Sub-Inspector H. R. Hallett	1885	
Sub-Inspector Cyril Hamilton	1878	Retired, 1885; died in London, 1901.
Sub-Inspector J. Hamilton .	1897	Appointed Sub-Inspector in Zululand Police, 1896; and transferred to Natal Police, 1897, on annexation, with rank of Sub-Inspector.
Sub-Inspector S. H. K. Hunt.	1890	Killed by natives at Hosking's Farm, Byrne, 1906.
Sub-Inspector W. Ingle .	1893	Drowned in Lake Sibayi, Ubombo, Zululand, 1910.
Inspector W. E. Ives . .	1885	Staff Paymaster; retired, 1910.
Sub-Inspector C. R. Jackson	1877	Appointed Sub-Inspector on joining.
Sub-Inspector J. D. Johnson	1896	
Sub-Inspector R. Keating .	1886	Retired 1903; died in Ireland.
Sub-Inspector C. W. Lewis .	1889	Now Adjutant of Volunteers in Cape Colony.
Sub-Inspector C. R. Lindsay	1890	Retired, 1912.
Inspector W. E. Lyttle .	1887	Died at Estcourt, 1910.

Sub-Inspector E. MacAndrew	1901	Paymaster.
Sub-Inspector J. McCarthy	1892	Superintendent of Water Police.
Sub-Inspector F. R. Mansel	1884	Retired, 1902.
Colonel G. Mansel, C.M.G. .	1874	Commandant Reserve Territory Carbineers, 1883 ; Commandant Zululand Police, 1887; transferred to Natal Police on annexation, 1897; retired, 1906.
Lt.-Colonel G. S. Mardall .	1879	Seconded to Natal Border Police as Senior Major, 1902 to 1903 ; appointed Inspector of Prisons, 1907 ; retired, 1911.
Inspector J. Marshall .	1897	Appointed Sub-Inspector in Zululand Police, 1888 ; transferred to Natal Police, 1897, on annexation, with rank of Sub-Inspector.
Inspector J. A. Masson .	1877	Retired, 1897.
Sub-Inspector W. T. Matravers	1888	
Inspector R. S. Maxwell .	1897	Transferred from Zululand Government Service to Zululand Police, with rank of Sub-Inspector, 1897; transferred from Zululand Police to Natal Police, on annexation, 1897, with rank of Sub-Inspector.
Inspector L. H. U. Meiners .	1885	
Sub-Inspector C. R. Ottley .	1890	Retired, 1910, medically unfit.
Sub-Inspector C. D. Pearce .	1894	First enlistment under the Police Act ; left the force, 1904.
Inspector A. G. Petley .	1880	Retired, 1902.
Inspector F. L. Phillips .	1876	Retired, 1908.
Sub-Inspector A. Pinto-Leite	1896	C.I.D.
Inspector A. Prendergast .	1879	
Inspector J. E. Rose .	1883	
Inspector F. H. S. Sewell .	1880	Transferred from Civil Service, with rank of Sub-Inspector on appointment ; retired, 1904.
Sub-Inspector A. Shackleton	1880	Died at Dundee from apoplexy, 1898.
Sub-Inspector E. J. Sherrall	1889	Superintendent of the late Railway Police.

Captain A. M. Smith .	1879	Late Captain 38th Regiment; entered Natal Civil Service as gaoler, Umsinga, 1879; appointed Governor, Central Gaol, Durban, 1893; retired, 1910.
Sub-Inspector W. Stean .	1874	Sub-Inspector and Adjutant; retired, 1895; died, 1912.
Sub-Inspector I. Strutt .	1883	Retired, 1905.
Superintendent G. E. Tatum	1881	Inspector and Superintendent Water Police; retired, 1905.
Governor J. R. Thompson .	1882	Appointed Governor, Maritzburg Gaol, 1894; retired, 1905.
Sub-Inspector J. F. Thurston	1898	Staff Veterinary Surgeon; resigned, 1899.
Sub-Inspector H. H. West .	1883	
Sub-Inspector F. B. Esmonde White	1890	

LEONAUR

ALSO FROM LEONAUR

AVAILABLE IN SOFTCOVER OR HARDCOVER WITH DUST JACKET

THE 9TH—THE KING'S (LIVERPOOL REGIMENT) IN THE GREAT WAR 1914 - 1918 *by Enos H. G. Roberts*—Mersey to mud—war and Liverpool men.

THE GAMBARDIER *by Mark Severn*—The experiences of a battery of Heavy artillery on the Western Front during the First World War.

FROM MESSINES TO THIRD YPRES *by Thomas Floyd*—A personal account of the First World War on the Western front by a 2/5th Lancashire Fusilier.

THE IRISH GUARDS IN THE GREAT WAR - VOLUME 1 *by Rudyard Kipling*—Edited and Compiled from Their Diaries and Papers—The First Battalion.

THE IRISH GUARDS IN THE GREAT WAR - VOLUME 1 *by Rudyard Kipling*—Edited and Compiled from Their Diaries and Papers—The Second Battalion.

ARMOURED CARS IN EDEN *by K. Roosevelt*—An American President's son serving in Rolls Royce armoured cars with the British in Mesopatamia & with the American Artillery in France during the First World War.

CHASSEUR OF 1914 *by Marcel Dupont*—Experiences of the twilight of the French Light Cavalry by a young officer during the early battles of the great war in Europe.

TROOP HORSE & TRENCH *by R.A. Lloyd*—The experiences of a British Lifeguardsman of the household cavalry fighting on the western front during the First World War 1914-18.

THE EAST AFRICAN MOUNTED RIFLES *by C.J. Wilson*—Experiences of the campaign in the East African bush during the First World War.

THE LONG PATROL *by George Berrie*—A Novel of Light Horsemen from Gallipoli to the Palestine campaign of the First World War.

THE FIGHTING CAMELIERS *by Frank Reid*—The exploits of the Imperial Camel Corps in the desert and Palestine campaigns of the First World War.

STEEL CHARIOTS IN THE DESERT *by S. C. Rolls*—The first world war experiences of a Rolls Royce armoured car driver with the Duke of Westminster in Libya and in Arabia with T.E. Lawrence.

WITH THE IMPERIAL CAMEL CORPS IN THE GREAT WAR *by Geoffrey Inchbald*—The story of a serving officer with the British 2nd battalion against the Senussi and during the Palestine campaign.

Lightning Source UK Ltd.
Milton Keynes UK
UKOW050019260612

195052UK00001B/206/P